MW00848851

THE TYPHOON TRUCE

THE TYPHOON TRUCE

Three Days in Vietnam when
Nature Intervened in the War

ROBERT F. CURTIS

CASEMATE
Philadelphia & Oxford

Published in the United States of America and Great Britain in 2015 by
CASEMATE PUBLISHERS
1950 Lawrence Road, Havertown, PA 19083
and
10 Hythe Bridge Street, Oxford, OX1 2EW

Copyright 2015 © Robert F. Curtis

ISBN 978-1-61200-329-0
Digital Edition: ISBN 978-1-61200-330-6

Cataloging-in-publication data is available from the Library of Congress and
the British Library.

All rights reserved. No part of this book may be reproduced or transmitted in any
form or by any means, electronic or mechanical including photocopying, recording
or by any information storage and retrieval system, without permission from the
Publisher in writing.

10 9 8 7 6 5 4 3 2 1

Printed and bound in the United States of America.

For a complete list of Casemate titles please contact:

CASEMATE PUBLISHERS (US)
Telephone (610) 853-9131, Fax (610) 853-9146
E-mail: casemate@casematepublishing.com

CASEMATE PUBLISHERS (UK)
Telephone (01865) 241249, Fax (01865) 794449
E-mail: casemate-uk@casematepublishing.co.uk

CONTENTS

This is a war story of the Vietnam War without war — for a brief time. There is very little shooting in this war story. Almost all of the shooting was directed at no one at all. This war story is based on real events and set in real places. Everything in this war story actually happened. All the people portrayed are real, too. My descriptions of their personalities are as I remember them the way they were then. All the conversations in this story are fictional, since I cannot remember that far back, but they might have happened the way I wrote them. This is not a story of combat, although combat happened before it and after it. In this war story warriors saved people, instead of killing them or contributing to their deaths. There, you can start reading now.

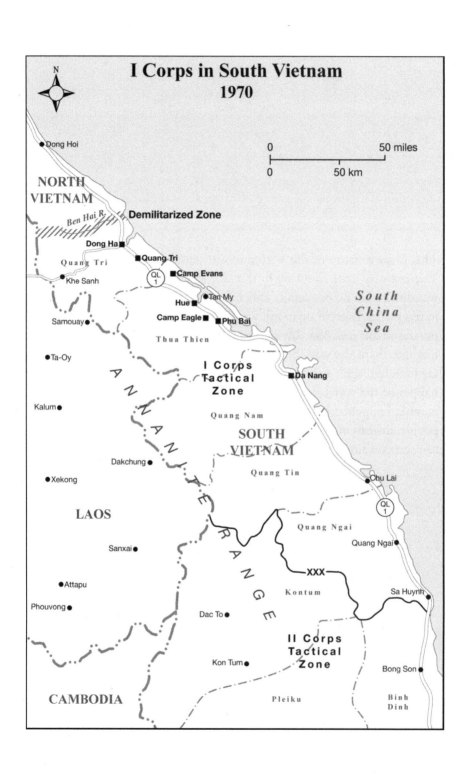

I Corps in South Vietnam
1970

N

Dong Hoi

NORTH VIETNAM

Ben Hai R.

Demilitarized Zone

Dong Ha

Quang Tri

■Quang Tri

Khe Sanh

QL 1

Camp Evans

Tan My

Hue■

Samouay

Thua Thien

Camp Eagle■ ■**Phu Bai**

Ta-Oy

Kalum

I Corps Tactical Zone

■Da Nang

Quang Nam

SOUTH VIETNAM

Dakchung

Quang Tin

Xekong

LAOS

Chu Lai

QL 1

Quang Ngai

Sanxai

Quang Ngai

XXX

Attapu

Kontum

Sa Huynh

Phouvong

Dac To

II Corps Tactical Zone

Kon Tum

Bong Son

CAMBODIA

Pleiku

Binh Dinh

South China Sea

A N N A M I T E   R A N G E

0   50 miles
0   50 km

This book is dedicated to the men of C Company, 159th Assault Support Helicopter Battalion, 101st Airborne Division (Airmobile): my friends and colleagues long time gone. The Air Medal Citation is a copy of mine, changed to show that all of the men who participated in the Typhoon Truce received the award for these actions.

PROLOGUE: RAIN UNENDING

Wars are suspended sometimes. Something intervenes and the war stops for a while. A holiday that both sides recognize might do it, as happened in the Christmas truce during early World War I, for example. Weather might do it, too, like it did during the Vietnam War in the fall of 1970. The latter was not a suspension on the scale of the WW I event, but still, it happened and the war stopped for three days. They never last, these suspensions, but life changes a bit for all the people involved while they are happening. Maybe the people change for the better, or maybe not, but, come what may, they don't forget what happened when their war stopped briefly.

In September and October 1970, in I Corps, the northern part of what was then South Vietnam, between Da Nang and the De-militarized Zone (DMZ), the monsoon came right on time. It was right on time, but the rain was far heavier than normal and far more intense than anyone expected, first because of a near miss by Category 5 Super Typhoon Joan. After smacking the Philippines, Joan took a right turn, passing to the east of Vietnam, but she was so big that she covered all the coastal lowlands in I Corps and on up into North Vietnam as she headed north to hammer China. Of course, it was raining in I Corps before Joan got there. The clouds had come in, low and dark as they always do, and for six weeks it rained non-stop. Before and after Joan, it rained, not a hard rain all the time, sometimes it was just a fine mist, but the rain never really stopped. As it fell, the water all over the coastal lowlands began to rise. Then, less than a week after Joan passed by, on October 25th, Super Typhoon Kate arrived.

Kate was a Category 4 storm, with top winds of 150 miles per hour. She nearly broke up as she was tearing apart the areas of the Philippines that Typhoon Joan had spared, but out over the open water of the Sulu Sea and then the South China Sea, Typhoon Kate built a lot of strength and a lot of rain. She hit the coast of South Vietnam near Da Nang. Kate's northern quadrant, the worse part of the storm, hit the lowlands north of Da Nang and to the east of Hue City, the old imperial capital, leaving the people there faced with both war and natural disaster at the same time.

No one but the foreign warriors fighting throughout the country had the resources to help the people who lived in the lowlands there, but the war had to stop, at least for a while, for that to happen. And stop it did, but for the men who took their helicopters out into the unending rain it really made no difference. Perhaps no one would shoot at them for a while, but the everyday dangers they faced remained, magnified by the low clouds and poor visibility. War or no war, complicated mechanical things like helicopters break down. Obstacles, like antennas and their guy wires, designed to add stability, are still there, you just can't see them through the rain and fog. You get just as tired, maybe more so, as you do on normal missions when you have to constantly stay clear of the clouds that now come nearly to the ground. None of that really mattered. They went out to help anyway, because rescuing people was now their mission and the mission must be done.

CHAPTER ONE

THE MEN OF PLAYTEX AND LIFE IN VIETNAM

WALKING FISH

"**A** fish just walked across the sidewalk in front of me," the tall, thin young man in the green flight suit and darker green rain jacket said as he came through the door of Playtex's Officers' Club. The three men already there, all pilots, just laughed and shook their heads in disbelief. A walking fish, really . . .

C Company, 159th Assault Support Helicopter Battalion (ASHB), 101st Aviation Group, 101st Airborne Division (Airmobile), was given the call sign "Playtex" in 1969, prior to leaving the United States for Vietnam. Their official motto was "Support Extraordinaire," but naturally, given the name Playtex, their unofficial motto became, "We give living support," echoing the women's underwear company's slogan. When C Company returned to the States after the war, the call sign was immediately changed from "Playtex" to the more politically correct "Haulmark." Political correctness had not yet been invented in 1969, so they were Playtex. None of the pilots or enlisted men in this story knew how or why the call sign Playtex came to be, nor were they curious enough to find out.

At any given moment, there were between 35 and 45 officers assigned to Playtex, all of them aviators. Of those, perhaps 30 would be available for flying at any one time. The rest had just arrived, were checking out, were sick, lame, or lazy or were on R&R (rest and recuperation) in Australia or Taiwan or Thailand if they were single, or in Hawaii if they were married. There were 200 to 250 enlisted men and, like the officers, maybe 20% were off somewhere else and not available for duty. For the first month or so after you joined Playtex, you were a "newbie," as in New Boy, whether you were a commissioned officer, a warrant officer, or an enlisted man. Second tour soldiers were not newbies; they already knew how to behave.

The oldest officer in Playtex was usually the CO (Commanding Officer), most often a major, but captains filled the job on occasion. The CO at the time when the floods came that October was a short, slim African American and the best commander many of the officers would ever have. He was the best because he trusted his officers to do their jobs, left them to do those jobs, and as long as they did their jobs properly, ran interference for them with the "higher ups" when necessary.

Early in his stint as CO of Playtex, the major called a formation of all the officers. When he spoke he said, "I am commanding officer of this company, but I'm not a Chinook pilot. I have been a Huey pilot for years, and truth be known, I prefer them to Chinooks. Chinooks are just too damn big and ugly. Yes, I had the Chinook transition course, but I really don't know that much about our mission and, as CO, I don't have time to learn. So here's what's going to happen; I am going to let the experts, you all, do the missions. I know you will do them well. When I fly, I will fly as a co-pilot and you can be sure I will be flying with the most experienced pilots, so that I don't screw things up too much. Meanwhile, I will handle the paperwork and keep higher headquarters off your collective asses. Company dismissed!"

And he did as he promised: the warrant officers flew the missions and never heard a word from above about anything. They would all miss the major when he left.

The pilots themselves came in two varieties: commissioned officers and warrant officers. The difference between the two was primarily education. Commissioned officers, in theory, had a college degree, or at least some college. They were expected to be more capable of handling all facets of military life, including administration. To the warrant officers they were all "RLOs,"—"Real Live Officers." Warrants, on the other hand, only required a high school diploma, or its equivalent, a General Education Development (GED) certificate. Warrants were expected to be technicians, highly skilled in one thing, in this case flying. Since commissioned officers always out rank warrants, the most junior 2nd lieutenant out ranked the most senior warrant officer. Socially, warrants and commissioned officers mostly stayed with their own groups, as did the enlisted men. It was much easier that way because you didn't have to remember who you had to call "Sir," instead of just calling them by their name.

The CO was probably between 35 and 40 years old, but that was really old compared to the warrant officers, who made up nearly all the rest of the pilots. The average age of Playtex's warrants was probably 21. The oldest of the warrants, CW2 Marvin Leonard, was 35 and considered a sage, due to his advanced years and vast experience. There were three captains: the Executive Officer (XO), the Operations Officer, and the Maintenance Officer. Below the captains, there were four 1st lieutenants, mostly holding down "assistant" jobs—assistant maintenance officer, assistant admin officer, etc. There were a few 2nd lieutenants too, but they were all warrants who had taken what was commonly called a "Penny Postcard" commission.

The Army was so desperate for officers in 1970 that any warrant could send in a request to the Department of the Army for a commission. If you had been a warrant for more than a year, you got a 1st Lieutenant's (1LT) silver bar in the return mail. If less than a year, a 2nd Lieutenant's (2LT) gold bar. The primary reason a warrant would take a Penny Postcard Commission was that it cut an entire year off the time owed to the Army. Take a warrant and you owed the Army three years. Take a commission and you only owed two, clearly showing the Army's view of the relative value of the two types of officers. Early release from service was something nearly everyone wanted in 1970, as witnessed by the acronym "US ARMY" on the patch over every soldier's left jungle fatigue pocket. All the soldiers considered it an abbreviation for "Uncle Sam Ain't Released Me Yet." Promotions came so fast in 1970 that it was nearly impossible for a commissioned officer to make it to Vietnam as an aviator and still be a 2nd lieutenant, since there was only a year between a gold bar and a silver bar. The schooling required to become an officer in Army Flight School took longer than it took to be promoted.

Playtex's warrant officers themselves came in two varieties: Warrant Officer 1 (WO1 or "Wobbly One"), the most junior rank, and Chief Warrant Officer 2 (CW2). A CW2 was someone who had been a warrant for over a year and had not screwed up badly enough to be passed over for promotion. It took a lot to screw up that badly and yet not get court-martialed. In the Army somewhere were also CW3s and CW4s, the oldest, most senior of the warrant officers, but there were none of these in Playtex. To graduate from Army Flight School and receive your warrant, you had to be at least 19 years old. If your grades had been good at Fort Rucker, Alabama, you might be offered Chinook transition, which took another six weeks, meaning you could be in Vietnam flying combat missions as an Aircraft Commander (AC) before you turned 20.

THE TECHNICIANS

The warrants flew the vast majority of Playtex's missions, rightly so, since they were the aviation technicians and, theoretically at least, the most qualified. It was a brilliant move on the Army's part, using warrant officers, men barely out of their teens, as the primary combat pilots in Vietnam. Their vision and reflexes were as good as they ever would be. Twenty-year-olds do not, as a rule, have a highly defined fear sense, particularly a fear of death. Death is something that happens to other people, not to them. Unlike the RLOs, they generally did not have four years of college behind them; instead they had an Olds 442, a Pontiac GTO, or a Chevy Chevelle SS396 in the parking lot back home, and car payments that came close to equaling their pay. They usually didn't have obligations beyond these car payments, i.e. no wife and kids back in the States. Most of all, they could fly eight to twelve hours a day, day after day, month after month, for a year. Their bodies were not yet too worn for such abuse, nor were their minds, but they would be if they survived, particularly if they survived two one-year tours. And here, in Vietnam, the Army gave these young men multi-million dollar high performance machines and sent them out with minimal supervision, a boy's second dream. Everyone knows what a boy's first dream is.

Referring to that first boy's dream, Playtex's base was named "Liftmaster Pad," sometimes informally called "Titty City" by the men of Playtex. It was actually a mini-airfield with a short runway suitable for lining up helicopters for takeoff on missions in the morning, a small control tower mounted on telephone poles where a single, bored air traffic controller worked, large tents for maintaining the aircraft, and steel parking revetments to hold the company's 16 Chinooks. On first viewing, the whole base at Liftmaster Pad was ugly: raw shacks on the sandy dirt with a scraggly banana tree here and there, but after a while you didn't see the ugly any more. It just was normal, not ugly at all. And that was how the war was, too—ugly at first, but after a while it was just normal.

Our story takes place in I Corps, the northern most part of what was then South Vietnam. Liftmaster Pad was on the edge of the coastal lowlands at Phu Bai, just a few miles south of Vietnam's old imperial capital, Hue City. A few miles to the west were the mountains where the fire support bases, the one's that Playtex supplied with ammunition for their howitzers and food and water for the men, were located. Liftmaster was located away from the rest of the 159th Assault Support Helicopter Battalion (ASHB). The other two Chinook companies, the "Pachyderms" and the "Varsity," as well as the Battalion Headquarters, were about a mile away from Liftmaster, next to the main runway at the Phu Bai airport. Liftmaster was out at the edge of the big American base clustered around that airport, close to the barbed wire and bunkers that protected the northwestern outer perimeter of the base. The men of Playtex liked it that way; being as far from headquarters as possible meant that they escaped a lot of "Army" things that went with being around senior RLOs, like saluting and wearing proper uniforms. Over on Phu Bai main, it was considered improper to walk through the company area naked to get to the showers, but no one at Liftmaster even noticed such things.

Of course, Playtex was not as far away from headquarters as the fourth company in the 159th ASHB, a CH-54 heavy lift helicopter company, call sign "The Hurricanes." They were 50 miles away from the rest of the battalion, at China Beach, down in the southern part of I Corps at Da Nang, down where the "round-eyed" American nurses, three big PXs, and Air Force Officers' Club at Da Nang airport were. On weekends there would be local lovelies outside the gate and discrete meetings might be arranged, between fancy dinners at the Air Force Clubs. None of those things were available at Phu Bai or Liftmaster, only the raw earth and buildings already starting to rot in the ever-damp air.

LIFTMASTER

If you arrived by helicopter at Liftmaster Pad, you would find yourself on the flight line, a short PSP (pierced steel planking, rectangular sheets of steel that lock together to make a temporary road or runway) runway, with steel revetments on one side and the company street on the other. As mentioned earlier, the revetments were steel walls about eight feet high and a foot wide, spaced far enough apart that you could easily taxi a Chinook between them. Liftmaster had 16 of them, one for each Chinook assigned to Playtex. Their purpose was to protect the aircraft from rocket and mortar blasts and shrapnel.

When you walked out of the flight line through the gate in the perimeter barbed wire by the tower and crossed the street, you were looking at the company headquarters and S-1 (admin offices). If you looked back, you would see a homemade sign hanging on the wire advertising Chinooks for sale at "Honest Mel's Used Hook Lot," an attempt at humor by two of the warrants. Once you were across the street, if you turned left at the Playtex sign, you would be looking at Playtex's outdoor theater where movies were shown most nights, the exception being, of course, when it rained. Someone built a shack at the back of the theater to house the projector and added a white-painted plywood screen at the front.

Anyone watching a movie had better use a lot of bug repellent, since lots of mosquitoes lived at Liftmaster, too. Some of them carried malaria, which is why there was a big bowl of pills by the mess hall entrance door. Monday through Saturday it was full of white pills and on Sunday, a larger red pill. The pills didn't prevent malaria, but they supposedly suppressed its symptoms. Who knows what they would do to the users when they were older. Like Agent Orange in Vietnam and atomic radiation in the 1950's, the U.S. military didn't pay too much attention to such things at the time. One immediate side effect of the pills was a mild case of diarrhea that lasted as long as you took them.

The seats at the outdoor theater were benches made from Chinook rotor blades—ones too shot up or otherwise damaged to be sent back to the depot to be repaired. One of them had a distinct dent about a foot from the end, deep enough to have damaged the rotor blade's spar, rendering it effectively destroyed. Once, while one of Playtex's Chinooks was dropping off a sling load in a saddle on an Army of Vietnam (ARVN) fire support base (FSB) in the mountains, an inattentive soldier walked down the side of the saddle near, very near, to where the helicopter was setting down its load. As he walked down the hillside, he apparently wasn't paying attention to the hovering Chinook; instead, he was shielding his eyes from the dirt its rotor wash was blowing up. In doing so he walked head first into the spinning aft rotor blades. His head disappeared instantly in a red spray, his body rolling on down to the bottom of the hill, blood spurting out as it tumbled.

Normally, this would not have done much, if any, damage to the rotor blade since human heads are relatively soft, but this ARVN soldier had his steel helmet on, and the impact badly dented the blade, even damaging the spar. The aircraft commander (AC) saw that the dead soldier's comrades weren't taking the accident well and, since they were all holding loaded rifles, rather than waiting to see what they would do next, he released the sling load immediately and flew away in the now badly vibrating helicopter. He landed at the next base about five miles away, and shut the aircraft down to see how much damage had been done. Too much, so maintenance came out and changed the blade, and since it was too damaged to repair, it became a bench in the theater. Whatever red had been on it was long since gone.

If you turned right at the Playtex sign and walked up the sidewalk, you would pass the operations bunker and the S-4 (supply) office. It was easy to tell which one was the operations bunker because it was the only building with sandbags around it. The sandbags had deteriorated now, ripped in places with weeds sprouting in the gaps. The S-4 was easily identifiable too, since it had a sign out front that read in big letters, "C Co Supply" with smaller letters underneath that announced modestly, "Support Extraordinaire," C Company's official motto. Behind the two offices was the enlisted living area. Continue on straight past the S-4, and you would come to the officer's living area.

Playtex's living area, both officer and enlisted was, of course, set out in an orderly, military fashion. All the buildings, except the ammo storage building, were SEA (Southeast Asia) huts, "hootches" to the men who lived in them. They were all one story, made of plywood, about 20 feet wide by 50 feet long, with tin roofs. The roofs all had been reinforced with sandbags on each side, connected with communications wire to help keep the tin panels in place during high winds. None of the SEA huts, enlisted or officer, were sandbagged on the sides to protect against incoming mortar or rocket.

This is not to say that there was no protection against "incoming."

There were sandbagged bunkers here and there between some of the hootches—basically half culverts with sandbags piled around them—for the men of Playtex to shelter in when the mortars and rockets started to fall, but the North Vietnamese Army (NVA) rarely bothered to shell Phu Bai. They would have to move through too much open land between the forest and the perimeter of the base for them to get within range for their rocket launchers or mortars. They would be spotted by the Americans well before they could get their weapons set up. Both sides knew full well that "what can be seen can be killed," and with the American artillery covering nearly all of I Corps, and Cobra gunships that could be in the air within minutes of being scrambled, the NVA knew they would have been pounded by one or both within minutes of being seen. So, the NVA didn't often bother with Liftmaster Pad.

Where there were no bunkers between the SEA huts, there were clotheslines. Rather than count on the Vietnamese laundry, many of the men hand washed their own clothes in the sinks by the common showers. When it was dry outside the clotheslines would be full of once-white tee-shirts, green shorts and socks, green flight suits, and green jungle fatigues, all flapping in the wind like the flags of the member nations outside the UN.

The SEA huts were put up by the Seabees (Navy Construction Battalions) in one furious rush, two years before our story begins. For some unknown reason, all the hootches were painted light blue, but the paint rapidly faded as the wood warped in the heat and humidity, leaving the walls mottled. The larger enlisted billeting area was close to the flight line, behind the company headquarters and other offices. All the enlisted hootches, except for the ones occupied by the senior non-commissioned officers (NCO), were split into two sections by a partition down the middle. Four enlisted men lived on each side. The sergeant major had his own half of one SEA hut, more space than any of the officers, except the CO.

Walk on to the right past the enlisted area and the theater, and you came to the officer's hootches. The officer's area was separate, surrounded by a privacy fence about five feet high made out of sheets of roofing tin. When the rains came that fall, Playtex's officer housing area felt it, too. Although built on land slightly higher than the enlisted area, water still stood everywhere in the officer's courtyard. The horseshoe pit was under water, as was the area around the stone barbeque grill, because after the first week of rain, the ground, pure sand or not, was too saturated to absorb more water.

The sandbagged bunkers between the rows of hootches were full of water too, not that it mattered, since hardly anyone used them. Even when the pilots, or at least those who had been there a while, heard mortar rounds coming in during the night they mostly ignored them, rolling over and going back to sleep. While the NVA didn't often shoot directly at Liftmaster Pad, when they did, they mostly shot at the antenna farm half a mile away; rounds never came close to hitting C Company's hootches. Battalion Headquarters, over at the Phu Bai Main, was not so lucky. In one attack, a 122mm Katyusha rocket, fired at random, hit the mess hall when it was full of men, causing many casualties. But in general, the NVA ignored Liftmaster Pad and Playtex's parked Chinooks.

Between the second and third rows of the officer's hootches, the Seabees had poured concrete all the way across instead of just putting in a sidewalk, like in the rest of the billeting area. The Playtex officers had scrounged some fiberglass matting and used it as a roof to cover the area, so it became the Officers' Club patio. Shady in the sun and dry-ish in the rain, the patio was always the second most popular off-duty gathering spot, after the Club itself, of course. In the middle of the patio was a homemade ping pong table: plywood cut to the correct size with "hundred mile an hour" tape (so called because it was sometimes used to cover bullet holes in rotor blades until they could be changed) covering the seams. Playing the seams on the plywood table became quite an art, but hurt your game on a real table. Chairs lined either side, so that the next player in line could give a running commentary on each game as it was played. There should have been a brass plaque on the ping pong table, because it once had the honor of saving a Playtex pilot's life.

One evening, the pilots in the Club heard someone on the patio yelling at the top of his lungs, "Help, help, dammit, somebody get out here and help me! NOW!"

CW2 Marvin Leonard jumped up from his bar stool and stuck his head out the screen door to see what was going on. There, on top of the ping pong table was WO1 Barry Fivelson, jumping up and down in near panic as he pointed frantically at one of the legs of the ping pong table. A small snake—a very poisonous Bamboo Pit Viper, a very angry, very poisonous Bamboo Pit Viper—was climbing the leg of the table to get to Fivelson. Fivelson didn't have his pistol with him, so he couldn't shoot it. Shooting at the snake wouldn't have been a good idea, since Fivelson was in the middle of all the hootches and who knew where the ricochets would have gone. That said, hootches or not, he would've shot at it if he could've. Leonard grabbed a hoe that was leaning against the wall of the Club, and dispatched the viper in short order. After having done so, Leonard then demanded that the snake's intended victim treat him to drinks for the rest of the month. Fivelson, the intended victim, claimed he had no idea what he did to piss the snake off, but all present agreed that it had been one pissed off Bamboo Pit Viper.

On one side of the patio was the Officers' Club, and on the other, some of the pilot's hootches. At the end toward the little courtyard inside the tin fence, was a red, white, and blue cast iron US Postal Service mailbox. It had been ripped down from a telephone pole back in California before Playtex left the States for Vietnam and now took the officer's letters home, instead of accepting some Californian's household bills. No one knew if there had been mail inside the box when it was "liberated" and, if there had been, if the letters inside had been re-mailed before the box left the U.S. Either way, the mailbox was a nice little touch of home there in the courtyard.

Speaking of courtyard: beyond the mailbox was a stretch of ground that served as the actual courtyard, but it was really just another patch of sand with a sickly banana tree here and there. It contained a barbeque grill and a horseshoe pit. Surrounding the courtyard was more of the tin privacy fence. The sidewalk through the courtyard led to a hole in the center of the fence, perhaps what might be considered a gate. Through that gate was the officer's latrine, a small screened hut containing a covered "three-holler." It was not exactly private; you could hold a nice conversation with two of your fellows while taking care of business. Outside the latrine were also two tubes stuck in the ground that formerly held powder for artillery, now serving as urinals. In the latrine under each of the three thrones, the waste fell into a half oil drum. Each of the receptacles was hauled out through a hatch in the back and burned in diesel fuel by a Vietnamese worker first thing in the morning every day. This event provided a good reason not to be on the Officers' Club deck in the morning, since the Club was usually right downwind from the burn site.

Walk on straight through the officer's area, past the ping pong table and the Officers' Club, and you came to the company mess hall. This building was divided into two sections, the larger for the enlisted men and the smaller for the officers. The food was the same on both sides, since whether officer or enlisted, you walked through a cafeteria line to get it. The drinks were the same too, re-constituted milk, weak ice tea, or bug juice, an ersatz "cool aide."

The mess hall cooks were all soldiers, but the cleaning and dish washing was done by Vietnamese, hired by the battalion admin office so that the men of the 159th ASHB wouldn't have to pull KP (Kitchen Police) duty. All of the food served was imported from the U.S., which meant that a lot of it was stale, canned, frozen, or otherwise preserved. The food would keep you alive, but it was real Army cooking, with all that implies. Still, given the resources they had to work with, the mess hall soldiers did well; there was plenty of quantity to keep young bodies going even if the quality might sometimes be lacking. The mess hall's hours were fixed, so if you didn't get there in time, it was C rations for you.

Next to the mess hall was the sand combat volleyball court, scene of many bloody, but non-lethal, battles. Mostly the battles were enlisted men verses enlisted men and warrants verses warrants, since no one wanted bad blood to develop between the two. Perhaps that was because everyone remembered that everyone else was armed. The deep, soft sand kept the injuries to bruises and sometimes bloody noses.

If you turned right as you left the officer's area, instead of heading straight for the mess hall, you came to the officer's showers. The water for the showers came from a small water tower, which consisted of a large black rubber bladder mounted on a platform about ten feet off the ground. Every other day, a truck would come by with water that was technically potable, but if you froze it to make ice cubes you could see streaks of dirt in it. If you froze it anyway, you couldn't use ice cube trays because you couldn't see the dirt in the cubes, and consequently your drinks tasted gritty. Instead, ice was made in a rectangular stainless steel pan stolen from the mess hall; that way you could just use an ice pick to break out the ice around the dirt before you put it in your drink.

About 1700 hours each day, one of the Vietnamese workers would come by and fire up two gasoline-powered emersion heaters in a separate steel tank to provide hot water for the showers. Sometimes the water was hot and sometimes it wasn't, luck of the draw, really. There was a similar rig down in the enlisted area, but it was much larger than the officer's. Larger or not, it still didn't work any better than the officer's did. If you got back late from flying or working, there would be no hot water at all, so everyone tried to time things so they could hit the showers no later than 1900 hours, not that it helped much. Still, even a cold shower was better than staying sweaty all the time.

It being Vietnam and all, none of the hootches, neither officer nor enlisted, were heated. It was not usually a problem, that is, until the monsoon season when it got chilly enough for a jacket. The hootch "windows" didn't have glass, only wire screening. On the outside of the screen was a sheet of plywood, propped open to allow air to circulate or lowered to keep out the rain. Because the hootches were not heated or air conditioned, when something got wet in the monsoon season, it generally stayed that way.

Since clothes could not be hung outside on the clotheslines between the hootches when it was raining, nothing could really dry, and everything quickly began to mildew, even leather boots. The officer's flight suits and jungle fatigues stayed damp, even when they tried to get them dry in the empty hootch that was designated a clothes-drying space. The "clothes-drying hootch" only worked in theory; since there was no heating and the humidity was 100%, the clothes that were hung there remained damp, no matter how long they were left hanging. The seemingly unending rain had effects evident in ways other than permanently damp clothes, such as mildewing beds and paperwork. It also got damn depressing after a while.

Back to the start of this war story: "A fish just walked across the sidewalk in front of me," the tall, thin young man said as he came hurrying through the door of the Officers' Club. The tall, thin young man, let's call him Strider, had been on his way to the mess hall, splashing through puddles and rain, when the fish walked across the sidewalk in front of him. It wasn't a really big fish, maybe about ten inches long, but it was a fish . . . walking.

Open mouthed, Strider ran into the Officers' Club to report what he had seen, but the three pilots sitting on the bar stools just laughed: first, attack snakes at the ping pong table and now, a walking fish in the courtyard. Right. As their laughter died down another one of the pilots walked in carrying a fish that he had also seen "walking" across the grass area by the horseshoe pit, the horseshoe pit that was now more the "horseshoe pond" than the "horseshoe pit." He sat the fish on the bar and it promptly began to walk toward the far end, away from the men, much to their astonishment. CW2 Steve Maas, the man who brought the fish in, proclaimed it to be an Asian walking catfish. They use their stiff whiskers as "feet" to move from one pond to another. They are quite common in that area of the world, but were a real novelty to the Americans who had never heard of, let alone seen, a walking fish. The catfish can breathe air for relatively short periods, letting it move from ponds that are drying up to ones still full of water, an excellent survival tactic. Right now they were apparently exploring new turf, like the new "horseshoe pit ponds" and "barbeque grill ponds."

If, when you entered the officer's area, you turned left instead of continuing straight ahead past the horseshoe pit and barbeque grill toward the Officers' Club, the first hootch you came to was home to three of the men central to this non-war war story: Strider, Jerry Cobb, and Dick Steiner. You could tell it was theirs by the Sears "Coldspot air conditioner" built into the wall by the door and the "Fly Navy" bumper sticker posted next to it.

THE ROOMMATES

STRIDER

Strider, the tall, thin young man who was the first to see the walking fish, was a brand new CW2, having just arrived in Vietnam and having been promoted from WO1 to CW2 only the month before. He was still a copilot and so had no good war stories, not yet anyway. He was tall at 6'4", skinny, and had black hair and big feet. Strider was of average age for Playtex's warrants, 21, but unlike most of them, he was married. At 18, with the draft and war looming, he wanted to experience as much of life as he could before the war took him—like, for example, he wanted very much to have as much sex as he could possibly get, always a boy's first dream. The best way to do that was to have a married life with his high school sweetheart. Out of that experience, he hoped, would come a child.

Strider got his bride and all that comes with marriage, and, especially when it's two healthy 18 year olds enjoying each other without reservation, that's quite a bit. The child arrived before Strider joined Playtex, but just barely. His son was born three weeks before he left the United States for Vietnam. He missed his wife and son desperately, like all the married young men he knew did. Unlike most of the first tour pilots in Playtex, he had a little more flight time through his experience as a flight instructor, having spent a year in the States between flight school and Chinook transition flying Korean War-vintage OH-13s at Fort Campbell, Kentucky. Strider had only been flying with Playtex for a few weeks when the rains began and wasn't sure yet when it was appropriate to be scared and when it was not. He had not lost the belief that aircraft commanders (AC), particularly Chinook ACs, could do no wrong. The last vestige of that disappeared when he became an AC himself.

Strider's two roommates, CW2 Dick Steiner and CW2 Jerry Cobb, were both accomplished ACs. After interviewing him to make sure he was a good guy and would fit into their lifestyle, they allowed him to buy one-third of the room from a departing CW2, that is, buy one-third of the substantial comforts, at least by Vietnam standards, built into the room. Strider's first contributions to the hootch's interior decoration were two posters sent by his wife, one of Peter Fonda and Dennis Hopper on motorcycles from the movie *Easy Rider* and the other of Alfred E. Newman from *Mad Magazine* dressed up as Uncle Sam with the caption, "Who Needs You?" These two posters went well with the rather incongruous poster of Snoopy dancing over the caption, "Today is the first day of the rest of your life" which hung next to the front door of the hootch. Indeed, when you went out that door with your flight gear it was the first day of the rest of your life, but the thought always occurred to Strider that it might be the last, too.

Normally, living quarters were just assigned to new arrivals and that was that, but the CO found it better to let the officer's more or less determine their own roommates, less friction that way. In this case, the living arrangement among the three worked well, since they were of a common temperament. Dick and Strider didn't drink too much and, while Jerry did, he kept his drinking mostly to the Officers' Club and didn't bring drunken behavior back to the hootch. Dick loved music, but he played his music softly or wore his headphones, so the other two weren't disturbed by it.

Strider smoked a pipe, tended to read science fiction novels or write letters home, so he, too, did not interfere with the others. Until recently he had smoked nothing but the "Red Death," unfiltered Pall Mall cigarettes in their red package, like his father did. The pipe seemed more sophisticated than cigarettes, so he thought he would try it. Turned out he liked it a lot and never went back to cigarettes, except when there was no pipe tobacco available. His pipe, tobacco pouch, and lighter fit nicely in his flight suit's lower right trouser pocket. Within a few days he had mastered the art of flying a helicopter while smoking a pipe, happily puffing away as he flew along. Like he did with cigarettes, Strider inhaled the pipe smoke; to his way of thinking, getting the nicotine hit was the only reason to smoke at all. It felt good.

All three roommates were willing to cook dinner in turn when they weren't flying, though the dishes tended to be rather basic when it was Strider's turn. Cobb smoked, so Strider's pipe smoking in the hootch wasn't an issue. Steiner didn't smoke, but never commented on the smell left by all the tobacco smoke clouding the hootch. Steiner was about the only pilot in Playtex who didn't smoke, but since cigarettes were 10 cents a pack, everyone could afford them, and since they were considered "cool," many who probably wouldn't have smoked in normal circumstances, did so in Vietnam.

CW2 DICK STEINER

The first pilot sitting in the Officers' Club when Strider came in to tell them about the walking fish was CW2 Dick Steiner. He was about 5'10" and at 22 already had thinning hair on top. He called himself "Super Jew," though Steiner showed no signs whatsoever of being a practicing Jew, or a Jew at all, for that matter. In fact, no one in Playtex knew or cared if he actually was Jewish. He seemed to say he was "Super Jew" for the shock value, though no one was shocked. Perhaps the only sign of Steiner's potential Jewishness was that as the Officers' Club officer, he refused to decorate for Christmas, against his beliefs, he said, but nobody minded that either, since there wasn't much Christmas spirit in Vietnam that year. . . .

One of the reasons neither of his roommates really cared what Steiner called himself, was because his "Care Packages." The boxes of goodies his family mailed him from the States were among the best anyone in Playtex received. Steiner's dad was a vice president at Hormel Meats and sent him an unending supply of the company's products. These goodies greatly boosted morale by vastly contributing to their ability to cook their own meals instead of relying on the mess hall or C rations. This "home cooking" saved the three of them from some of the violent rounds of diarrhea that most everyone else got from dining in the mess hall. For a couple days after it struck, some of the pilots had to fly wearing homemade diapers, much to their chagrin. The missions must be done and, since the aircraft could not land in the middle of hostile territory to satisfy nature, diapers it was, much to the amusement of the three roommates.

Beyond care packages, Steiner had the first cassette tape player anyone in Playtex had ever seen. Nearly everyone else had huge reel-to-reel tape players, but the little cassette player seemed far more sophisticated somehow, even though it had nowhere near the power of bigger reel-to-reels. After a rest and recuperation (R&R) week in Taiwan, Steiner had an excellent collection of all the latest pop albums on cassette. The albums were pirated, of course, but they still sounded pretty good to helicopter pilots already losing their hearing to the roar of their aircraft's engines and transmissions. A good copy LP went for one dollar in Taipei and for another dollar you could get the same songs on cassette. Everyone put in a list of albums they wanted and Steiner's star rose even higher when he came back with all of them. He had no problem letting anyone copy them to their systems, so long as they let him copy any of theirs he wanted.

The speakers for Steiner's stereo system were mounted on the wall above his bed, spread out three feet apart for maximum stereo effect. Between them he hung a Vietnamese conical straw hat he had bought at the Gook Shop, the casually racist name for the Vietnamese sundry shop, as his little decorating contribution to the decor.

Unfortunately for Steiner, Jerry Cobb had bought a homemade Vietnamese crossbow from the Gook Shop which he hung on the wall over his bed as his contribution. A quiver full of bamboo arrows came with the crossbow and hung on the same hook. One evening as they sat there contemplating life, Strider and Cobb decided that the hat made an ideal target for the crossbow, but when they fired, they discovered that the arrows had warped and seldom went anywhere even vaguely close to where they were aimed. In fact, the first three arrows Cobb fired missed the hat entirely and hit the plywood wall within inches of Steiner's speakers, sending Steiner into an apoplectic fit, threatening their domestic harmony. The problem was solved by moving the hat from between the speakers to the back of the entry door to the hootch, which, after the other pilots found out about, also cured the problem of people walking in without knocking.

Steiner's job as club officer was critical to the Playtex pilot's morale. The Officers' Club was not part of the PX system and so was not an "official" club, but rather an informal one. Playtex's officers liked it like that, because that meant there were no silly formal rules, like no hats on the bar, no weapons in the Club, etc. After the barmaids quit (more about them later) it was strictly self-service and you could dress as you like, or, for that matter, not at all, since you had to pass the Club to reach the showers. It was not uncommon to see an officer having a drink wearing only a towel, if even that, since walking to the showers could generate a powerful thirst.

You could play poker in the Club for as high stakes as you could (or thought you could) afford, and drink all you could hold for 10 cents a beer and 25 cents for a mixed drink or a soft drink. Even at those prices the Club was profitable, though most of the profits went for new bar glasses which usually lasted less than a month. Somehow they always got smashed quickly. Best of all, the Playtex Club was open 24 hours a day, 7 days a week, 365 days a year. All the pilots went into the Club every day because the operations officer kept a list of who would be flying posted there, near the front door. This greatly improved business—why not have a drink, since you were already there anyway?

As club officer, Dick would collect all the officers' booze ration cards once a month. On his first day off, he would sign out a Chinook, load a jeep into the back of it, and fly it to Da Nang. He would park it with Playtex's sister company, The Hurricanes, at China Beach and drive the jeep out the gate to make the rounds of the PXs to buy any bar items, like glasses, the Club needed. For his last stop he would visit the big Class VI (liquor) store at the Da Nang Air Force Base and buy all the hard stuff needed for another 30 days. Mostly he would buy vodka, gin, bourbon, and scotch. Of course, he added selections of his own choosing for the bar game "7/14/21."

In 7/14/21 all the players roll the dice in turn, with only aces counting. Roll an ace and you must roll again. The seventh ace rolled named the drink, like, for example, a mixture of crème de menthe and Amoretto or something equally disgusting. The 14th ace bought the drink and the unlucky roller of the 21st ace drank it, preferably in one gulp. Cobb, experienced drinker that he was, once lost three times in a row and had to quit the game due extreme distress (e.g. throwing up four times in a row).

Steiner also bought 151 proof rum for "flaming hookers." Flaming hookers are quite simple, really: take a shot glass full of 151, light it off, and drink it while it's burning. You got extra points for setting the glass down empty, but still on fire. Many mustaches were removed by flaming hookers, even if you took the precaution of having a "Crash truck," a fellow pilot with a wet towel, standing by to put out the flames when you inevitably spilled it down the front of yourself.

Steiner bought the beer by the case locally at Phu Bai's PX. The beer was in steel cans shipped from the States and was often flat when opened, but no one cared, since it was usually cold and more importantly, had alcohol in it. Playtex drank far more beer than any other kind of alcohol since it was cheap and the supposedly potable water supplied by the Army was disgustingly gritty.

More important than being club officer, Steiner was an excellent AC. He did his missions and did them well. He never complained when asked to fly more, even when he was very tired. He probably should have complained, but he didn't.

JERRY COBB

The "shortest" of the three, that is to say the one with the least time remaining until his tour in Vietnam was over, was CW2 Jerry Cobb. Unlike all the other Playtex warrants, except one, Cobb was on his second tour in Vietnam as a helicopter pilot. He had flown Hueys the first time and was tired of being in the middle of a giant flight of assault helicopters flying into hot landing zones (LZ). He wanted something different this go, something that didn't involve Hueys hauling infantrymen, a.k.a. "grunts" around. Cobb was also a born rebel, a fighter against the establishment, i.e. the executive officer (XO). To Strider, Cobb was at least a minor deity, since not only was he an AC, he had been an instructor pilot (IP) at Fort Rucker, Alabama, between Vietnam tours. Strider's short stint as an IP in OH-13's at Fort Campbell, Kentucky, before he came over to Vietnam, gave him a hint that being an instructor did not make you all-knowing, but being a Fort Rucker IP and a Chinook AC, well, that was entirely a different thing. He listened carefully for words of wisdom from Jerry Cobb.

When Strider arrived in Playtex, Cobb had a Poncho Villa mustache, big and proud. The XO told him to shave it to Army regulation size, meaning it could not go past the corners of his mouth. Cobb went to the S-1, the admin office of the company, and pulled the regulation on grooming. He discovered that, while it did say a mustache couldn't go past the corners of the mouth, it did not say how long the mustache could be, so Cobb waxed his straight out. At its peak it was nearly two inches long, looking like giant nose hairs on his upper lip. The mustache made the XO livid, but like the CO promised, he kept the XO off Cobb's back so that Jerry could fly the missions, and the mustache stayed. It stayed until Cobb got tired of it a couple weeks later, but before he shaved it off completely he checked the regulation again. It did not say the mustache had to be even, so he shaved off the right side, leaving the left side sticking out, still looking like deranged nose hairs. Two days later, tired of this particular game and ready for a new one, Jerry shaved and the mustache was gone completely, never to return.

Cobb was also the leader of the Phu Bai Glee Club, an informal singing group, nearly always made up of inebriated warrants. The Glee Club met in the Officers' Club whenever Jerry felt like singing. After numerous beers, Jerry would break out his guitar and start playing, mostly country songs. He could play any tune, and was happy to do requests. He also wrote music. His own favorite work, first sung by the Phu Bai Glee Club, was "The Mang Yang Song," named after the mountain pass where the Viet Minh destroyed a major French convoy in the last battle of that war in 1954. On his first tour in Vietnam, he had been part of a relief effort for another flood and almost crashed in the Mang Yang during bad weather. Right afterwards his unit was transferred south to the Mekong Delta. In 1970 you could still see the French graves when you flew up the valley that held the Mang Yang, hundreds of little depressions in the soil. Legend had it that the dead were buried standing up, facing France.

The Mang Yang Song
I was flying down to Quinn Yan,

Just to help a little bit,
Carrying some rice and all that shit.
But the weather in the pass,
It was right down on the grass,
And I've only got 200 pounds of gas.
Oh, I nearly lost my ass,
In the mouth of Mang Yang Pass,
The weather it was 300 and 2.
Oh, my cheeks were hugging,
And my pucker string was tugging,
And I thought that my flying days were through.
Oh my dear old daddy Gray,
Are you sending me away?
Down to the Delta, where I'll die quick?
Oh, I'm going across the country,
In a big old Caribou,
And I'm never coming back to old Pleiku.

The Glee Club met in the evening starting about 2100 hours and continued until the XO, who lived next door to the Officers' Club, would come in to break it up, usually somewhere around midnight.

"All of you go to bed NOW. Right NOW! GO!" the XO would yell. The XO tried to be a hard ass, but he was really yelling because he knew that some of those Glee Club members would be up before daylight and off at dawn on eight or more hours of missions. Young men or not, they needed sleep to continue to function without killing themselves and their crews. The mission must be done and it is done better when the crews are at least semi-rested, not hung over, or, technically, still drunk.

"Fuck you, you son of a bitch!" Cobb would yell back, usually followed by a bar stool thrown across the room. It was major insubordination, near mutiny in fact, but again, the XO knew that the CO would not do anything about it. Cobb might drink too much, but he was good at his job and always got the missions done, no matter how late he'd been up leading the Glee Club. Funny thing was, Cobb and the XO actually got on quite well at other times. They often flew together, always with Cobb as AC and the XO as copilot. Strider suspected, but didn't know for sure, that the XO was concerned about Cobb and was checking to make sure his drinking wasn't hurting his performance.

THE HOOTCH

These three, Gerry, Dick, and Strider, were not among the damp ones when the rains came, since they had planned ahead for the inevitable weather contingencies. No, their boots and clothes were clean and dry at the start of each day, monsoon or no monsoon. No mildew grew on them no matter how wet the day might be.

Back before the rains came, they made many trips to the Phu Bai garbage dump and salvaged the Styrofoam slabs that the 2.75" folding fin aerial rockets (2.75 FFAR), the ones the Cobras fired, had been packed in for shipment from the States. The three of them used the Styrofoam to insulate the walls of their hootch, closing them up completely with plywood, the windows too. For ventilation and cooling in the ten months of hot weather, they had a Sears Coldspot air conditioner, scrounged from who knows where, built directly into the wall by the front door. For the cooler nights they had a small space heater that worked nicely in the enclosed living space. The room thus insulated, it was warm and dry during the monsoon and cool and dry the rest of the time, making their hootch a popular place for socializing with their fellow aviators.

This hootch wasn't Strider's first. When he arrived at Playtex, he only knew one of the pilots from before and that individual was not his favorite person in the world, so he accepted without comment the XO's assignment of a hootch with one of the Penny Post Card Lieutenants as a roommate. His first roommate was disconcerting, to say the least. At first meeting, he seemed normal enough, but that sense of normality passed on the very first evening when Strider came in after dinner to find all the lights in the hootch off, the only illumination provided by the flickering dials of his roommate's reel-to-reel TEAC tape player.

The roommate had large speakers mounted on the far wall of the hootch to better get the stereo spread of the sound. He didn't like to listen through a headset, but so as not to offend Strider, he turned the volume down to where it was merely loud, instead of deafening. The tape player was state of the art, with an auto reverse, meaning that you could play both sides of the tape without having to turn the reel over manually. The song he was playing when Strider came in was Steppenwolf's version of the Hoyt Axton song "The Pusher," made popular in 1968 in the film *Easy Rider*, an odd choice for a pilot, Strider thought, especially the part about all the drugs the singer had taken. After the song completed it started again. After the next time it completed it started once again. Strider's roommate had recorded it over and over so that it would play for an hour and a half straight.

But thankfully, that wasn't the only song Strider's roommate had recorded. The next night he put on Kenny Rodgers "Ruby Don't Take Your Love to Town," also recorded over and over for an hour and half of continuous replay. On the third day, before hearing his roommate's musical selection for the evening, Strider went to the XO to ask, beg if necessary, for a hootch change. The XO recommended he "apply" to move in with Cobb and Steiner, since their third roommate had completed his tour and would be departing in a few days. After his "application" was accepted, and after paying $150.00 to the departing roommate for his share, Strider moved in. He liked his new "home" a lot from the first day, particularly after his less than ideal musical experience in the other hootch.

Even so, nice hootch or not, he was still not sure about life in Vietnam, because on the second night in his new home, as he lay in his bed, he woke to a soft "boom" in the distance. Moments later there was a slightly louder "boom," followed shortly by a very loud "BOOM" that shook the hootch. Strider sat bolt upright in bed and yelled out, "Is that mortars?" Cobb sat up in his bed, listened to the next in the series of booms and said, "Yes." With that, he lay back down and promptly went back to sleep. Steiner, apparently, didn't even wake up. Strider decided if Cobb and Steiner could sleep through a mortar attack, so could he. This must not be one of those times when you were supposed to be afraid. It was time for Strider to start building "cool" points, so he pretended to be asleep until the mortar impacts were long past.

It wasn't only the insulation, air conditioning, and heater that kept the three comfortable in their hootch. They had the only real porcelain bathtub in C Company, perhaps in all the 159th ASHB, perhaps in the entire 101st, maybe in all of I Corps. It was a full-size, pristine white enamel one, normal enough for the States, but downright elegant for a SEA hut hootch. They also had a 20 gallon electric water heater brought from the

States when Playtex deployed, so they didn't have to depend on the inherently undependable immersion heaters used in the rest of the officers showers. Another prize, undoubtedly the finest after the air conditioner, was a Maytag wringer clothes washing machine, also the only one in the company. These three comforts were pure and true luxuries all, and combined, gave the roommates comforts that not even the CO of Playtex enjoyed. They did not brag about these things, or even mention them to their brother pilots, for that matter. Rubbing in non-flying things to your fellows was not cool.

You could put the plug in the tub if you wanted to take a bath, but the roommates rarely did, since the water, while deemed potable, wasn't exactly strained before being loaded into the company water tank. You could see the dirt in the water if you ran a tub full and it felt gritty when you sat in it. Hiding the dirt under bubble bath would have been unmanly, although Strider would admit, he had at least considered it when he was particularly tired and stiff after sitting in the cockpit seat for eight hours in a row, and so showers it was.

To take a shower you first filled the washing machine with warm water. When you were ready to shower, you connected the washer's drain to the hose that lead to the shower head and then turned the washer on to the "drain" cycle. You just had to get out of the shower and turn it off before the washer's tub was completely empty, so that you would not damage the pump by running it dry. Spare parts for the washer took a long time to get to Liftmaster from the States, so damaging the washer was severely frowned upon. The water, of course, just drained out onto the ground at the back of the hootch, since there was no sewer system anywhere in Playtex's area.

Also hooked into the hot water heater was a white porcelain sink that did double duty as both a kitchen and bathroom sink. Shave in the morning, wash the dishes at night, very nice indeed. The water did not have to go through the washing machine to use the sink, so turning on the hot water faucet and having hot water was an unparalleled luxury in Playtex, right up there with the air conditioner and washing machine itself. The water from the sink too, drained out directly on the ground, again, not a problem.

Beyond being a pump for the shower, the washing machine worked very well at its prime function of keeping their clothes clean. Unlike the clothes the other pilots sent to the base laundry, the three roommate's white clothes were not all gray or worse, pink, from something red being thrown in with the white stuff. After the three washed and put their clothes through the wringer, they put them in their own personal clothes dryer.

The three built a closet on the wall by the entrance door where the fourth bunk should have been, and installed four 200-watt light bulbs, spaced evenly along its interior length. Over the light bulbs they put up screen to keep them from touching the clothes, a potential fire hazard. After adding some clotheslines, they had a perfect clothes-drying closet. It took about three hours per load for the clothes to go from wrung out wet to completely dry. The clothes were always very stiff since no fabric softener was used, but that was OK because they were well and truly dry. The three kept quiet about the closet, too, so no one else would ask them to share and they didn't offer. Strider wondered why no one got suspicious about why they always had clean, dry clothes, but he certainly wasn't going to ask anyone.

Strider had another use for the clothes-drying closet that was near and dear to his heart. Strider had big feet. Unfortunately, not only were they size 14, his feet were also very narrow, AA or A, depending on the shoe. Ever since he had been 14 years old his feet had been that size and since then, he had rarely been able to just walk into a store and buy shoes—stores just didn't normally carry size 14 narrow shoes, anywhere. When he got to the Army, Strider discovered to his delight that his big, narrow feet were no problem at all. Combat boots in 14 narrow fit him perfectly, almost like they had been custom made. When he was assigned to Vietnam, he heard stories about boots rotting to pieces in the damp and the fear grew in his mind that his boots would rot. After they had fallen apart, he would not be able to get more and would have to suffer for his entire tour with too-small shoes. To assuage his fears of sore feet, Strider brought three pairs of new combat boots with him to Vietnam in his duffle bag. At the end of each day, he would take off his wet boots and put them into the clothes-drying closet, removing yesterday's now toasty dry pair. He would polish them before putting the now dry pair under his bed. He would pull out the third pair and put them next to his locker, all ready for the following day's wear. It seemed to be working well, since none of the three pair showed any wear or evidence of rot. So far . . .

As alluded to earlier, when missions didn't interfere, the roommates took turns cooking dinner instead of eating in the mess hall. They were well prepared. In addition to their other comforts in their back room, they had a full-sized refrigerator that also came from who knows where, to store the perishable food they had scrounged. On the counter they had built, they also had a hot plate and an electric skillet to work with when cooking the good things that the refrigerator and their storage shelves held. Between their pooled care packages and what they could scrounge, they ate very well indeed.

What they could not scrounge, they could procure through other methods. Once, Steiner had been hauling an external load of 6,000 pounds of frozen steaks in boxes of 20 each from the Main Supply point at Camp Eagle over to the Phu Bai airport, when, just as he was about to set it down, the load "accidently" released from the cargo hook and fell the last 20 feet. The sling burst open on impact, the boxes of steaks spilling out onto the runway. For a moment, all activity stopped at Phu Bai, that is, stopped until everyone realized just what had been in that sling load. In the next moment, men appeared from everywhere, all running to grab a case or two of steaks. Strider, who "just happened to be in the area," managed to retrieve one case himself. This promptly joined their other food in the back-room refrigerator.

Steaks were rare, though, so dinner was usually pizza or some concoction, such as hamburger and baked beans with catsup and bacon on the top (Dick's alleged Jewishness not withstanding) or some vaguely Jewish dish Dick would cook using his special care packages. Steiner introduced both Cobb and Strider to gefilte fish, something they were not sure they had missed before they knew about it. That said, after the third time they had it they began to look forward to it. If the three needed some ingredient not available through care packages, such as fresh baguettes or a more high-toned wine than that sold at the Class VI store, they would sometimes ask their Boeing Technical Representative to buy it for them in town when he was next out, which was nearly every day. The Boeing Tech Rep was a civilian and liked working in Vietnam. He had been in-country for five years now, working down south at first and then coming north when the CH-47Cs were introduced. As a civilian he could go anywhere he wanted off the base, for example the markets and bakeries in Hue City, while the Playtex officers were restricted to the base unless on a mission.

The Tech Rep had an M-151 jeep that he had purchased somewhere, not an unusual thing in and of itself, since many military jeeps somehow wound up as civilian vehicles in Vietnam. At another base where he had been working before he joined Playtex, the men from the aircraft paint shop stole his jeep one day. They returned it three days later painted lipstick pink. Far from being offended, the Tech Rep liked the new color scheme so much he had a Vietnamese shop make a matching pink and white stripped surrey top, complete with fringes, to replace the original GI issue, olive drab (OD) green canvas. The tech rep then drove that lovely pink jeep all over the country for the next three years and was never bothered by the Viet Cong (VC), or anyone else, for that matter. Perhaps everyone believed that a man in a pink jeep could not possibly be a threat.

Because he was such a valuable resource in procuring materials not otherwise available, the Tech Rep had a standing invitation to any event in their hootch, including dinner, whenever he wanted to come. It didn't hurt that he always brought a nice bottle of French wine when he did.

About two weeks before the start of the monsoon, Steiner had read an article in *The Stars and Stripes* about the upcoming typhoon season. He figured from the article that there would be major damage to the hootches if a typhoon hit, given how flimsy they were, so he and Strider went outside to inspect their roof. It didn't look good, with nails popping through the tin here and there, so they climbed up and hammered them back down. Then they noticed the sandbags that had been put on the roof when the SEA huts were originally built had mostly rotted; holes in them let the sand run out to the point where they were just about useless. Strider had never been in a hurricane or a typhoon, but he had felt the rotor wash from a Chinook when hooking up practice sling loads at Fort Rucker during Chinook transition training, wind equal to a Category 2 hurricane. Wind like that would take that roof right off, no problem, unless they made it stronger.

Between the two of them, they decided to take their own pre-emptive action on their roof, to "typhoon proof" it as much as they possibly could. So, after a visit to the company supply office, they had a roll of communication wire (normally used to connect field telephones together), 30 sandbags, a wheelbarrow, and a couple of shovels. They got Cobb to help them, but even so, it took the three of them a whole day to fill the new sandbags and lift them one at a time to the roof. They used the new sandbags to replace the ones that were worn out from sun exposure, tying two new sandbags together with the communication wire, putting one bag on each side, way down where the tin overhung the outer walls. The tin roof, thus weighed down with new sandbags and re-nailed, gave them confidence that they were ready for typhoons, or at least as close to ready as they were going to get.

None of the other Playtex pilots prepared for the eventuality of the high winds a typhoon would bring. It just didn't seem important, not when you could do things like take a life-sized blowup girl doll, an "inflatable date" sent to one of the pilots as a joke (maybe, maybe not), and put her up on the roof of the Officers' Club on a cot. After they got her up there, they filled her with water so she wouldn't blow away, and left her there. It looked exactly like she was nude sunbathing, safe from prying eyes on the ground, but not from helicopters in the sky. The boys then opened a few beers and sat on the Officers Club deck to see what would happen next.

Within15 minutes the first Huey flew over, then banked suddenly after it had passed, circled around and came back in a low pass for a second, closer, look. After that, word must have spread quickly through the aircraft companies, because helicopter after helicopter flew low over Playtex's Officers Club. The bathing beauty couldn't be seen from the ground, so the XO, whose room was next door to the Club, couldn't figure out why, all of a sudden, so many aircraft were buzzing the Playtex compound. It continued right on until it was completely dark that evening, but did not resume the next morning like they thought it would. When the boys climbed up to see what had happened, they were sad to see she had sprung a leak and was now completely flat, no longer fooling anyone.

But, no inflatable dates for the three roommates—they spent their time getting ready for heavy weather, when not preoccupied with flying or cooking or singing, that is.

CHAPTER TWO

THE 159TH, THE AIRCRAFT, AND THE MISSION

THE 159TH ASSAULT SUPPORT HELICOPTER BATTALION (159TH ASHB)

The lieutenant colonel commanding the 159th ASHB didn't really do much actual "commanding." He didn't lead his men into battle and rarely flew with them. Even when more than one aircraft was required for a mission it meant Chinooks doing sling loads, one after another, but not in a massed aircraft formation assault like the Hueys did; it was impossible to "lead" this mission in any way that would show that you were in charge. Instead, what he tried to do was set the leadership tone for the company commanders under him, but the company commanders were there for such a short time that it was hard to set much of a tone in anything. The Army wanted everyone to get "command time," and to make sure this happened, rotated the company commanders quickly. Playtex, for example, went through three commanding officers in less than 12 months in 1970–1971.

To tell the truth, most of Playtex's warrants thought the battalion CO was afraid of Chinooks, big ugly things that they are. He was an armor officer, a tanker by trade, trained on M-48's and M-60s at Fort Knox, Kentucky, and loved the sound the tanks made when they crashed through woods, treads raising clouds of dust. He could not figure out how he wound up commanding a transport helicopter battalion, instead of a nice cavalry unit. Yes, he could fly the damned Chinooks and did fly one once or twice a month, but he didn't have to like it. He certainly did not like to see them try to do the things that other, more agile helicopters did routinely, like mass formation flights.

Once, after a rare mission that required four of Playtex's aircraft to fly together, the pilots decided that on the way back home they would fly a "Parade" formation low pass over the runway at Phu Bai, basically right in front of the battalion commander's office window. They really just wanted to say hello to their friends in their sister companies, The Pachyderms and The Varsity who were based on the runway at Phu Bai, so they called both on their company radio frequencies to tell them what time they would fly past to ensure a maximum viewing audience. They did not consider the fact that the battalion CO might not like it, because they never thought of the battalion CO at all. So, after the mission was complete, all four aircraft went into Camp Eagle for fuel. The AC elected flight lead, by popular acclamation, took off out of the fuel pits first, quickly followed by the other three Chinooks. It was only about six miles from Camp Eagle's fuel pits to Phu Bai, but that gave them plenty of time to join up in their "Parade" formation before they got there.

A "Parade" formation is supposed to be one that looks good from the ground, with the aircraft two rotor diameters away from each other when properly done. The pilots decided they would do an "echelon right" formation, meaning a "V" with one aircraft to the leader's left and the other two to his right. All the pilots in the flight had done parade formation flying in flight school over a year ago, but unfortunately, that was the last time they had done it. Chinooks don't fly in formation as they carry their normal external loads to mountaintops, so the pilots were very rusty, very rusty indeed, when it came to looking good in a formation flight.

The tower operator at Phu Bai was surprised when lead called "Phu Bai Tower, Playtex 540, flight of four Chinook three miles north requesting permission for a low pass on the main runway." He sounded very amused when he cleared them for the maneuver. "Playtex 540, cleared as requested. Report one mile." Immediately after giving the clearance, he called the other agencies around the airfield—the weather observers, the operations people, etc., so they could get into position to observe the show. He also called the crash crew, just in case.

Shortly, the wobbling group of four Chinooks came into view. Far from the tight parade formation flown by the combat assault Hueys, where every aircraft was "locked" into position without moving no matter what maneuver the lead aircraft did, the Chinooks were anywhere from a cringe-inducing one rotor diameter apart, or less, to four or five rotor diameters away from the next aircraft. It might have been called a "nuclear formation," given that two of the aircraft were so far from the other two that one atomic weapon would not have destroyed all four. But then, as they came over the edge of the airfield, the two far away helicopters suddenly came rushing up at their companions, resulting in flares to reduce speed, sudden turns to keep from hitting an aircraft in front. From a distance, it appeared they were see-sawing, noses up, then down, but not necessarily in unison. The lead Chinook, who could not see what was going on with the other aircraft, descended serenely down to 50 feet above the ground and continued straight down the runway.

The pilots from the Pachyderms and the Varsity were rolling on the ground in laughter at the sight of the four Playtex Chinook's "parade" formation as it flew down Phu Bai's runway. The battalion CO, who just happened to be looking out his office window at the runway when the formation went past, was not amused. As they passed, he stood in open-mouthed horror, expecting one of the aircraft to run into another at any moment and rain pieces of flaming aluminum down on the runway. It didn't happen, but as soon as they passed, he was on the phone to the COs of the Varsity, the Pachyderms, and Playtex, forbidding formation flight of any kind by aircraft in his battalion effective immediately!

Playtex's CO took the heat from the battalion CO, and as he promised, he kept it from scorching any of the pilots in the "parade." He did later tell his operations officer to inform all his pilots that there was to be "no more parade formation flying," particularly where the battalion CO could see it.

No, the battalion CO didn't really "command." Instead, he was the head of an administrative conduit that passed the missions from the 101st Airborne (Airmobile) Division Operations Department on to the company operations departments. The battalion CO's operations officer did get to decide which company got which missions, but the major in charge of operations mostly passed that duty to an unfortunate CW2 that worked as permanent night duty officer for him. He was permanent night duty officer because it seems that early in his tour, while still a copilot, this particular CW2 pulled the wrong engine off-line in a Chinook after the other one failed in flight, leaving that aircraft with no engines at all. No one was killed in the ensuing crash, but the Chinook was a total loss and the CW2 never flew again in Vietnam, or anywhere else, for that matter . . .

The 159th ASHB was an air force in and of itself, larger than the entire helicopter lift capacity of most of the countries in the world. The lieutenant colonel commanding had four helicopter companies at his disposal: three 16 aircraft companies of Boeing CH-47C Chinooks and one 12 aircraft company of Sikorsky CH-54A (Tarhe) Flying Cranes. Spare parts of all types were readily available, as were replacement aircraft when one was lost in combat or an accident. With the aircraft came the pilots and men to maintain them. They too were replaced almost immediately when lost.

On any given day, each of the three Chinook companies could put an average of 10 of their 16 aircraft in the air, with the other four undergoing routine maintenance and the other two on some sort of unscheduled work. With little notice the maintenance officers could get all 16 airborne at once, though if they did, it would be a sure bet that at least one or two of them was in the air strictly on faith and probably being flown by one of the maintenance warrants, trained to handle dodgy aircraft. Having all 16 turning at once was a rare event, since most days each company would only have six or seven aircraft out on missions, with another two ready as back up for the primary aircraft, should they have a mechanical problem on start or while out working.

The fourth company of the 159th ASHB, the Hurricanes, was completely different from the other three. As mentioned earlier, they were not at Phu Bai, but 50 miles away at China Beach, just north of Da Nang. They flew Sikorsky CH-54A Flying Cranes, helicopters that were not quite as mechanically reliable as the Boeing CH-47 Chinooks. One might say that when it came to aircraft readiness, they often weren't. They broke down easily, but the Crane Company could get enough aircraft airborne each day to handle their missions, most of the time. Delicate things, the CH-54s looked like ungainly giant grasshoppers on their long legs. They were also slow, carried little fuel and, because they did not mount door guns, required an AH-1 Cobra escort wherever they went.

The Chinook companies really didn't like working with the Hurricanes on the same mission, because even though the CH-54s could carry more weight than a 47 in one load, the Chinook was faster and carried more fuel. If the landing zone was any distance from the pick-up zone, with their superior speed the Chinooks could do three loads for each one the 54s completed. Even then, it was not unusual for the Crane to drop out of the mission due to mechanical problems; if it did, there was rarely a backup aircraft to take its place. This left the Chinooks to complete the mission alone, which they would have done anyway if no Crane was assigned, so why bother with CH-54s in the first place?

The lieutenant colonel commanding the 159th ASHB also had six Hughes OH-6 LOHs (Light Observation Helicopter, pronounced "Loach"), but the little egg-shaped helicopters weren't used as scouts. They were instead administrative aircraft, originally assigned two each to the individual Chinook companies to be used to fly small parts for broken aircraft away from base, transfer maintenance crews to different locations, and other administrative functions.

Basically, the LOHs were little sports cars, out of place in a big cargo helicopter world. That being so, the battalion commander considered them too dangerous to be left in the hands of the Chinook companies, so he had them all assigned permanently to Battalion Headquarters. With the LOHs right there, the headquarters folks could get their flight time without bothering the Chinook companies. He was certainly right about keeping the battalion staff from bothering the Chinook companies for flight time, because they could not fly enough to maintain the proficiency required by mountaintop missions. He was also probably right about the LOHs being too dangerous to be left in the Chinook company's hands, as we will see later in this story.

THE AIRCRAFT

Playtex and her two sister Chinook companies—A Company, the Pachyderms, and B Company, the Varsity—flew the CH-47C Chinook, the newest model Chinook that the Army owned at that time. The earlier "A" and "B" model Chinooks were also deployed with other companies in Vietnam, but they had far less capability in lift capacity and range than the "C". While the Chinook was listed as a medium lift helicopter, as opposed to the Marine Corps' heavy lift CH-53s and the Army's CH-54As, it is a really big aircraft as helicopters go. The cabin will hold two M-151 Jeeps or one jeep and a trailer. It will seat 33 troops, but will take all the people you can pack in if they are standing. It will routinely carry 8,000 pounds of cargo, internally or externally.

All of the 159th ASHB aircraft were given a call sign based on the last three numbers of the aircraft's serial number, for example, Playtex 506. Playtex 506 was a CH-47C with the serial number 67-18506. The first two numbers indicated its year of manufacture and the last three it's call sign. One of Playtex's aircraft serial numbers ended in 009, so naturally its call sign was "Balls Niner." Like all Chinooks, it had been manufactured by Boeing Vertol in Ridley Park, Pennsylvania, a suburb just south of Philadelphia.

The CH-47C was very fast for helicopters, with a top listed speed of 170 knots. They would cruise comfortably at 140 knots, but get one up around 160 and things were not comfortable at all. The vibration levels greatly increased at that airspeed and the increased vibration started breaking things. At about that speed, stress usually causes the hanger bearing on the shaft that connects the two rotor systems to start failing. They had to be replaced before the next flight, because if a significant number of the hanger bearings failed, it could lead to the de-synchronization of the two rotor systems, resulting in the rotor blades hitting each other and the aircraft coming apart in flight, an always fatal event.

Being so fast meant that a Chinook carrying an internal cargo load could easily outrun the AH-1 Cobra gunship escorts thoughtfully provided by division operations whenever they knew for certain the Chinooks would be fired on. Fully loaded with fuel and ordnance at full power, the Cobras could only manage 120 to 130 knots, far less than the Chinooks. However, Playtex's Standard Operating Procedures (SOP) limited the Chinooks to 90 knots with an external sling load, its normal mission load, so the Cobras would fly round and round the Chinook they were escorting on the way to the drop zone, laughing all the while. Ah, but on the return leg, after the sling load was dropped off, the Cobras would have to watch the Chinook disappear in the distance, since there was no SOP limit on speed without a load. At 120 the Cobras would be right beside the Chinooks. At 130 they would start to fall behind. At 140 the Chinooks would begin to pull away and at 150, it was no contest. The Cobras would meet up with the Chinook again on its next sling load and, boys being boys, the dance would begin again.

Fast though they may be, as helicopters go, Chinooks are still slow in absolute terms. Many jet fighters are near stall at the Chinook's top speed.

As such, the Chinook is a big, slow, easy target for anti-aircraft guns, or for that matter, anyone with a gun.

The Chinook is not maneuverable, either. Its bank angle is limited to a paltry 30 degrees, meaning it makes wide turns, leaving the enemy more time to lock their weapons on it. In Playtex's C models, if the pilot banked it any more than 30 degrees, stress cracks would begin to develop in the fuselage. Stress cracks were always a problem on any aircraft, but the C model Chinook was especially prone to them.

Jerry Cobb, trying to describe how bad the problem could be, told Strider this: After a long day of flying sling load missions, Cobb was headed to the fuel pits at Camp Eagle for one last refueling before heading back to Liftmaster when he, and the rest of the crew, heard a loud BANG— something very rare over the usual roar of the Chinook's engines and transmission. Explosive engine failure? Anti-aircraft fire impacting the fuselage? Alarmed, Jerry started slowing to best single-engine speed as both pilot's eyes immediately went to the caution and warning panel and the flight engineer ran to the aft to check the transmission area, but there were no caution lights and nothing unusual in the aft pylon area. Jerry decided to continue on into the fuel pits. After landing, the flight engineer stepped off the rear ramp and said, "Jesus, Mr. Cobb, come look at this!" The three feet by four feet left work platform that is mounted on the side of the aft pylon was completely gone. The area around the forward lock had cracked, allowing the work platform to partially open at 140 knots and the slipstream immediately tore it off. Fortunately for the crew, it had missed the aft rotor blades as it sailed away, since something that big and heavy could have taken the blades right off, killing them all.

For a big aircraft, the Chinook's cockpit was not all that big. The Huey's cockpit actually felt bigger because it had opening entry doors, while you had to climb into the Chinook's cockpit from a narrow companionway between the cockpit and the cabin. The AC sat on the left side and the pilot (copilot, actually) on the right. All the buttons on the Chinook's control stick had exactly the same function as those on a Huey's, making transition between the two aircraft types easier, since all Chinook pilots were also qualified in Hueys.

The Chinook's cockpit also had an interesting feature in the emergency doors on each side—they were spring loaded. The handle used to activate the door jettison was located on the top of the door and looked very much like a nice place to hang your flight helmet while you were getting situated, but all the pilots learned early on not to touch that handle unless you really wanted to use it. If you inadvertently pulled the jettison handle, the doors went flying away very rapidly and were generally destroyed, something that made the aircraft's flight engineer and the maintenance officer very unhappy with the offending pilot. Of course, in a crash they usually automatically ejected themselves, saving the pilot a step as he exited the aircraft in an emergency, always a good thing.

In Playtex's aircraft, the windshield and cockpit windows often leaked in the rain, an inconvenience perhaps, but more comfortable than when it was hot and dusty outside. Wet will dry, but hot and sticky stays hot and sticky. Before the rotors began turning in hot weather, the cockpit would leave the pilots soaked in sweat before the day even began. So the first thing they did after they got the auxiliary power plant on the line was to close their eyes and then turn on the heater blowers to get some air moving. Since the Chinooks were going to Vietnam and the jet fuel-powered cabin heaters would have been dead weight, they were removed, but the blower fans were still intact and their ducts remained down at the bottom of the emergency doors. Of course, the ducts filled up with sand blown in during landings at dusty zones, so the first time you turned them on in the morning they filled the cockpit with stinging sand, blown at high speed right into the pilot's faces. Still, the pilots thought it was worth it to get some air moving in the normal heat and humidity; they just closed their eyes, hit the switch, and didn't complain.

Underneath both pilot's seats were relief tubes. The idea was that to take a piss, the pilots could remain comfortably seated and relieve themselves into the red plastic funnel-shaped opening at the top of the relief tube. The exit point for the relief tube was in the aircraft belly just under the cockpit. There were two problems with this arrangement. First, the urine covered the belly of the aircraft, requiring the crew to clean it every day to prevent corrosion to the aluminum skin. Second and most important, if the aircraft was doing an external load, and the flight engineer was watching the load through the hell hole (the hatch in the center of the cabin floor above the cargo hook) while the pilot was using the relief tube, the urine would go directly in his face.

To prevent either of these things from happening, the flight engineers would routinely turn the relief tube exit around, so that instead of allowing the urine to escape, it would allow ram air to blow the contents directly back on the offending pilot. Pilot's, of course, quickly learned this maneuver and avoided using the relief tube, unless it was a dire emergency. Old pilots, however, rarely shared this bit of knowledge about the reversed drain point with new copilots, so new pilots sometimes wound up holding a full relief tube that would not drain. This awkward problem usually ended with the new pilot getting wet and smelling bad until he could change his flight suit, a situation always greatly amusing to ACs and the enlisted air crewmen.

On one of Strider's first flights with Playtex, during pre-flight, the ACs noticed that the flight engineer had not turned the relief tube exit point around on the left side of the aircraft, meaning that this one would actually work, if used. Later in the day, while the aircraft was carrying a sling load, the AC took a canteen of water and poured it down the relief tube. In a flash, the flight engineer was up from the hell hole and running to the cockpit with a big wrench in his hand to wreak revenge on the offending pilot/pilots, but he pulled up laughing when he saw the AC holding the canteen up.

All Playtex's aircraft were painted a nice flat green when they left the factory in Pennsylvania, but the longer they were there on Liftmaster Pad, the more they looked like they had a skin disease, since the paint would peal from oil and grease. Sand would erode it in other places. Maintenance always put touch-up paint on the bare spots to prevent corrosion, but their touch ups never matched the original paint. Then, too, patches over bullet holes came out a different color no matter how hard the paint shop tried to match it.

To show what company they belonged to, each 159th ASHB Chinook had a triangle painted on both sides of the forward pylon work platform, just below the forward rotors. The Pachyderms had a red triangle, the Varsity a white triangle, and Playtex a blue triangle. All the Chinooks in the 159th ASHB had a big 101st Airborne Screaming Eagle on the work platform on both sides of the aft pylon. Huey pilots would tease the 159th ASHB pilots that the Eagle looked scared back there.

In flight, the cockpit belonged to the AC, but the cabin of the aircraft was the territory of the flight engineer. He owned it and did everything back there. Without him the aircraft was useless and the pilots knew and respected that. He kept it ordered and configured the way the mission required it to be, as well as supervising the crew chief and door gunner. He too knew that the mission must be done and did everything in his power to make it so.

THE MISSION

The mission must be done.

The mission must always be done because that was the reason everyone, even Chinook crews, were in Vietnam. The mission was the only reason the Army owned aircraft at all. For that matter, the mission was the only reason there was an Army.

Playtex's mission was "Assault Support," meaning that their primary job was to bring sling loads of ammunition, fuel, food, and water to the artillery fire support bases scattered throughout the mountains to the west of the coastal lowlands. There were other missions, of course: recovery of downed aircraft, flare drops, passenger transfers, napalm drops, chemical drops, and carrying around the "People Pods" originally designed to fit under the long legs of a CH-54 Flying Crane.

The People Pod carry was one of the most hated missions for Playtex. Originally built to give the CH-54 a passenger carrying capability, the Pods had now been converted to mobile command posts. Because they were light and had a big surface area, the Pods would easily swing from side to side when being carried as an external load, making any forward speed beyond a fast hover impossible. The Cranes could not carry them themselves, even if they were designed to, because they had an annoying habit of accidently dropping the Pods from great heights, hence the prohibition on carrying passengers in them. So, the Chinooks were stuck with hovering along with these giant boxes under them, hoping all the time the People Pod would not swing up and smack the Chinook's belly, quite possibly taking the helicopter out of the sky.

Other missions notwithstanding, 90% of the time the Chinook's mission was transporting sling loads of ammo, fuel, food, and water from Camp Eagle, Camp Evans, and Quang Tri to the FSBs in the mountains. They would pick up the sling loads and then fly west, setting them down as close as possible to where they were needed, trying to save some work for the artillerymen on the mountaintop. Sometimes the North Vietnamese Army (NVA) would shoot at the Chinooks as they set down their loads, but the grunts would be watching; if the NVA fired, they had better fire and run, because artillery rounds would be coming in their direction momentarily.

The artillery on those mountaintops, mostly 105mm gun batteries, with a few 155mm here and there, provided 24-hour fire support cover for nearly any area in I Corps where the grunts operated. If the grunts moved to where the existing FSBs could not provide the cover, another mountaintop would be cleared and a new FSB established. After the engineers had flattened off the mountaintop to make room for the guns, the Chinooks would come in with a double sling load. The lower sling load would be artillery ammunition and the upper, the 105mm howitzer. The Chinook would set the ammo down and then slide over and set the gun down next to it. It was possible for the gun crews also to come in with the load. After setting down the ammo and then the gun, the Chinook would slide to the side, land, and debark the gun crew. Normally, though, because the mountaintops were so small, it was difficult to find a spot big enough for the Chinooks to land, so Hueys would bring in the gun crew before the Chinook arrived. Either way, done right, the gun could be firing within ten minutes of being dropped.

Because the mountaintop FSBs were so remote, only rarely were there roads leading to them. Even if there had been roads, resupply convoys moving on them would have been easy targets for the NVA, just as the French had been for the Viet Minh in 1954, so everything came in by helicopter. Because this was so, you couldn't just stop flying in the monsoon, you had to adjust, because the helicopter's missions must be done if the artillery was to do their mission of supporting the grunts.

The missions must always be done because the men on those FSBs counted on you for everything and you couldn't let them down. Every day the Chinooks would bring loads in slings beneath the helicopter, ammo and fuel, mostly, but sometimes pallets of C rations and soft drinks. Sometimes the Chinooks would bring Special Purpose Packs (SPP), a pallet load of things the PX usually carried, writing paper, razor blades, candy bars, soap, things that the men on the fire bases needed, but couldn't get since there were no PXs on mountaintops in the middle of nowhere. Everyone, including the Playtex crews, liked SPPs, to the point where a box or two of them from the SPP pallet might just disappear before the pallet reached the FSB. Strider's first pipe came from an SPP.

One day at the end of a mission, the crew in the pick-up zone (PZ) where they had been picking up their sling loads all day, asked Strider's Chinook to land. When it did, two of the men from the PZ brought over a box and gave it to the flight engineer. It was an SPP that was extra, one from a broken pallet and they wanted to give it to the Chinook crew because they had worked extra fast that day, completing the mission in time for the hook-up crew to get a little extra rest. Back at Liftmaster, after they had shut down for the day, the flight engineer opened it up. As the boys were looking through the goodies in the SPP, Strider saw a pipe, one with a filter inside. Bundled with the pipe were two pouches of tobacco and an extra box of filters. Etiquette dictated that the enlisted men got first cut and anything left was for the officers. The pipe was not taken, so Strider claimed it.

Being big and slow targets, Playtex's Chinooks usually flew high—well, high by helicopter standards—to avoid the possibility of ground fire from the VC and the NVA. A 7.62mm rifle bullet from an AK-47, or a light machine gun, is accurate up to 1,500 feet above the ground. A 12.7mm round from an anti-aircraft machine gun is accurate up to 3,000 feet. A 14.5mm round from a heavy machine gun is accurate up to 4,500 feet. Helicopters can't fly high enough to get above anything bigger than 14.5mm, such as the 23mm, 37mm, or even the 57mm anti-aircraft guns the NVA had in some of the deeper jungle areas they controlled. Keep in mind that "accurate" fire didn't mean that you couldn't be hit above that altitude: it just meant that you were above tracer burnout. Since the gunner couldn't see where the bullets were going, it was much more difficult for him to hit the target. Once, Strider counted six bullet holes from an AK-47 or light machine gun, in one of the main fuel cells after a day's mission. No one heard them hit, and since the tanks were self-sealing, no fuel was lost—it might have happened first thing in the morning or on the last mission of the day.

The mission was always the most important thing, the only thing, really. The mission must be done, period.

To make sure all the missions were completed, Playtex Operations always had spare aircraft standing by to replace ones that developed mechanical problems on morning startup. If six aircraft were required for the morning launch, eight would be ready for takeoff at launch time. If one of the scheduled six aircraft had a mechanical or electrical failure, the aircraft commander would simply leave the copilot to shut down the broken bird and move over to one of the running backups. No time was ever lost launching the aircraft.

If, as often happened, an aircraft had a mechanical problem during the day while flying missions, the maintenance department would bring another Chinook to the pilots where they were. Maintenance would give the good aircraft to the pilots and then stay and fix the broken one for the return flight. If that procedure was going to take too long, another Playtex aircraft already airborne would be tasked by operations to start working that mission. No one ever complained about being assigned additional missions during the day. That was their job and the mission must be done.

Long afterwards, Strider discovered there were mission priority codes. In Playtex, the pilots didn't know that there was any alternative to completing a mission, or even that there might be mission priorities of "routine," "urgent," and "mandatory." As far as Playtex and all of the 101st were concerned, all the missions were mandatory. Period.

The mission must be done.

CHAPTER THREE

MONSOON FLYING

T
he Playtex pilots would normally climb to around 6,000 feet above the ground as they flew between their pick-up zone and their drop zone or landing zone. Besides avoiding ground fire, the crews also enjoyed a break from the high temperature and humidity. If it's 95 degrees at the surface it will be around 77 degrees at 6,000 feet—very comfortable, almost as good as air conditioning. But there was no climbing during the monsoon, because the clouds prevented it; they were often as low as 300 feet off the ground in the low lands. In the mountains, where the fire support bases (FSB) were, you couldn't tell how high they were, really, because the clouds and the ground joined together into a white mass.

The Playtex crews would often launch from Liftmaster Pad even when the weather was too bad to get to the FSBs in the mountains. Operations would have them forward deploy to other bases like Camp Evans, up 40 miles north of Hue City, or Quang Tri, 80 miles north, or even Dong Ha, nearly on the DMZ. There they would wait for a break in the weather, for when the clouds would lift enough to get into the FSBs with their food, ammo, and ironically, given that it had been raining for weeks, water.

Smaller helicopters, Hueys and LOHs, would constantly check the routes between the mountains and Camp Evans, Quang Tri, and the other PZs, for the Chinooks' benefit. The pathfinders and the air traffic controllers on the FSBs would also call in weather reports from their individual locations, but their reports were sometimes regarded with suspicion by the Playtex pilots, since they tended to make things sound better than they actually were. The Hueys and LOHS, on the other hand, were actually flying in the same weather that the Chinooks would be, so their reports were more trusted. Sometimes 159th ASHB Operations would send one of the Chinook pilots along with the Huey or LOH crews for a firsthand look at the weather. That was a job for a copilot, not an AC.

WEATHER CHECKER

Today's weather checker copilot was Strider. The Huey came into the field at Camp Evans where Strider's Chinook sat, waiting for clearing skies. When the Huey AC signaled for him to board, he ducked under the rotor disk and ran to the right side of the helicopter. He climbed into the back of the Huey, moved over to the seat between the pilots and plugged his helmet into the helicopter's intercom so that he could hear what was going on. What he mostly heard for the next 45 minutes was the sound of silence.

While things were usually relaxed in a Chinook's cockpit, the entire crew of this Huey was relaxed beyond words, so calm they seemed bored. Were they doing a bid for maximum cool points from the Chinook pilot? A clue that they weren't was that instead of moving their pistols over between their legs for a little more protection (more psychological than real) against rounds coming up through the floor, like the Chinook pilots routinely did, both Huey pilots had taken off their holsters containing their .38 revolvers and had hung them on the side of their seats. If they crashed, the odds of getting their pistols out of the wreckage were slim, since usually, if you weren't wearing it when you went in, you wouldn't have it at all. They would not do that for effect, just to impress a Chinook pilot, so it must have been what they normally did. Either that or they had decided that this was not a combat mission at all, just a little joy ride into weather too bad for fighting. Strider decided that must be the case since neither Huey pilot wore a "bullet bouncer," the ceramic and steel body armor that was issued to all aircrew.

The Huey's crew chief and door gunner were relaxed too. Both had leaned back into their positions on the right and left sides of the Huey, appearing nearly asleep behind their machine guns. If the entire crew could act bored, so could Strider. He would out-bore them, in fact. The AC in the left seat gave Strider a "thumbs up," which he returned to show that he was ready to go. The AC lifted the Huey into a three-foot hover, then lowered the nose, added power and they took off, heading west toward the mountains and the clouds. Hueys had seemed so big back at Fort Rucker when Strider learned to fly them, but now after Chinooks, this one seemed almost tiny.

At first they were staying low, the AC keeping the Huey skimming the tops of the trees at 100 knots, something Chinooks never did unless absolutely forced, like now when the clouds were so low. Strider knew that flying close to the treetops was a good way to avoid ground fire, because you were gone before the enemy had time to get you in their sights, but the Huey crews seemed to enjoy being low, not just in bad weather, but as a routine way of getting around. Even in good weather they could often be seen way below the Chinooks; the Chinooks stayed high as much as they could because big helicopters carrying sling loads are not very maneuverable and are easy targets. From above, there was beauty in the green Hueys flashing just above the jungle, young men in their expensive toys, showing the world that they were invincible—until they discovered they were not invincible. One of Strider's first missions was to recover a smashed Huey on a mountainside. The Huey crew had apparently either misjudged the height of the ridgeline or had been caught in a down draft and had flown right into it. He never found out if the crew survived or not, but it reinforced to Strider that, unless forced by weather or orders, flying low was not healthy.

After a few moments to allow Strider to strap in, without a word to his crew, the Huey AC added power and climbed the aircraft directly into the low clouds above them. The world went suddenly white at around 400 feet as all reference to the ground disappeared. Strider thought that at this point, the AC would call the Air Force radar unit that provided coverage in this part of I Corps and tell them what they were doing, but the Huey crew made no radio calls, they just continued to climb into the clouds. If there was an aircraft in the clouds with them, the Huey's crew was counting on that aircraft's radar to keep them clear. Or, they were counting on luck. Strider decided it was luck, some sort of fatalism on their part that he did not share.

At 7,000 feet, the Huey broke into the clear, with bright sunshine that nearly blinded everyone on board as it reflected from the white cloud tops below them, hitting them so hard that everyone wished they had their sunglasses on. Seeing the sunshine made them all smile. It was the first time they had seen it in weeks. Since the highest mountain in the area only went up to a little over 6,000 feet, all the mountain's green tops were hidden in the clouds below them. The blue sky above and the sea of white clouds below them were beautiful, particularly after all the rain.

"Looks like the ceiling is above 6,000. I don't see any breaks in the clouds over the mountains east or west. OK, let's go back down," the AC remarked to his copilot and Strider. Without a further word, the AC turned the Huey back toward the east, to where the coastal lowlands were, lowered the power, and they began to descend back into the white at a steady 500 feet per minute and 90 knots of airspeed.

Surely at this point he will call the Air Force radar, Strider thought to himself. The Huey would need a radar approach into Phu Bai, 40 miles or so to the south to get safely down from on top of the clouds. Looking at the Huey's fuel gauge, Strider could see that it would be close, since they only had about 50 minutes of fuel remaining and Phu Bai was at least 20 minutes away. The Huey AC called no one. Instead, the aircraft just continued to descend at a steady 500 feet per minute, the standard rate of descent, and the crew remained as calm and quiet as they had been throughout the flight. Strider watched the barometric altimeter unwind: 5,000 feet, 3,000 feet, and then 2,000 feet. If they had cleared the mountains there was no danger of inadvertently flying into the ground, not yet anyway. The ground over the lowlands never reached more than 150 feet or so above sea level once you cleared the foothills, which they had hopefully done. Strider tensed, looking for the darker part of the white cloud in front of them that meant they were just about to fly into a mountain, but it never came. Everything just stayed a uniform white.

As the Huey passed 1,000 feet, the AC added a little power and reduced their rate of descent to 200 feet a minute. At 500 feet on the barometric altimeter, the clouds began to break up, trees becoming visible below them. By 300 feet, the Huey was in the clear, although the visibility stayed at less than a mile. The AC seemed to recognize where they were, because instead of staying at 300 feet, he dropped down to the treetops again and as he did so, turned the aircraft left toward the northwest. In a few minutes Strider saw the main north-south highway in South Vietnam, QL1, pass underneath them and in a few more minutes, they crossed the barbed wire around Camp Evans. Immediately after that, the AC landed the Huey near the parked Chinooks and Strider was back in the LZ where the flight had started 30 minutes ago.

Throughout the entire flight, Strider had said not one word, but he decided this was one of the times when you are supposed to be afraid, even if you can't show it without losing all your cool points. You have to trust the crew doing the flying, even if you think they are crazy, suicidal maniacs, which Strider most assuredly did.

Strider thought so with good reason. Playtex lost an aircraft and a crew of five men a year earlier when another aircraft descended out of the clouds right on top of them. There were no survivors in either crew to say what happened exactly, but apparently the fixed wing descended directly into Playtex 513's rotor blades, destroying both aircraft. Pieces of the aircraft and the crews were spread out over quite a distance on the ground, Strider had been told. It took a long while to recover them all, well, most parts of them all.

Besides descending down on top of other aircraft, there were other dangers—radio towers, for example. There weren't many, but there were some radio antennas in the area, some reaching up from 50 to 300 feet or higher, but no matter how tall they were, all of them waited for a passing helicopter to fly right into them or their guy wires.

Strider resolved then and there that hereafter, he would never fly as a passenger in a Huey again, unless ordered and there was no other choice.

Maintaining his cool points, such as they were, Strider exited the Huey, ducking under the rotor blades. As he walked away, he turned and waved to the crew before he headed back to his Chinook. All the Playtex pilots were gathered there, waiting on his report. He told them "no go," leaving out the part about suicidal Huey pilots, so the Chinook crews went back to their aircraft and continued to standby. When a break was reported or actually came, the Chinooks would scramble to start their engines, hover over to the pick-up zone, and try to move as many loads as they could before the clouds came down again, but for now it was just wait and wait some more.

The Playtex crews were living temporarily in hootches borrowed from a Huey company there at Camp Evans instead of commuting back and forth between Liftmaster and their hold point. This gave them an extra half hour to get out to the mountains when there was a break in the weather. The hootches didn't have the comforts of Strider's back at Liftmaster, but at least they did have beds, showers (sometimes with actual hot water), and a mess hall to give them a break from C rations and having to sleep on troop seats in the back of a Chinook. Lunch in the mess hall there at Camp Evans gave Strider a glimpse, more of a flash back, really, to two years ago, before he was a soldier.

LOOSE LIPS

That day, after the Chinook crews had their lunch, the weather still had not cleared, so instead of going back to their helicopters, the waiting crews sat in the mess hall telling lies and war stories, not that there's much difference between the two. Eventually, the conversation turned to where they all had joined the Army. When it was his turn, Strider said that he had enlisted in Covington, Kentucky. As he did so, a voice from the next table over said, "Covington? Why, I bet I signed you up myself."

Strider looked over at the next table and recognized the speaker as the Army recruiter who had indeed signed him up. He had been a staff sergeant in January 1968, and now, in October 1970, he had been promoted to sergeant first class (SFC). He was older, with a little more weight around his middle, but the same man for sure. Strider remembered that after he had talked to the Marines and was turning to leave the recruiting station, this man had smiled at the Marine Corps gunnery sergeant and then said to him, "Hey kid, how would you like to be a helicopter pilot?" starting him on the path to where he was right now.

Strider slowly slid his chair back and stood up, his face grim and his right hand going slowly toward the holstered pistol on his belt. The SFC's mouth dropped open and he instantly turned very pale. Strider left the pistol alone and with a laugh, walked over to the next table to shake his hand. The former recruiter was rooted to his chair, pale and speechless. He shook Strider's hand, but would not talk. Instead, he quickly got up and left the mess hall in a rush. Perhaps it wasn't a good idea to call attention to the fact that you had been a recruiter when the men you were talking to were actually in a war zone . . .

As the SFC hurried out the door, Strider turned back to the other pilots and remarked, "You know, some people just don't have a sense of humor," followed by howls of laughter from his fellows. Cool points gain for sure.

LAST DITCHES

If the clouds didn't lift and the situation became desperate for the men on the fire bases—like running low on ammo, food, or water—the Chinooks would have to get to them regardless of the clouds. In a last ditch effort, the Playtex pilots would pick up their sling loads, fly low level to the base of the mountain that held the FSB, and then hover up the mountain side in the cloud. Looking down, the pilot could see the tops of the trees, giving him enough visual reference to continue upward. Looking up through the windshield and seeing only white, no reference could tell you whether you were upright, in a turn, climbing, or descending. Look up too long, and since there is no reference, you are guaranteed to lose control of the aircraft. "Too long" in this case could be as little as 15 seconds. The Chinooks only did this for extremely critical, life and death missions, since it was just too difficult for anything less. In addition to difficult, it was also extremely dangerous, but the missions must be done and if this was the only way, so be it.

Of course, the mission did not end until you were back at Liftmaster, so you had to get back somehow. The problem was that after hovering up the mountain in the clouds, the crew could not go back down the same way they came up. You couldn't hover back down because in a hover, the aircraft's nose is up, leaving you looking directly into the clouds, with no reference at all if you were trying to go downhill. If you still tried this, the risk of inadvertently sticking your aft rotor blades into the trees was very high. No, instead of trying to hover down, the pilot would have to do an ITO (instrument takeoff). An ITO from a mountaintop meant taking off looking only at your flight instruments while climbing as rapidly as you could without outside visibility until you were above the highest mountain. When the aircraft reached a safe altitude, 6,000 feet or higher, the pilot would then call the Air Force for a vector to the precision radar approach control at Phu Bai, assuming that the radar was operational.

An ITO from a mountaintop was something Playtex crews were loath to do for a couple of reasons. First, Phu Bai was usually a long way from the FSBs where the loads were dropped, adding hours to the mission day and sweat to the pilot's faces if fuel was low. Second, and probably most important, Playtex crews were, by and large, lousy instrument pilots. The Army was in such a rush to get pilots to Vietnam that training in instrument flying back at Fort Rucker was minimal. Instead of a Standard Instrument Card, like pilots in all the other services held, Army pilots straight from flight school held a Tactical Instrument Card that allowed them to fly in instrument conditions only in Vietnam. When it came to instrument flying, the joke was that since Army pilots' Tactical Instrument Cards were blue in color and had a hole punched in the center, before flying, the pilot was supposed to hold the card up to the sky and if the color of the sky through the hole was the same color blue as the rest of the card, it was safe to take off. If it was not, the pilot should stay on the ground until they were the same color.

Since the Army pilots' missions in Vietnam usually required daylight visual flight rules (VFR), Tactical Instrument Card or not, the pilots had almost no instrument flying practice except the little bit of training they got in flight School. Even when they did practice instrument flying, they did not do so with the aircraft actually in the clouds—too dangerous, they thought. Instead, the pilot would wear a hood to restrict his vision to the instrument panel. Of course, most of Playtex's pilots cheated when flying simulated instruments by peaking around the hood, thereby negating any training value. All this meant that instrument flight, while routine to the Marine Corps, Navy, and Air Force, was more often an emergency procedure for the Army warrants flying Playtex's Chinooks.

Dangerous or not, ITO required or not, instrument flight required or not, Playtex's pilots would hover up the side of the mountain in the clouds if that was the only way to get the load up there. The mission must be done, but they all hoped they didn't have to do it that way.

EVEN THE BAD GUYS GET THE BLUES

The clouds and rain made it more difficult for the North Vietnamese Army (NVA), too, since they also got wet and cold, while watching mildew grow on everything they had. Since they had less chance to keep things dry than their American and ARVN enemies, their equipment rotted quickly. The NVA were hard men, but that didn't stop the tropical rot. The wooden stock on a captured AK-47 hanging on the wall in battalion operations had rotted almost in half from being constantly wet. Even so, the barrel of the weapon was clear and bright on the inside and its action worked smoothly, so it would still shoot quite nicely if a target presented itself.

Not only did the constant wet make it uncomfortable for the NVA just to live, it also became more difficult for them to attack the helicopters, since without radar, to shoot a target, you have to see it. When the Chinooks flew low over the treetops because of low clouds and poor visibility, the NVA did not have time to lock onto them as they passed. They might hear the helicopters coming, but even if the helicopters flew directly overhead, they just would not have time to get their weapons sighted and fire before they were gone. It must have been very frustrating for them.

When the clouds weren't low, the NVA would sometimes set up their guns on higher ground, allowing them to see low-flying helicopters coming in plenty of time to fix aim. Sometimes they would use tracer bullets, the green glowing rounds showing them where their fire was going. Of course, tracer bullets work both ways. Tracers allow you to see where your bullets are going, but at the same time they let the other side know where they are coming from, making you a target in return. Sometimes the NVA would pull the tracer rounds out of the belts of machine gun bullets to prevent this from happening, but this wasted ammo since it took more rounds to kill a helicopter when you couldn't see where the bullets were going. But in the monsoon season it was nearly impossible to set up such ambushes, tracers or no tracers. The weather made it impossible for the NVA to attack the Americans because they could not see them, but the Americans couldn't see the NVA to attack them either.

After the rains started, the pilots in the 101st knew the NVA was having trouble targeting their helicopters when they stopped finding bullet holes in their aircraft at the end of the day. The mortar rounds stopped falling on the FSBs, too. The NVA just could not see their targets on the mountaintops well enough to aim the mortars effectively. Since they had to hand-carry every round of ammunition hundreds of miles down the Ho Chi Minh Trail from North Vietnam, the ammunition was just too precious to waste on blind firing. But then, the NVA lived there in the mountains and they knew full well the weather would eventually get better, just as they knew the helicopters would still be there when it did, flying out toward the mountains with their sling loads for the FSBs. The NVA, besides being hard men, were patient men. They would wait.

ONCE STARTED

As the October days passed, the rains kept falling, and in the lowlands, the water in the streams and paddies began to rise. Although the pilots could not get enough altitude to see very far, it was apparent from casual observation as they flew that the situation for the Vietnamese living in country villages was getting critical—the land was just disappearing beneath the water. It wasn't sudden, like when a dam breaks or a river rushes over its banks. The water just kept slowly rising, slowly, but never stopping in its rise. Soon the dikes between the rice patties were no longer visible in some places. The roads in the rural areas were nearly gone, too, invisible under the brown water. The villages would be next.

One day as he flew the 40 miles north from Phu Bai to Camp Evans, Strider noticed two water buffalo tethered by their nose rings to a post in a field a few miles from the base. The first time he saw them, he wanted to snap a picture, because the entire tableau looked exactly like an old time travel poster for Asia—black buffalo against the green of the village, with a few palm trees in the background. Somehow he never got around to taking that picture, even though it was always a routine flight and he could have easily talked the AC into circling around to get in the best position. A few days later, when the rains got heavier, he saw that the village was empty as the waters started to cover it. The water buffalo's owners had apparently fled the rising water, leaving the buffalos tethered instead of freeing them. Now the buffalo were in trouble. At first, the water rose to their bellies, then as it rose still more the buffalo were floating. The next day when Strider's Chinook flew past the village on the way back to Phu Bai, both water buffalo had drowned. Unable to free themselves, their bodies floated with their heads under water, still tethered to their post.

CHAPTER FOUR

OCTOBER 16, 1970

SHOW TIME

"**H**ey, guys, we've got a USO show coming tonight! They start at 2000. Well, it's not really a USO show, but, even better, it's one of those Pilipino shows with girls," Cobb announced happily to the five or six pilots in the Officers' Club.

Strider had learned by now not to ask questions when he wasn't sure what everyone was talking about—not cool, it was just not cool. Besides, usually all would be revealed immediately. The guys weren't big on keeping secrets.

"I saw one in Pleiku on my first tour!" Cobb continued. "If the band's going to start playing at 2000 hours, we've got to get the club set up. I figure we can put the stage over there by the door out onto the patio and get some more chairs from the mess hall. We've got to get rid of the poker tables, at least for tonight, so that we've got room for everybody in here."

Ah, a live sex show, with a little live music thrown in, Strider thought. He had never seen one, but he had heard rumors and bragging by other pilots about such shows. Vietnam certainly was turning out to be an education for a Kentucky boy. Strider wondered who had booked and paid for this show. He knew it wasn't Steiner. The club officer was just too squeaky clean, at least from what Strider knew of him, for such things. In any case, it certainly wasn't the Army or the USO. Their shows were all pure American apple pie stuff, with only mild sexual innuendo of the Bob Hope semi-dirty-old-man type, not real live sex acts with real live audience participation. Well, from what Strider had heard, the girls tried to get the audience to participate in the shows, but with little success, usually. Americans, at least when sober, seemed to rarely do such things—particularly when there were cameras about, as there were sure to be tonight since everyone carried them.

"Before show party! My hootch, 1800 hours!!!" Jerry shouted. "Everyone bring your own booze and if anybody's got boxed pizza mix, bring that too. Our duty copilot is cooking." So much for the "sober" part, Strider thought. The duty copilot would be Strider, since he was the only copilot who lived there. Although the three had agreed they would all discuss it before inviting more than one or two people over, Cobb had not cleared a hootch party with either Steiner or Strider, but, what the hell, it would be fun. Maybe . . .

The pilots started arriving at the hootch well before 1800 and, as Jerry requested, they all brought various kinds of wine, whiskey, vodka, but mostly beer by the case. The beer, as already noted, was mostly flat and tasted of the steel can it came in, but it did have alcohol in it and that was the point, really. Strider had the electric skillet fired up early and hit the hootch's own stash of boxed pizza to get started. He opened one of the canned hams and cut up a can of mushrooms for toppings, but he knew it really didn't matter what was on the pizza; the guys would eat anything set out in front of them, as long as they didn't have to cook it and it didn't come from the mess hall. Within half an hour, the sound volume in the front room grew to the point where no one could clearly hear anything anyone was saying. No matter though, because the conversation became less coherent by the minute.

By 1900 everyone was very well lubricated, including Strider. After the third pizza, he quit cooking and joined the party in the front room of the hootch. There were so many people there by then that the party had spilled out the front door and onto the sidewalk in front of the hootch, rain or no rain. Strider did notice that none of the senior RLOs—neither the CO, nor the XO, nor the operations officer—were to be seen. "Plausible deniability" was the term invented later to cover such situations. "Party? What party? I was over at battalion doing paperwork, so I never heard about a party. Sorry I missed it. Was it a good one?"

As he left his hootch for the Officers' Club, Strider put on his brown felt campaign hat, the same kind drill instructors (DI) and state troopers wore back in the States. His, however, was not a real military or police campaign hat. Though the label on the inside had been removed, it appeared to be a Boy Scout hat, like the one he had in Boy Scout Troop 57 eight years ago. Strider had no idea how the hat wound up in Vietnam. He picked it up out of a pile of junk at a base that was closing and was very pleased to find that it fit him exactly. Instead of wearing it flat brimmed, like a DI or state trooper, Strider used a set of Army Aviator Wings and a CW2 bar to pin the brim up in the front, like Gabby Hayes used to do with his cowboy hat in old western movies. On the side of the hat he put a button he bought years before at a novelty shop in Cincinnati; the button was red and said in white letters, "Kill a Commie for Christ."

The campaign hat was Strider's dress up party hat, worn only on special occasions, like meetings of the Phu Bai Glee Club or Philippine "USO" shows, though once, when he was standing duty officer, he forgot he had it on. While he was inspecting bunkers out on the base perimeters, he wondered why he got a few strange looks from the sentries, that is, until he glanced in the mirror of his jeep when heading back to the hootch. No one said a word about the non-standard headgear though, not even the sergeant of the guard. In return Strider did not mention the marijuana smoke billowing up out of all the bunkers.

The last pilots still hanging around the hootch departed for the Officers' Club by 1945. When they got there they found that all seats were already taken, leaving standing room only in the back. Strider was the last of the pilots to arrive. The room was so crowded that he barely fit through the club's door. When he did get in, he noticed that the last pilots out of the pre-show party had joined the back row of men, the ones jammed up against the bar, and they were all copilots. The ACs had claimed the stage front seats by virtue of seniority and were ready for the show to begin.

The band began playing loud, tinny-sounding rock music, and shortly thereafter, the two girl singers/dancers made a grand entrance from their hiding place outside on the club's deck. They were small girls, short and skinny under their blond wigs, with tiny breasts, breasts that were barely covered by what appeared to be sequined black bras. Over the black bras they started out wearing a type of gauzy, dirty white jacket. Their white go-go boots came nearly to their knees. Strider noticed that they appeared to have bruises on their legs, and though they were smiling as they danced and sang, they did not look happy. Nor to Strider did they look sexy. To Strider it wasn't sexy at all, it was just sad, the young men there to fight a war watching the unhappy girls trying to be sexy, singing and dancing poorly in the shabby Officers' Club for a bunch of drunk Americans. The girls began to dance to some song that was vaguely familiar, but Strider was feeling very woozy all of a sudden. He had no idea when things started to get blurry, but they were now getting that way fast. He stood up to go outside for some fresh air, but someone handed him an open beer as he rose. Instead of drinking the beer from the can, he took off his campaign hat and poured the beer into it. To much shouting and laughter from the other pilots, he began to drink it directly from the hat. After that, nothing about the evening was quite clear.

CHAPTER FIVE

OCTOBER 17, 1970

MUCH PAIN, NO GAIN

Strider woke up just as it was getting light. His head was pounding and his whole body shivering with cold, a rarity in Vietnam. His bed seemed very hard and scratchy this morning. When he opened his eyes, he saw why. He was not on his bed, instead he was stretched out on the concrete sidewalk on the outside of the tin fence around the courtyard, not far from the latrine. He was soaking wet, not surprising since the rain hadn't stopped in weeks, and he was wearing his boots, trousers, and tee-shirt, but that was it, since he seemed to have lost his shirt somewhere. His head was "Condition One," the classic hangover, the worst kind. It was the head pounding, throbbing behind the eyes, a mouth-tasting-vile kind of hangover. Had he been throwing up? He must have been, given the way his mouth tasted. His arms were covered with mosquito bites, probably his face and neck too, since he did not have a hat on. Who knew mosquitoes bit in the rain? Dimly he remembered filling his hat with beer, drinking it while spilling it all over himself, and then trying to take pictures of the girls on the makeshift stage, by then dancing bare breasted to off-key music from their three-piece band. Then, nothing . . .

The pounding sounds in his head were augmented by the sound of Chinooks taking off from Liftmaster Pad on their morning missions. "Oh, shit. Was I supposed to fly today?" Strider wondered, but it was too complex a problem to answer right now. Right now he had to collect himself and get off this concrete. Looking at the mosquito bites covering his arms he wondered if he would get malaria, another issue too complex for right now.

Strider slowly picked himself up off the sidewalk, painful as it was. He really, really had to pee and, fortunately, had been lying right next to one of the pipes stuck in the ground that served as a urinal, so he didn't have to travel far to do so. He managed to piss without getting it all over himself, a major accomplishment given his condition, but moot really, since he was already soaking wet. He hoped he was wet from the rain, but couldn't tell for sure. Business of the moment completed, he turned to head back up the sidewalk to his hootch. As he lurched toward the hole in the tin fence that opened to the officer's courtyard he saw the operations officer coming toward him, probably headed for the urinal himself. He was smiling quite happily as he walked through the rain.

"Ah, Strider, you were supposed to fly today, but in light of your extraordinary performance last night I have decided to give you the morning off. Report to me this afternoon, I've got some paperwork you can do while everyone else is out fighting the war," the operations officer said, his smile trying to turn into a grim look, an effort that was not succeeding. It was clear that it was taking a mighty effort to suppress a smile.

Straightening up as much as he could, Strider came to a semi-position of attention and said, "Yes Sir, I'll be there," each word making his head hurt worse.

Extraordinary performance? What extraordinary performance, Strider wondered as he walked into his hootch. Oh God, did 2LT Taylor have his movie camera going? He was usually walking around filming something every day, but Strider couldn't remember if Taylor was there or not. Strider realized he had to find out what happened, especially since he remembered nothing. Wait, what about Fivelson and his 35mm? What about everyone else's cameras? What about his own camera?

When Strider opened the door to the hootch, Cobb and Steiner were both gone, probably flying, and, as Strider expected, they had not made a move to clean up from last night's party. That would be copilot work. Empty wine bottles, beer cans, and various food remnants were heaped on the dining table and scattered around the room. The floor was sticky with spillage. Ignoring it all, Strider tried getting into bed and going back to sleep, but that wasn't happening, too much head pounding for sleep. He was too dirty, too. Instead of staying in bed, he went into the back room and after taking three aspirin, started the hot water going to fill the washing machine so he could take a shower. While it was filling he ran shaving water into the sink. "I wonder where my flight suit shirt got to," he thought as he shaved. Thirty minutes later, showered and dressed in a clean, dry flight suit, he began cleaning the room.

After half an hour of cleaning, the hootch was no longer completely disgusting, so he wandered over to the Officers' Club, the spot where he last knew for sure he had his shirt on. He found it in a corner behind the bar, wadded up in a ball and still wet with last night's beer, but in a small victory over adversity, his government-issue Skilcraft pen was still in its pocket. He was comforted by a black-ink pen in his shoulder pocket, thinking that whatever one signed with an issue Skilcraft pen made the thing seem more official. Strider's Instamatic camera was there too, parked in a dry spot underneath the shirt and seemingly no worse for wear, though half a roll of film had been taken. He wondered, taken of what? Along with the shirt and camera, his campaign hat was there too, wet, crushed and shapeless now, but with wings and CW2 bar still in place. The "Kill a Commie for Christ" button was gone, a casualty of the "USO" show, no doubt.

After putting hat and shirt back in his hootch to dry, Strider went to the operations bunker, where, as the operations officer promised, he was put to work, checking mission sheets and other paperwork that he had not heretofore known existed. He was amazed at how closely operations tracked what the company did—how many missions were flown and by whom, how many flight hours in the last 30 days each pilot had, where they were shot, and what was doing the shooting, etc. Perhaps there was more to the Army than merely flying. The operations officer's reputation grew in Strider's estimation, as he realized how much of the paperwork load the operations officer took to keep it off the pilot's plates.

By dark, Strider's work in operations was complete and he was back to semi-normal, with only a slight headache remaining to remind him of how much he drank before the "USO" show. He fixed a tuna/mac/cheese casserole for dinner just like "Leave it to Beaver" June Cleaver did for Ward, and had it ready when Cobb and Steiner came wandering into the hootch back from the day's flights.

He could almost hear them saying, "June, June, I'm home." "In here, Ward."

When they came in, Strider was glad to see that both his roommates were the worse for wear after last night, too. They had just not gone quite as far as Strider had, probably because they had more experience at these things, he supposed. Then again, maybe they were just smarter. But, whether smarter or not, they were dog-tired. At least Cobb and Steiner cleaned up after supper—pity for the poor newbie? Probably, or maybe the newbie no longer was a newbie in their eyes.

Before he called it a night, Strider went to the Officers' Club to check the crew assignment's board. He saw that he would be flying with Steiner the next day, and since they were number two in the list, it promised to be at least six hours in the air, maybe even eight, depending on how many missions operations assigned them. Strider wouldn't know for certain until Steiner let him see the mission sheet in the morning, since only ACs, not copilots, got them in advance. It didn't really matter though; whatever the number of missions and however long it took, they would complete them. The mission must be done.

Strider wrote his daily letter to his wife and laid out his gear for the morning before he went to bed. The room was quiet, no music tonight. Steiner was lying in bed, reading. He had been very quiet all evening, even less talkative than usual. As Strider went in the back to take his shower, Cobb went out, guitar in hand, probably going singing and drinking at the club, as usual. Strider didn't give it too much thought; it was just what Cobb did. Still, how could he do it night after night? Strider knew he couldn't, since he still had a headache from the party. Before he turned out his light, Strider turned on the rotating fan over his bed to keep the mosquitoes away and reflected on events. Ten months to go . . . but who's counting?

hough Strider's head was still hurting the next morning when the duty clerk provided the wake-up call at 0430 hours, he was ready to fly. At breakfast, no one said a word about missing yesterday's morning launch or "extraordinary performances." At one time or another, nearly everyone in Playtex had done something similar, so Strider knew he was now just another one of the boys. He later learned that the operations officer had known from past experience that at least one pilot would be in no condition to fly after the party and, with his advance approval, had put the CO on the schedule as backup copilot. Better to let the pilots blow off steam now and then, than to push them too hard, lest they break.

Strider never did that again, it was entirely too much pain for no gain at all. He also still did not know exactly what went on at one of those shows.

PLAYTEX 820: ROOMMATES GO FLYING

Strider figured right about the hours that he and Steiner would get. As daylight broke over Liftmaster, they took off to the north in Playtex 820, lifting into the rain and fog that just seemed to get worse every day. Since they were number two on the priority list, they had six missions listed on the sheet, each one with many sorties. It was a long day, with many trips to the FSBs carrying ammo and fuel swinging below their Chinook. Their last few loads were water, since the rain was too hard to catch for drinking out on the FSBs. There were probably so many more missions than usual scheduled in order to build up stockpiles before the weather got too bad to bring in more ammunition, water, fuel, food, etc.

Even so, the length of the day had more to do with sitting around than flying. Sometimes between sorties they had to wait for weather. Then the weather would clear and they had to wait for the loads to be ready for pick-up. Since other Chinooks were working the same PZ, it almost resembled a traffic jam at some points, with aircraft in a high hover as they waited for those in front of them to get out of the way. They also had to wait their turn in the fuel pits as other 159th ASHB Chinooks needed to refuel, too. All that aside, it was just another day until the real drama came while they were waiting for maintenance to bring them another aircraft after their Chinook broke down at Camp Evans.

As the days had passed and the weather steadily deteriorated, battalion operations began holding aircraft at the different supply bases throughout Northern I Corps: Camp Eagle, Camp Evans, Quang Tri, and Dong Ha. The bases all had to be ready to launch the Chinooks to haul the loads to the FSBs as quickly as possible, whenever there was a break in the weather. Since those holding bases weren't really set up for long term Chinook operations, parking became a problem, with aircraft shutting down wherever space was available on some of the bases, at designated areas at others. Playtex's holding area was Camp Evans.

After numerous reports that it was getting very dangerous out there, battalion operations sent word to "hold all aircraft on the ground for a couple hours before trying it again." The battalion CO had visions of aircraft going missing all over the area in the bad weather and it was a vision he did not like, so he told the operations officer to pass the word. Playtex's CO was relieved that they were getting a break. Even though he trusted his pilots' judgment, he knew that they would go to the wall to get the mission done. That was what they did, complete the missions. Sometimes, though, they needed an adult to tell them to back off for a while.

When Steiner got the word from Playtex Operations that there was a weather hold, he took the aircraft into the fuel pits at Camp Evans. He had the crew top off the fuel cells to bring their total to 8,000 pounds; when they were finished, he flew over to the holding area to shut down. The aircraft from their sister companies would be holding at Camp Eagle and Quang Tri, since battalion liked to keep aircraft for the same company working in the same general area, easier for them to reallocate missions if an aircraft broke or was damaged. One holding area, one of the two assigned to Playtex that day, was at Camp Evans. This particular holding area had four landing spots available.

Three of the spots at Camp Evans were fine for landing Chinooks, nice and flat with lots of spacing between them. The fourth spot, however, was only marginally safe and was normally used only as a last resort. It was loathed by the aircrews, because it had a pretty good slope in it, about 10 degrees, causing the pilots to have to land uphill, with the front wheels touching ground first. This added a real degree of difficulty, since a Chinook's rear wheels normally touch first. When the front wheels touched first, the pilots had to basically balance the aircraft until they were ready to take the power off and let the rear wheels settle heavily onto the ground, a very unsettling maneuver. When the pilots did get the aircraft on the deck, they were sitting uncomfortably nose high, far higher than normal, and damned uncomfortable. All the drama of landing on that particular spot earned it the name "the Crash Pad," though no one actually crashed there—yet. Steiner and Strider were the second aircraft into the holding area, so they got one of the two remaining flat spots, leaving the Crash Pad and the final flat spot open for whoever was next.

As Steiner landed Playtex 820 on the holding pad, the master caution light, the big red light above the dash, came on. Looking at the caution panel capsule lights, the panel in the center of the dash that tells the pilots which system is out of normal range, they both saw it was the "Forward Transmission Chip Light," indicating possible impending transmission failure, an always fatal event in Chinooks, and helicopters in general for that matter. Since they were on the ground already, there wasn't much immediate danger, so they just shut the aircraft down to check it out. This allowed the flight engineer to unscrew the plug and pull it out from the bottom of the transmission to examine it.

The chip detector is basically a magnet mounted in the bottom of the transmission oil tank. If a flake of metal or some metal fuzz comes off one of the gears inside the transmission, the magnet catches it as it circulates in the transmission fluid, thereby closing an electrical circuit and lighting the master caution light and the corresponding capsule light. If it is just a little fuzz, the flight engineer may just clean the plug off and put it back.

If, after they restart the aircraft and the light doesn't come on, all is well and they can continue with the mission. In this case, when the flight engineer pulled the plug, he found a very small sliver of metal, not just fuzz. Time to call the maintenance department and let them deal with it; meanwhile, the crew of 820 was just stuck there.

Since they were well out of the line-of-sight, getting the maintenance department on the radio was impossible from Camp Evans, so Steiner walked over to one of the buildings close to the pad to use their telephone. While he took care of that, Strider and the rest of the crew stayed in the aircraft, eating cold C rations, again. Fifteen minutes later when Steiner returned, he told them it would be at least an hour before they could get someone up to Camp Evans from Liftmaster, which he figured really meant it would be two or three hours before maintenance got there. Steiner, too, then settled down to a lunch of C rations. When he finished, he stretched out on a section of the troop seats and took a nap there in the back of the "Boeing Hilton." It struck Strider that a nap was an excellent idea, so he followed his leader's lead and stretched out on his own chunk of seats. He must have fallen straight asleep because he saw it was 15 minutes later when both he and Steiner were awakened by the sound of Playtex Balls Niner (009) landing on the last flat spot in the holding area. That left only the crash pad open for whoever was unlucky enough to be the last aircraft in.

Strider tried to go back to sleep, but sleep would not return, which was just as well since about half an hour later, they heard the sound of another Chinook coming in to land. It wasn't, however, maintenance coming to rescue Steiner and Strider with another Chinook, as hoped. Instead it was Playtex 831, also coming in to hold on the ground until the weather standby was lifted or operations called off flights for the day.

PLAYTEX 831

The pilots of Playtex 831 were CW2 Jerald Carter and CW2 Joe Savick. Carter and Savick seemed to everyone like they were brothers or at least first cousins. Carter was so proud of his two sons in Colorado that he would happily bore you to tears with family stories at any opportunity. Savick was the same about his wife in Alabama: beautiful woman, had excellent taste because she married him, etc. Carter and Savick graduated from Army flight school two weeks apart, had arrived in Vietnam on the same day, were assigned to the 101st Airborne (Airmobile) on the same day, attended the same Screaming Eagle Replacement Training Center (SERTC) class, and finally, had arrived in Playtex on the same day.

To Strider, they were more than mere brothers; as far as he was concerned for all practical purposes, they were fraternal twins. They had to be fraternal, not identical, because even though their body types were similar, they looked nothing alike in the face. Of course, they dressed exactly alike, like twins might, but then all the pilots dressed exactly alike in green two-piece flight suits, black combat boots, etc. They also roomed together, like twins might, sharing one of the smaller hootches just down from the Officers' Club. Unlike most of the small hootches, there was also a third roommate living with them: a pet lizard they named Ralph. Ralph lived in their clothes closet and had his own private entrance through a hole in the bottom of the door. His job was to keep the hootch free of bugs and he did it fairly well, so they didn't mind his occasional barking in the night. Besides, it's always nice to have someone to keep an eye on things when you are out flying all day.

THE AC

Carter hadn't been an aircraft commander for very long. It took him a bit longer than most because he was stuck with one of those responsible ground jobs that cut into the amount of time available for flying, so getting the required Chinook time and Vietnam flight time, along with his ground job, extended the effort. He should have been the supply officer because he was a born horse trader: take for example, his method of keeping his hootch cool during the ten months of hot, humid weather. Other pilots had tried cooling their hootches with varying degrees of success, since air conditioners that worked were very hard to come by and vent fans just didn't work well in all the humidity. Carter decided that if he couldn't find a working air conditioner, he would take cooling to the next level. He never said what he traded or who he traded with, but somehow he scrounged a walk-in freezer unit from parts unknown.

As Strider walked through the officers' area one day, he saw the back wall of Carter and Savick's hootch had been partially cut away. A forklift was busy positioning the freezer unit into the hole, with Carter intently supervising the effort. Strider walked over and looked at the control dial on the freezer unit. He saw that its warmest setting was 40 degrees F. When he pointed this out to Carter, who, with his roommate, was busy hooking the unit up to the overhead electric lines, Carter just laughed and said, "We'll just use more blankets." Strider was not sure this was a good or even workable plan, but minor details like that did not deter Carter.

As Savick later told it, that night he woke at 0200 realizing he was freezing, literally, not figuratively, freezing. He said he could not feel his feet, but he could see his breath as he threw off the three blankets on his bed and ran out of the room into the tropical night. One of the other Playtex pilots had gone around to the back of their hootch after they had called it a night and turned the control dial on the freezer unit from 40 degrees above zero to 10 degrees below zero, just to see what would happen. The unit worked exactly as advertised and was well on its way to -10 degrees when the occupants of the hootch finally woke up to their near-death experience. How would the CO explain two pilots freezing to death in their sleep in Vietnam, Strider wondered?

Carter turned the dial on the freezer unit back up to 40 degrees and removed the temperature control knob to prevent anyone from turning it down again. It made no difference, since the next night someone used a pair of pliers to turn it back down to -10 degrees once more. After that, in a more conventional approach to cooling, Savick bought an air conditioner from a pilot in another Chinook company and installed it in their hootch's back wall in place of the freezer unit. Carter borrowed the forklift from the maintenance department again to remove the freezer unit. He had it loaded on a duce and half (2.5 ton truck) and it disappeared from Playtex, headed to parts unknown. Carter would not say what he traded it for, but the betting among the warrants was that it was something good. When you brought it up, Carter would just smile.

But today he wasn't horse trading, he was commanding Playtex 831 and he was visibly happy that the aircraft was safely on the ground at Camp Evans. He was not comfortable with the low cloud and poor visibility, particularly back in the higher terrain where the FSBs were. His real job kept him on the ground a lot and his missions had so far all been daylight VFR. He had not had time to practice even a little IFR flying, even the simulated kind. He dreaded the possibility of inadvertently getting in the clouds and then having to get back down again.

THE COPILOT

A good Catholic boy from Akron, Ohio, Savick seemed to always be two weeks behind Carter in flying. As noted earlier, he had graduated Army Flight School two weeks behind him, finished Chinook transition two weeks behind him, and even though they arrived in Playtex the same day, Savick made AC two weeks after Carter. Not to say that this bothered him, because it did not. Flying seemed to be incidental to Savick, because he had found his true calling in the Army as armory officer and as motor pool officer. To Strider, he seemed to be more at home stripping weapons, inspecting them, and putting them back together than he was in the cockpit of a Chinook. Similarly, he took to the motor pool with a flare not seen before in Playtex.

To Savick, the motor pool officer's job was just icing on the cake. The way he ran Playtex's small motor pool foreshadowed potential big doings in logistics later in his life, since it was apparent to all that he fully understood the law of supply and demand. It was far more difficult to sign out one of the company's jeeps than it was to sign out a Chinook: the aforementioned law of supply and demand in action. There were 16 Chinooks in Playtex, but only three jeeps. Being able to sign out one of the jeeps, load it in the back of a Chinook and head off to a PX in Da Nang, was an aircrew's dream day off, but it was difficult to achieve, as dreams often are. The jeeps were needed for official things—when maintenance needed to do runs over to the depot to pick up small parts for the aircraft, for mail runs, and in case the CO wanted to go over to Battalion Headquarters— so Savick had to ration them carefully. That said, no one in Playtex found it odd that somehow there was always a jeep available when the motor pool officer wanted one or when the Officers' Club officer needed one for a booze run down to Da Nang. Those were just normal things in the life of Playtex.

THE FLIGHT ENGINEER

Specialist 4th Class (Spec 4) Mike Crawford was Playtex 831's flight engineer. He had worked very hard for that position and, like all flight engineers, he took the job very, very seriously. He was constantly checking everything on his helicopter to keep it in the best possible shape for missions. When his Chinook was a backup aircraft, he was even known to suggest quietly to ACs, as they walked onto the flight line, that perhaps they should find something wrong with their assigned aircraft and take his instead. Because he took such pride in his aircraft, some of the ACs might have even taken him up on it, even if they wouldn't admit it. He was, like most flight engineers, Spec 4, but he was on the list to make sergeant instead of Spec 5. While a Spec 5 and a sergeant are both E-5s and get the same pay, a Spec 5 is considered a technician, while a sergeant is considered a leader, an important distinction for someone like Crawford who was looking forward to making the Army a career.

An Oklahoma boy, Crawford saw the Army as a way to stay out of the flat red lands of home for his wife and himself, a way to see the world as they started a family. He found seeing it from above in his own helicopter was particularly nice. His hard work had paid off well, so far, since he was on the list to be an E-5 sergeant at 20 years old, two years sooner than most men made it. He loved the fact that pilots depended on him to make sure their machines were ready. They also depended on him to quickly and accurately direct them over the loads and get them in and out of the landing zones in one piece. They were a team, Playtex 831's crew; everyone in the crew lives in each other's hands every day, and Crawford led the enlisted portion of that team.

All that said, Spec 4 Crawford would leave the Army today, if it meant he could leave Vietnam at the same time. Careers in the Army were in the future and right now, he was very tired of Vietnam. Rain, rain, never ending rain, something unknown back home in Oklahoma where it seemed sometimes it would never rain again. He never said that out loud, though. He would get through the rain somehow, as long as he could keep on being flight engineer of his beloved Playtex 831.

THE CREW CHIEF

It's a long way from La Puente, in Los Angeles County, California, to Liftmaster Pad in I Corps, Vietnam, but to his surprise, Spec 4 Ray Trujillo made it that far a lot more quickly than he thought he would. About 5'8", solid build, dark hair and friendly eyes, Trujillo had many friends in not only Playtex, but also in the Varsity. To his surprise, he actually found himself enjoying his tour in Vietnam. Like nearly all 19-year-old men, he loved fast cars, but now he found fast helicopters even more interesting, particularly now that he was well on his way to becoming a flight engineer on his own Chinook. Crawford was getting "short" and Trujillo had every reason to think that the maintenance officer would soon move him up to take Crawford's place. He had worked very hard to get to be a crew chief and would work just as hard to have the finest Chinook in Playtex when he got the chance.

In his mind, Trujillo had already designed the art he would paint on the armor plate when Playtex 831 became his. He had a friend in the hydraulics section of the maintenance department who was a real artist, a painter. He could paint anything and would happily do the actual painting on the armor plate of his Chinook, based on a photo Trujillo had of his girlfriend back home. Nothing too racy, but man, was she a beautiful woman and her picture on the armor plate would add grace to an otherwise ugly green Chinook. He missed her a lot. Sometimes he regretted not getting married before he left, but it was way too late now. Maybe in eight months when he got home . . .

THE DOOR GUNNER

The door gunner, Private Willie Oaks, was an apprentice mechanic, fresh in-country and so new to Chinooks that he didn't know about magic spots to take a piss under turning rotor blades. As all new guys did, he had soaked himself thoroughly on his first attempt, this very morning. He was being good natured about the ribbing he was taking, especially in light of the flight engineer's words that everyone had done the same thing at least once. Besides, all three of the enlisted crewmen were soaked from refueling the Chinook in the rain, so maybe all that rainwater had washed away the piss. At least Oaks hoped it had.

Like Strider, Oaks was a Kentucky mountain boy. When he turned 18, right after he finished high school, he enlisted in the Army to get started in life. Kentucky mountain men often did that, more as a way out of the hills and coal mines than from burning patriotism, although they were patriotic by their nature. Oaks grew up in Lee County, right next door to where Strider's people lived in Breathitt County. In fact, Strider's grandfather preached at a church in Lee County. His grandfather had baptized Strider in a muddy farm pond just down the road from the Lee County church when Strider was 12 years old. When Strider heard Oaks mention in a weather hold BS session that he was from Beattyville, Kentucky, he was amazed: someone from so close to home right here in the same Chinook company.

One day after missions were complete, Strider asked Oaks if he knew of his preacher grandfather, but he did not. Further discussion disclosed that Strider's grandfather was Church of Christ, while Oaks' people were Church of God; religious differences that could not be reconciled kept the two groups apart socially. Neither Strider nor Oaks could have told you what the exact differences between the two churches were, but whatever they were, they were real to the people from the mountains of Kentucky. From what Strider's grandfather had told him, religious differences there were sometimes settled with guns, so it was better not to get too into it in a place where everyone had an automatic weapon, not just a pistol or bolt action rifle.

At this early point in his tour, Oaks had some vague interest in becoming a crew chief and maybe later a flight engineer, but right now being a door gunner was his idea of heaven. Clean the machine guns, install them, sometimes shoot them, all the while watching the world go by from the window of a Chinook flying over Vietnam. How far was that from the coal mines of the Kentucky mountains? He might miss the mountains occasionally, but this was all right for now.

THE WEATHER HOLD

Playtex Operations told Carter to join the other company aircraft at Camp Evans to stand by for a break in the weather, so after refueling, he took the aircraft to the holding area to wait. When Playtex 831 arrived, as last in, Carter's only choice for a place to park—a Hobson's choice really—was the Crash Pad. As Strider watched 831 come in, he could see the crews in the other three Chinooks already parked in the holding area doing the same thing he was doing, i.e. hanging out their windows to watch the show as the late comer tried to settle his aircraft down on the sloping stretch of land.

The watchers were all disappointed. Carter must have been flying and concentrating very hard on being smooth, since he knew that the other three crews would be watching and ready to razz him if he bobbled. The Chinook touched down lightly on its front wheels and then settled back smoothly onto its rear wheels, firmly on the ground. This took a level of skill that new ACs, like Carter, rarely had. There was no drama at all, much to everyone's disappointment. Even so, no one would say "good landing" to Carter: that might give him a big head. In a few minutes, 831's parking brakes were set, the engines came off-line, the rotor blades slowly spun to a stop and finally the APU wound down. Playtex 831 was at rest with its sister aircraft until it was needed again.

Having finished their lunch and nap, Steiner and Strider decided to walk over to Playtex 831 and see what the late arrival had to say. Maybe Carter knew something about Playtex Operations deciding that they wouldn't be able to get into the FSBs today and therefore could come back to Liftmaster. It was not likely, though, since in everyone's opinion, not even operations knew what operations was going to do. Strider didn't think that was fair, really, since Playtex Operations could not move without orders from 159th ASHB Operations, who in turn could not move without orders from 101st ABN (AMBL) Division Operations. Still, eventually someone would decide when they could call it a day. But then, in one way it was moot for them, since right now Strider and Steiner were stuck at Camp Evans with a broken aircraft, weather hold or no weather hold, until maintenance either brought them a new aircraft or cleared this one to fly.

Just as Playtex 820's crew had done earlier, Carter, Savick, and the aircrew men immediately settled down to a C ration lunch in the aircraft's cabin, everyone selecting their favorite meal from the case Crawford always kept in his private stash. Crawford had a case of soft drinks stashed, too, so for once it wasn't just canteen water with lunch. Everyone in 831's crew was in a good mood as Steiner and Strider climbed aboard, laughing about something the door gunner had done that morning. They weren't saying what it was, but Oaks looked sheepish. Whatever he had done, it couldn't have been too bad since he was laughing about it along with the rest of his crew.

It wasn't very comfortable sitting in the back of Playtex 831. Besides everyone being wet and cold, they had to sit at an odd angle, since in addition to the aircraft's normal nose up attitude when it was on the ground, there was the added slope of the Crash Pad to contend with. The pilots were leaning uphill as they sat in the troop seats talking with empty C rations containers on the cabin deck in front of them. It was almost like the days of flying the old bubble helicopters when they were in training back at Fort Wolters: when you were out of trim your downhill butt cheek went numb.

The enlisted crewmen had no time to sit and talk after they finished their C rations, because Crawford had them up and checking the aircraft so it would be ready to go when they got the call to take off again. Like all the other flight engineers shut down at Camp Evans, it was his aircraft and he was going to make damn sure it was ready to fly when the call came to launch again.

ROUTINE MAINTENANCE, PLAYTEX 831

As he checked out the area around the aft transmission, Crawford noticed that the utility hydraulic system fluid sight gauge showed that the fluid was a little low, a minor problem, but one that should be corrected before they went flying again. To service it he would have to release the pressure in the accumulator tank, meaning that someone would have to manually pump it back up to normal pressure, so that they could start the auxiliary power unit (APU) when they were getting ready to start the engines. The system re-pressurization was a tedious job that required 15 minutes of vigorous manual pumping on the handle back by the aircraft's rear ramp, but that's what crew chiefs were for. Crawford had several cans of spare hydraulic fluid stored in the box with the rest of the miscellaneous bits and bobs that all aircraft have onboard for just such reasons. He got a couple of the cans, dumped the utility pressure, and started to open the reservoir to begin refilling it. Trujillo, as the crew chief, watched, knowing full well the pumping came next and he would be the one doing it.

Then, for no readily apparent reason, and much to everyone's surprise, with an audible thump the aircraft's brakes released and the Chinook began rolling down the hill, backwards with the crew, pilots included, still in the aircraft's cabin.

The aircraft's brakes are completely separate from the utility hydraulic system, so depressurizing it should have had no effect and indeed, it did not, but the fact that the helicopter was rolling downhill out of control was real. No one had thought to put chalks behind the wheels because they weren't something that Playtex's Chinooks routinely carried.

For a second, everyone just froze in place. Then, as the aircraft gathered speed bumping along backwards, Carter leaped up and ran uphill through the cabin for the cockpit. The brake pedals are on top of the rudders, so you have to be in the cockpit to set them. He got through the companionway without too much difficulty, but getting into the left seat was harder. Even under normal conditions, it took a few contortions to get your body into the seat, but given that the Chinook was at a much higher nose attitude than normal, and was moving, it was nearly impossible. Even so, Carter managed to get in, but as he did, his foot hit the cyclic control stick so hard that he bent it forward slightly. It didn't matter, as the five seconds it took to get there meant he was too late to get the brakes on before the aircraft hit something. That something was a drainage ditch next to the road that ran along the bottom of the Crash Pad.

With a large thump that knocked everyone in the cabin off their feet then sent them tumbling into a heap under the aft transmission, the Chinook stopped rolling backwards. As it did so, the aircraft settled left rear low, leaving it unnaturally nose high and leaning about two feet down on the left side. Savick, Steiner, and Strider had all been sitting down and managed to hang on to their seats, so they were fine. Strider wasn't too sure about the three crewmen lying in a tangle under the aft transmission, but when they managed to separate themselves from the scrum, it was clear that they were fine. As it later turned out, they didn't even suffer a decent bruise among them.

Crawford dropped the unopened can of hydraulic fluid as he fell on the ramp at the impact of the Chinook with the ditch, and was immediately covered by the other crew members as they tumbled aft, both of them landing on top of him. When the motion stopped, he quickly separated himself from the tangle of men in the back, got to his feet and ran uphill through the cabin for the right side front crew door. There was no exiting via the rear of the aircraft, since the partially opened ramp was now blocked from opening fully by the muddy dirt of the road. He crawled under the right door gun, leaped from the crew doorstep onto the mud at the bottom of the crash pad, and ran for the rear of the Chinook to see how much damage had been done.

In a moment, those still inside the cabin heard Crawford yell, "Son of a bitch!"

When he got to the back of the aircraft, Crawford saw the left rear wheel had broken off entirely, leaving the sponson resting in the muddy dirt of the ditch, with a bit of crumpled sheet metal above the broken bit. The partially open ramp was holding its position just above the surface of the road, not actually touching it, but it was close. Crawford was shortly joined by the rest of 831's crew, as well as Steiner and Strider. Moments later Playtex 820's three crewmen arrived at a run, carrying the fire extinguishers from their aircraft in case they were needed. They weren't needed. There was no fire; instead of the crackle of flames, there was only the sound of the soft rain hitting the now lopsided Chinook, adding more fluid to the mud all around the Crash Pad and the ditch where 831 now rested.

In a few minutes, the crews of the other two Playtex Chinooks were also standing next to 831's crew, all staring at the broken wheel and the crumpled metal. To Strider they looked no different from a crowd of bystanders at a car wreck. Why is it, he wondered, broken things are more interesting to some people than whole things? Why does everyone come running at the sound of an impact? But, then, Strider thought, he would do the same if he wasn't already here.

As broken as it was, the crew of Playtex 831 could only stare at their aircraft; there was nothing they could do to fix it now. Fortunately, the ramp had not hit the road. If it had, it would have acted as a lever and bent the fuselage, something that could well have made the aircraft a complete loss. As things were, Playtex 831 looked fixable, though it wouldn't be easy. Everyone immediately had an opinion on how to fix it. Maybe they could jack the aircraft up or something and replace the sheared off wheel and strut. Maybe they could get a crane to lift it so they could replace the strut. Or, maybe they could start it up where it sat and fly it back to Liftmaster for repair. Maybe . . .

No matter what, Carter knew they weren't doing anything with the Chinook until maintenance had a look at it, and probably not even then. All present agreed that the maintenance officer would not be pleased.

BROKEN BITS

Two hours after it rolled down the hill, the maintenance officer and the maintenance chief were there at the Crash Pad with a team evaluating Playtex 831's condition. As best as they could tell, Crawford was right, the fuselage was straight and there was no damage to any of the mechanical parts or rotor system, except to the landing gear and a little bit of wrinkled skin just above it. No, Playtex 831 was just fine, except, of course, for the broken off strut, resulting in a much higher than normal nose attitude.

Oh, yes, the utility hydraulic system was a bit low on fluid.

The maintenance officer also brought a quality assurance (QA) inspector with him to look at the transmission chips from Playtex 820. Looking at the small metal sliver that the flight engineer had taken off the chip detector plug, QA determined that it was probably nothing serious, just normal wear. After cleaning and reinstalling the chip detector plug, QA had Steiner and Strider ground run the aircraft for 20 minutes. The chip detector light did not come back on during that time, but the QA man had the crew shut it down anyway, so he could pull the plug for one final check. Again, there was nothing, no fuzz or slivers of metal, so Playtex 820 was cleared to fly.

While all this was going on, Playtex Operations had decided there would be no more missions that day, so everyone should go back home to Liftmaster. Everyone holding there at Camp Evans was greatly relieved that there had been a decision at last.

Carter, Savick, and Oaks, 831's door gunner, climbed into 820 for the trip back to Liftmaster. There was nothing for the pilots to do, since the broken Chinook was maintenance's aircraft now, not theirs. Carter was carrying the KY-28 radio scrambler and Oaks was carrying both machine guns. Neither radio scramblers nor door guns were of any use in a broken helicopter. Crawford and Trujillo, being the flight engineer and crew chief, would stay with their aircraft to help the maintenance team any way they could, not that they could do anything at this point. To Strider, Crawford looked very sad as he regarded his now broken aircraft.

Leaving the maintenance team to do their evaluations of Playtex 831, the maintenance officer also climbed in the back of Playtex 820 and rode down south to Liftmaster Pad. He didn't bother to plug his helmet into the ICS. Instead, he slumped down in one of the troop seats and appeared to sleep the entire trip, gathering him major cool points in Strider's mind. Or, instead of cool, was he was just being naturally taciturn? Then again, maybe he was just tired. Strider couldn't remember the maintenance officer ever saying anything at any of the officer gatherings or when he was having a beer in the Officers' Club. At official events, he always left the talking to the maintenance warrant officers who worked for him. Since he didn't socialize in the Club, you never knew what was on his mind.

Forty-five minutes and one fuel stop later, Steiner landed Playtex 820 back at Liftmaster. Before he could taxi 820 back into the revetment, the maintenance officer climbed into the companionway between the pilots and indicated to Steiner he wanted out. Steiner held position while the maintenance officer exited through the ramp. He walked across the runway toward the CO's office, but before he cleared the runway, he turned to wave at Steiner and Strider. Standing there clear of the rotor blades, his face still neutral as he waved, he left them once again with no idea what he was thinking. Who could understand RLOs? Strider noticed the maintenance officer slipped a little on the wet PSP as he walked away. Must have been some spilled oil to make it that slick in the rain.

After Playtex 820 was shut down and the blades had stopped, Carter, Savick, and Oaks walked off the ramp toward the company area. Carter and Savick both turned to wave, like the maintenance officer had. Carter, the AC, looked sad as he waved; it must have been because his aircraft was still at Camp Evans and, as AC, was at fault. Savick just looked like Savick. Oaks didn't look back. He just trudged across the ramp, a machine gun in each hand, headed for the armory to clean the weapons and call it a day.

CHAPTER SEVEN

OCTOBER 24, 1970

RECOVERING PLAYTEX 831

F irst thing in the morning, the maintenance officer sent a team of personnel, including the Boeing Tech Rep and the maintenance chief, back up to Camp Evans to see if they thought the plan that the evaluation team had come up with the day before would work. They were on site at 0830 to get started. After an hour of looking at the aircraft, looking at the plan, and talking to the Boeing Tech Rep, the maintenance chief briefed the maintenance officer on the situation and the options.

First, the aircraft could not be repaired on the spot. The dirt was too soft to allow it to be jacked up enough for the broken wheel to be replaced without the risk of the jack collapsing and doing further damage to the aircraft. The aircraft would have to be moved to a hard surface, preferably Liftmaster Pad, for the repair to be started. There were two ways to get Playtex 831 to a hard surface: one, since there was no ground crane available that would lift that much weight, have another helicopter, either a Chinook or a CH-54, lift it from where it was sitting to a level spot where it could be repaired or, two, fly it out.

If they tried to lift it with another Chinook, they would have to strip 831 down to make it as light as possible by removing the engines, rotor blades and pumping all the fuel out. Even then, the Chinook that would be lifting it would have to burn down to minimum fuel to be able to pick up that much weight. The maintenance officer was against this idea: the last time they tried it using a Chinook, Playtex 499 successfully did the lift, setting the other Chinook down quite nicely, before running out of fuel, crashing after complete loss of engine power, and becoming itself a total loss. That left two destroyed helicopters to deal with, instead of only one. The only positive side of that incident was that no one was seriously hurt in the crash of either Chinook. Still, this was not exactly the desired outcome.

On the other hand, a CH-54 could easily lift 831 with only minimal stripping required, but getting one scheduled would take at least a week, even though the Hurricanes were a sister company in the 159th ASHB. Even then it was quite possible that the mission would be canceled due to higher priorities. In any case, it would take a long time to get the CH-54 in place and the maintenance officer wanted 831 operational as soon as possible. Other than the broken landing gear, it was in fine shape, with at least 90 hours available until its next scheduled major maintenance event. After considering both possibilities, the team recommended that it be flown out directly to Liftmaster.

After some deliberation with the Boeing Tech Rep and the maintenance chief, the maintenance officer accepted the team's recommendation: fly Playtex 831 out of its muddy resting spot on the Crash Pad back home to Liftmaster Pad. In the team's opinion, it could be done safely, even if getting it started up and running would be a little more tense than normal. Once back at Liftmaster they would land the aircraft's left rear on a pile of mattresses to prevent further damage to the fuselage. Then, they would jack it up enough to do a temporary fix on the strut, just enough of a fix to move it to a revetment where a permanent repair could be done. After a full analysis of the damage, they would then get it ready for operational flight again. How long that would take was unknown, since they didn't know how many broken bits there were and they didn't know if they could readily get the replacement parts, given that left wheel struts were not normal wear and tear items.

It was obvious that the left rear wheel was indeed broken off, since it was lying loose next to the sponson, but after digging around it a little, they could see that it was a clean break, with the mounting bolts sheared off without too much damage to the mounting point. Had it been the right wheel, things would have been different since the right wheel is power driven for steering the aircraft during ground taxi, while the left just freewheels. Breaking off the right wheel would quite probably have done damage to the airframe instead of just ruining the wheel. Other than that, it appeared that there was only superficial damage to the aircraft's skin. The position of the ramp had been just high enough to keep it from contacting the ground and truly destroying the helicopter.

The only tricky part of flying it out was getting 831 started without having the aft rotor blades flex down and hit the fuselage, which would pretty well total the aircraft. The team considered this a real possibility, since the nose was abnormally high, at least 5 degrees higher than it would be if the aircraft were sitting on level ground, but the Boeing Tech Rep was optimistic that it could be done safely. They briefly considered putting a piece of plywood on the side of the aircraft where the blade would hit, so that if it did, the blade would "bounce" over the fuselage, but the maintenance officer decided against it on the grounds that it might actually cause more damage if the blade hit it and the plywood went flying.

The maintenance officer, after discussing the idea with the team, decided that instead of plywood, they would change the aircraft start up procedures. The pilot would start number one engine, the one on the left side, and instead of leaving it turning the rotors at idle RPM while he started number two engine, as per normal starting procedures, he would immediately take number one engine directly to full flying speed. This would, in theory, get the rotors spinning fast enough to prevent their flexing down excessively. The Boeing Tech Rep agreed that this was the best option they had. Still . . .

Carter had tried to join the maintenance team headed up to Camp Eagle that morning, but was told "no" by both the operations officer and the maintenance officer. He wanted to fly it out since he had signed for 831 when it rolled down the hill, but the maintenance officer vetoed the idea. The maintenance officer wanted a pilot with maintenance check flight training to do the flying, so that he would have a better idea if it truly was safely flyable for the trip back home. Carter, much to his dismay, would have to watch with everyone else when it came back into Liftmaster. The maintenance officer himself and his assistant maintenance officer, a specially trained warrant who only did maintenance check flights and not missions, would do the flying back down south.

PLAYTEX 831 RETURNS TO LIFTMASTER PAD

Even though they were fairly certain it would work, the maintenance chief had everyone move well back out of the way before the maintenance warrant began the start-up procedures, just in case it didn't. The maintenance warrant was by himself in the aircraft's cockpit for the run-up, with even the flight engineer standing well back in case the blades hit the fuselage and pieces started flying. The watchers heard the APU come on line, followed shortly by the sound of number one engine spooling up. Then, there was the rush of the rotor blades as the maintenance warrant threw the engine condition lever directly from "Idle" to "Fly," instead of starting number two engine before he moved it.

The rotor blades did not hit the fuselage. The start-up was completely normal, even if very quickly done. To the crew watching, Playtex 831 looked very odd, rotor blades turning at full speed as it sat there with its tail in the ditch and its nose far higher than it should have been. It looked like the aircraft should be moving backwards at 30 or 40 knots.

When the run-up was complete, the maintenance officer signaled that the rest of the crew was clear to board. The ramp couldn't be opened because it was too close to the road, so the maintenance officer and the flight engineer climbed in through the crew door after the run-up was complete. There would only be the three of them on the trip back to Liftmaster— the two pilots and the flight engineer (no crew chief or door gunner), in case there was damage to the aircraft they had not found in their inspections. No use risking more people than necessary.

Playtex 506, flown by Maas and Fivelson, had brought the maintenance officers and their team to Camp Evans. Now, with 831 running, their mission was to follow the cripple back home in case it developed problems en route. In back, they had a couple of mattresses for 831 to land on if it did have a problem before it got to Liftmaster. Maas would stay well back from them as they flew, not to be in compliance with the battalion commander's "no formation flying" order, but more from common sense. Why risk getting too close to a damaged aircraft? When Maas saw 831 safely turning, he started 506 up and called for the maintenance team to board. When everyone was onboard and strapped in, Maas lifted the Chinook into a normal 20-foot hover. He then held the aircraft there while waiting for 831 to take off, so that he could keep an eye on them as they flew south.

It was raining, of course, but for once the visibility was more than a mile and the clouds were at least 500 feet above the ground. It should be an easy flight back to Liftmaster, at least they all hoped it would be.

With the reduced crew settled into their positions and the takeoff checklist complete, Playtex 831 was ready for lift off. The maintenance officer took the controls and when the flight engineer called "ready in back," he lifted the helicopter quickly, but smoothly, off the ground and into a 20-foot hover. There was a little backward drift caused by the abnormal nose high attitude as they lifted, but he quickly corrected for it. The helicopter did not show any signs of difficulty breaking free of the mud, nor did it show any unusual characteristics after he stabilized it in a hover. It just felt like a normal Chinook, even if its left cyclic control stick was bent noticeably forward and it was missing its left rear wheel.

After a call to Camp Evans aircraft control for takeoff clearance, the maintenance officer lowered the nose for a perfectly ordinary takeoff. Again, everything was normal on climb out, with no unusual vibrations or other indications of problems. Maas, in Playtex 506, waited 30 seconds before following 831 in takeoff. In a few minutes, both aircraft had cleared Camp Evans's barbed wire and were headed south following the highway QL1 back to Liftmaster at 500 feet above the ground.

The battalion CO had, of course, been briefed by Playtex's CO on what was happening with Playtex 831. He had contemplated taking one of the OH-6s and flying up to Camp Evans to watch events, but decided against it. His Chinook companies already gave him ulcers when they did their normal operations, never mind unusual ones like this. Why make the worry even worse by watching a broken aircraft lift off? He could have, of course, prevented them from flying it out and ordered them to request a CH-54 lift, but Playtex's CO was adamant that their plan would work, so he left them to it. He did tell his operations officer to let him know when they were 30 minutes out from Liftmaster Pad, so that he could have a jeep bring him over to watch the landing. The call came at 1030 and thirty minutes later he was standing on Liftmaster's PSP with Playtex's CO looking for the two inbound aircraft.

Liftmaster had quite a crowd of observers gathered by the entrance to the runway. All the pilots not on the flight schedule turned out, rain or not, to see what was going to happen next. Even the XO left his beloved paperwork to watch the landing. The pilots were laughing about whether or not the two maintenance pilots could hold a steady enough hover to actually put the broken left gear mounting point on the mattresses, the normal back and forth banter between the operational pilots and the maintenance pilots. Of course, neither group wanted the other one's job, so it was friendly banter, mostly.

Playtex's CO stood with the battalion CO, talking softly about something as they waited, but the pilots could see they were not laughing and joking about it, whatever it was. They did not disturb them, because you could never tell how RLOs were going to react to anything. The best thing warrants could do with RLOs, especially senior ones, was to leave them alone and not push your luck, lest you find yourself nominated as the next night duty officer at battalion operations.

As per the maintenance officer's direction, the S-4 had scrounged five surplus mattresses from the 101st's division dump and had them piled just off the Liftmaster runway. The maintenance chief decided five mattresses were too many, so at the Boeing Tech Rep's recommendation, they put down one mattress on the PSP and over that three wooden pallets. Over the pallets they added another three mattresses for cushioning, figuring that this should be enough to keep 831's fuselage from settling all the way to the ground. They also had jacking equipment standing by so that they could jack the aircraft up off the mattresses as soon as possible and get to work replacing the left landing gear. The landing spot they decided on was off the runway; Liftmaster Pad would remain usable while 831 was repaired sufficiently to tow it completely out of the way.

Strider, on the flight schedule with Steiner, was to start-up a backup aircraft instead of flying missions today, and was among the observers. Their aircraft, Playtex 820, had not been needed for the morning launch, so after the mission aircraft departed, they shut it down and went about their daily activities. Steiner headed off to operations to see how things were going, while Strider stayed on the flight line to watch 831 come in. He did not join in the banter among the pilots, but instead listened with great interest. Gallows humor was in the air: Would they crash on landing? How many maintenance pilots does it take to hover an aircraft in a stable position? No one knows, because it's never been done before, etc.

Strider had heard about aircraft coming in minus landing gear, but had never actually seen a helicopter come in with a missing wheel. He had seen a picture at Fort Rucker of a Huey that had somehow lost one skid and came back to land successfully on a pile of mattresses like the one currently on the pad at Liftmaster. He suspected this three-wheeled landing was going to be a non-event. As he saw it, Playtex 831 would do a normal approach to a hover, stabilize at 20 feet, and then come down onto the improvised landing aid, and shut down. He supposed that after it got on the ground, it was possible it would slide off the mattresses, but even that was highly unlikely. To his mind the maintenance pilots were more skilled at this sort of thing than the operational pilots were, though he would never say that out loud, lest he be ostracized.

Looking around, Strider saw many cameras ready to record all the action. Of course, 2LT Taylor was there with his movie camera, but no Fivelson with his 35mm. Ah, yes, he was copilot in 506 today, so he couldn't be here taking pictures. Too bad he was flying, since Fivelson seemed to enjoy taking pictures at least as much as he did being in the cockpit. Pictures are there for years, while flying is gone when you shut the aircraft down. Strider did not bother bringing his Instamatic camera, since he knew that someone with a 35mm would be happy to share if anything exciting happened. Even a bad 35mm picture was better than a good Instamatic one.

In a few minutes, the watchers could see Playtex 831 coming toward Liftmaster from the direction of Camp Eagle, with Playtex 506 following at a discrete distance. It went exactly like Strider thought it would: 831 shot an approach to a hover, made a straight descent, ending with a gentle touch down. The maintenance pilots had landed the Chinook without incident and ten minutes later, 831's rotor blades stopped turning, its APU went off-line and all the lookers, Strider included, went back to their normal routines. While there may have been a subdued disappointment among the onlookers that they didn't get any good pictures, Strider did notice a very relieved look on both the battalion CO and Playtex's CO's faces as they walked out through Liftmaster's gate.

With 831 safely on deck, it was 506's turn to land. After Playtex 506 taxied into its revetment, Trujillo exited and walked over to where Crawford was standing back behind 831. As they stood there, Oaks, who had been among the watchers, also joined them. All three were looking at 831 sitting there sadly with the spot where its left rear wheel should have been, now resting on its mattresses, when the maintenance chief walked by. He stopped and said to them, "Sergeant Crawford, I want you and Trujillo to go over to 866 and start getting it ready for tomorrow. The flight engineer left on emergency leave this morning and since 831 is going to be out for a while, 866 is your new aircraft, at least temporarily. Oaks, you will be flying with them tomorrow as gunner, so you give them a hand." With that, the maintenance chief walked away, leaving all three surprised, but happy, men.

They wouldn't be grounded after all. Apparently, any blame for 831's mishap was outweighed by the immediate need for trained and well performing aircrews. Crawford went onboard 831 to gather his gear before heading over to the maintenance office to start reviewing 866's records. As he walked away, the other two crewmen joined him, peeling off as they got to their new aircraft's revetment. Crawford and his two crewmen would make sure 866 was ready for launch at dawn tomorrow morning. They would also make sure that it would be an aircraft the pilots would want to fly, like 831 had been.

Steiner had not been watching 831's arrival, because he had been in the operations office talking to the duty officer about a possible new mission he would be assigned. Looking out through the door and seeing Strider walking back toward their hootch, Steiner called him over. Battalion operations wanted more aircraft available in the pick-up zones, so Playtex Operations had just added Steiner and Strider to the flight schedule. Their mission was to go north and wait up there in case the weather improved enough to fly missions to the farthest FSB north. In fact, this FSB was so far north that it was right on the DMZ and therefore, was in range of many NVA weapons.

Steiner was not optimistic about getting any loads to it; if the weather was bad over the lowlands, it was bound to be worse up there on the mountain where the FSB was, but a mission was a mission. On the bright side, if they did get off, the weather would make it impossible for the NVA to shoot at them.

Operations wanted them off no later than 1300 and since it was only 1100, they had time for a quick lunch in the mess hall before they took off in Playtex 820 for their holding point at Dong Ha, just south of the DMZ. Both Steiner and Strider packed a few things, change of underwear, shaving gear, extra pipe tobacco, etc., for a stay of overnight to a few days. When they got to the aircraft thirty minutes later, the crew had it ready. After a quick review of the pre-flight inspection they had done earlier in the day, they started it up, taxied out, and took off to the north into the rain. Visibility couldn't have been more than a mile and a half as they passed Camp Eagle, and showed no signs of improving.

PLAYTEX 820 GOES NORTH

As Steiner figured it would be, the flight up was a mess. The low clouds kept them from climbing above 500 feet, sometimes forcing them down to 300 feet or lower. The poor visibility slowed them down to 100 knots instead of their usual 120 as they flew the 60 miles north. Even though they were flying right in prime ground fire range, they didn't have to worry too much about getting shot because QL1, being the main national highway in that part of South Vietnam, was mostly secure. Given all the Army of the Republic of Vietnam (ARVN) and U.S. forces in bases along the highway, it was not likely the NVA would be in position along the road for an ambush, although it could always happen. They took no hits on the way, so if anyone did shoot at them, they missed. At least the navigation was easy on this mission, no maps required. All they had to do was fly straight up QL1 until they reached the two bridges, one railroad and one highway, at the town of Dong Ha, turn right, and there was the PZ where they would be waiting. If they missed the turn and went too far north, they would come to the collapsed bridges in the middle of the DMZ and find themselves in North Vietnam, real "bad guy country."

Steiner told Strider that it had happened once to one of the ACs going to this same LZ. He got disoriented doing an ITO from the LZ and went north instead of south. When he broke out of the clouds, he saw a four-lane highway below. The only problem with this was that South Vietnam doesn't have any four-lane highways in Northern I Corps. Realizing immediately that he was in North, not South, Vietnam, he quickly climbed back into the clouds and turned east until he was well out over the sea. He then turned south until he was definitely over South Vietnamese waters again. The AC was very lucky—if the NVA had shot at him, they missed and he got away with it. Not to worry, though, they weren't going to fly into North Vietnam today.

On the flight up, they remained strictly on the right side of the road as they went north, just as if they were driving a car back home. It is a rule that pilots learn early on: when following a linear feature, such a road or railroad, treat it the same as if driving a car in the U.S. and keep to the right. Sure enough, just after they had passed Camp Evans, a flight of five Hueys appeared headed in the opposite direction, also keeping to the right side of the road. The lead Huey flashed his landing light in greeting as they passed, a salute that Steiner returned. Strider idly wondered if the rule was the same in the United Kingdom or, since they drive on the left, was it reversed?

The bridges at Dong Ha appeared right on schedule. Steiner landed 820 and they were shortly shut down in the big field that served as a pick-up zone (PZ) and holding area. A Pathfinder came out to greet and direct them to the SEA hut that was the home of base operations. When CW2 Alex Kelley came back from talking to operations, the entire crew was pleased to find out that here in Dong Ha, for once, they would not be sleeping in the Boeing Hilton. A helicopter unit that had been stationed right next to the PZ had pulled up stakes and departed a week ago, leaving a group of SEA huts, complete with bunks, available for whoever would like to use them.

Steiner wanted the crew together, so with Dong Ha Operations approval, all five of them moved into the hootch closest to where their aircraft was parked. It appeared that Dong Ha was slated for transfer to the ARVN soon, since the empty hootches had not been torn down. That said, the hootches weren't being maintained and their deterioration had been rapid, with holes in the floor and a leaky roof already. Still, leaky roof or not, the beds were dry and the screens kept the mosquitoes out, mostly.

Though there was still a fair-sized U.S. force at Dong Ha, there were also large holes where units had been withdrawn in preparation for turning the base over to the ARVN. Even with fewer forces, there was still a lot of helicopter action in the area, as shown by the three Hueys shut down in the PZ when they landed. They were probably working with a grunt unit deployed in bunkers around the PZ area, perhaps taking them out for sweeps around the perimeter. This was good because it meant that, even if Dong Ha was closing, at least there was still good security at the PZ. The Playtex crew could see infantry on guard around the landing zone, so their aircraft would be protected tonight without the crew having to do it themselves. Even so, the door gunner volunteered to sleep in the aircraft to prevent any target of opportunity pilfering by the local units. Steiner told him it would not be necessary, since the flight line seemingly had good security, but thanked him for the offer.

As it got close to dark, it was obvious that they would not be flying any missions to the FSBs today. The weather was just too foul, with the same poor visibility and fog that had been there all day still obscuring the hills to the north. In any case, a night mission would be impossible since they would be unable to find the FSB in the fog and rain. Steiner made a telephone call back to Playtex Operations to give them a status report, while the crew checked out the helicopter.

After the crew completed the turnaround inspection ensuring that the aircraft would be ready for tomorrow's missions, they closed it up tight, with the machine guns stowed inside, the ramp up, and the crew door closed. Next, they went to what appeared to be Dong Ha's last remaining mess hall for dinner, where Steiner and Strider joined them. It was typical mess hall food, but no one from Playtex 820 complained, since even mess hall food beat the hell out of cold C rations eaten in the cabin of the aircraft.

After dinner, Strider walked back to their hootch through the rain with the rest of the crew. He only stayed a few minutes before he went outside to smoke his pipe one last time before turning in. He also wanted to get away from the other men for a little while. He liked them all and enjoyed their company, but needed a break from them now and then. He found a spot under the eve of one of the hootches that was out of the rain and, sheltering there, loaded up his pipe. As he lit his pipe, he noticed one of the Huey crews leaving the mess hall, headed for the hootch they had selected for the night. As they walked past Strider, one of the pilots did a double take, turned, and spoke to him.

"Strider? What the Hell are you doing here? Last time I saw you, you were going to Fort Campbell." The pilot said with a laugh.

Strider saw with surprise and a bit of pleasure that it was one of his classmates from flight school. In fact, they went farther back than that. They had both been in the Second Platoon, E Company, 5th Recruit Battalion, at Fort Polk, Louisiana, for Army Basic Training before the buses took them to Fort Wolters, Texas. Strider still remembered their battle cry, "E, Five Two, Best by Test! All the way, Drill Sergeant!"

Right now Basic Training seemed to be about 100 years ago, even though it had only been a little less than two. They laughed, shook hands, and clapped each other on the back, all the things men do to show pleasure at seeing a friend. His friend had gone to Vietnam to fly Hueys long before Strider's turn came, and now he was nearing the end of his tour. They each made the usual jokes between pilots who fly different aircraft, Strider calling out, "Skids are for kids, wheels are where it's at," while his friend countered with fat, ugly aircraft jokes about the Chinook. After five minutes they were out of things to talk about, so they shook hands and went their separate directions. Strider never saw him again.

CHAPTER EIGHT

OCTOBER 25, 1970

PLAYTEX 820 HAS A TINY PROBLEM

Around noon, all Playtex's aircraft were recalled from standby at the various holding zones around Northern I Corps back to Liftmaster Pad by company operations. They came in from Camp Evans, Camp Eagle, Quang Tri, and Dong Ha, throughout all the PZs in the northern part of South Vietnam, until all 16 Chinooks were parked in their revetments. Of course, Playtex 831, broken as it was, was being cannibalized for parts to keep the other 15 Chinooks operational, but at least it was in its revetment like all the others. Some of its parts were ones that aviation supply had not yet been able to bring up from the depot in Saigon, so at least the broken wheel allowed the maintenance officer to get two of the other aircraft ready to fly. Fifteen out of sixteen isn't a bad readiness rate in any aircraft company or squadron.

Steiner and Strider were late getting the word to come back home due to some confusion on Playtex Operations' part as to what unit they were staying with and how to contact them. Late word and late starting at Dong Ha, the furthest north PZ, made them the last aircraft back home. They took Playtex 820 into Camp Eagle's fuel pits to top off the tanks before returning to Liftmaster, which added even more time to their return. It was just before 1600 and starting to get dark when they finally landed in the fuel pits. Everyone in the crew was tired, damp, and very ready to call it a day, as soon as they topped the tanks off.

As they usually did, Steiner and Strider sat in the cockpit while the crew refueled the helicopter, with the flight engineer supervising while the crew chief filled the right main fuel cell and the door gunner filled the left. As the two pilots sat there watching the fuel gauges climb on the two main fuel cells, number one engine, the one on the left side of the aircraft, dropped off-line. It did not shut down completely, it just went to "Idle" RPM, even though the condition lever, the handle that controls its speed, was in the "Fly" position. The number two engine continued to operate normally, keeping the rotor RPM right where it should be. Steiner and Strider both looked at the gauges on the dash when the sound of the engines changed, but could see nothing wrong, except number one engine wasn't running at the speed it should be. Steiner told the flight engineer to stop refueling immediately.

The flight engineer also heard the engine drop off-line and before Steiner said a word, had already signaled the crew chief and door gunner to stop refueling. He then turned, ran up the ramp and on up to the cockpit to see what was going on. Steiner and the flight engineer conferred, but could think of no reason the engine would do that by itself. Steiner tried pulling the engine condition lever that controlled its speed back to the "Idle" position manually and then bringing it back to the "Fly" position several times, but that had no effect. He tried pulling the circuit breaker for the automatic control and adjusting its speed manually, again with no effect since it only works when the engine is in the "Fly" position. The flight engineer checked the controls he could see from the back, but he could find nothing wrong. What to do now?

Both pilots knew what they should have done at this point: finish shutting the aircraft down where it sat and call back to Liftmaster Pad for the maintenance department to come fix the aircraft. That would have meant a wait of at least an hour for maintenance to get there in another Chinook. When it arrived, Steiner and Strider would then swap places with the pilots in the second Chinook and fly it back over to Liftmaster. The rest of the aircrew would wait with their broken bird until it was fixed, no matter how long that took. The crew would miss dinner and their long day would get even longer.

In frustration at a broken aircraft after a very long day, Steiner said over the ICS "Fuck it, "Everyone back into the aircraft right now."

With all aboard and the ramp up, Steiner ran number two engine, the normally operating one, as high as it would go, bringing the rotor RPM to 10% above its normal speed. When it was going as fast as it could, he slowly lifted the Chinook into a 20-foot hover. It took everything the good engine had to do it, but the aircraft made it to 20 feet without the rotor blades dropping very much below normal speed. Of course, there was no additional power left to get the helicopter into the air as he normally would, so takeoff would be a problem.

Fortunately, the refuel pads at Camp Eagle were on the top of a small hill, giving Steiner a little space in which to trade altitude for forward speed before an immediate climb was required. Once he had enough speed to get nice, clean air not disturbed by their hover through the rotor blades, say around 20 knots, they would be fine, provided, of course, that nothing else went wrong. Screw it up even slightly and they would certainly crash, hitting the barbed wire around the perimeter of the base before impacting the ground.

Steiner eased the aircraft gently forward, starting the takeoff. He could not pull more power without dropping the rotor speed, potentially slowing it to the point where he would be risking the generators and stability system coming off-line, probably followed by flying the aircraft into the ground, so it was a very slow, steady movement. As the Chinook began to move forward, it settled slightly as helicopters normally do when you take off without adding at least a little additional power, but then came the shudder as it went from a hover into forward flight.

The aircraft was flying now instead of hovering. They cleared the barbed wire around Camp Eagle by 10 feet, enough that any observer would think they were just doing a normal takeoff, not a single engine one. Steiner stayed low, not attempting a climb until the airspeed reached 70 knots, then he pulled a little back stick to hold 70 and they began to climb at a few hundred feet per minute. Still holding around 70 knots airspeed, Steiner got the Chinook to 500 feet. At 500 feet he traded the climb for airspeed and let the helicopter accelerate to 100 knots as he turned it back toward Liftmaster Pad.

Steiner would not have tried to fly back with a single engine if Liftmaster had not had a short runway. With a short runway, he would be able to do a slow speed running landing, keeping his airspeed up while using less power, and leaving the possibility of a missed approach should something go wrong at the last second. If it had been a helicopter landing pad, he would have had to do a to-the-ground-approach, an approach directly to landing without hovering, and also without the possibility of going around for a second try if anything went wrong. By doing a running landing, he could keep his speed up and at least have the possibility of a wave off. Only a possibility, but better than nothing.

Nothing did go wrong. Steiner lined Playtex 820 up with the Liftmaster's short runway and touched down with about 10 knots forward speed. He held the nose up off the ground after touchdown to remove the last remaining ground speed and brought 820 to a stop.

Strider noticed that when their rotor wash hit the control tower mounted on its telephone poles, it rocked quite a bit, swaying enough to generate a look of alarm in the tower operator's face through the plexiglas 20 feet above them. The tower operator didn't say a word on the radio, though; he too had his "cool" to maintain. No one inside the aircraft said anything either. When they were taxiing to their revetment, Steiner looked over and winked at Strider. The flight engineer and his crew were grateful to Steiner that they were back at Liftmaster, instead of shut down in Camp Eagle's fuel pits. They were grateful because, even though their day was not through until the aircraft was operational again, at least they would get chow tonight.

As soon as they were safely on the ground, Steiner called maintenance on the radio to report the engine problem. Everyone in 820's crew would later swear to the maintenance officer that the engine dropped off-line just as they were about to touch down at Liftmaster, so that Steiner would not get in trouble for doing a single engine takeoff when they had been safely on the ground. Not that the maintenance officer was fooled by their story. He knew in his heart that Steiner had flown back on one engine, but he accepted the lie. He too was glad to have the aircraft back without all the hassle of fixing it in Camp Eagle's fuel pits, because he had just received word from Battalion Headquarters that a typhoon was on its way.

Both pilots in Playtex 820 were just as glad to be back at Liftmaster as the crew was. They were soaking wet. The windshields on both sides leaked, not much, but just enough for the water to soak Strider's back and Steiner's legs. Both had shut their side windows but somehow a little water came in there, too. These leaks went well with the drip, drip, drip of water from the overhead panel on top of Strider's helmet. The crewmen in back were much wetter than the pilots, as always. They tried to stay out of the wind, but with the side hatches removed to make room for the door guns, it was pretty well impossible. Then, too, when they had to go outside to refuel the aircraft, the parts of them that had been dry got soaked and had no chance to dry again.

Everyone onboard 820 was tired, not from a long day of flying missions, but just tired of being wet and cold, tired of unending rain. Unfortunately, as they knew, the day was not yet over.

LIFTMASTER PREPARES FOR SUPER TYPHOON KATE

A maintenance crew was waiting for them as they taxied 820 into the revetment, not to figure out what was wrong with number one engine, but to get the helicopter secured against the rising wind. Fixing the engine problem would take second place to getting the aircraft ready to ride out the approaching typhoon. All hands, even the officers and the administrative soldiers from the S-1 and S-4, had turned out to get Playtex's aircraft secured, putting extra tie-down ropes on all six of the rotor blades on each Chinook to keep them from being damaged from flapping up and down in the wind. They even put the window back in on the port side of each aircraft's fuselage where the left machine gun was normally mounted. All the aircraft covers, the ones on the engine air intakes, and the other tubes and pressure sensors, were installed and double-checked for security.

The maintenance officer had borrowed sixteen "duce and a half's" (two-and-a-half-ton trucks) from somewhere and had them parked in front of the revetments to break the wind, but this was not all he did. He walked the flight line again and again, making sure all loose objects that might blow into the aircraft were removed or tied securely down. He asked the maintenance chief to assign men to patrol the flight line, even though he knew that the flight engineers and crew chiefs would sleep in their aircraft until the storm passed, making sure their helicopters stayed safe and that no rotor blades came loose from their tie downs. The Chinooks were, after all, theirs, not the maintenance officer's, no matter what he might think. Their crews would protect them as best they could, and besides, there was a very practical reason to sleep on the flight line. Protecting their aircraft by remaining in them kept the sergeant major from assigning them other hurricane preparation duties in the company area.

DOMESTIC MATTERS

By 1800 hours, everything throughout Playtex's company living area and Liftmaster Pad was as secure as it was going to be. The men not on flight line patrol duty had all gone to dinner and then back to their hootches to see what would happen next. Steiner went to the operations bunker to turn in the KY-28 and the escape and evasion gear, while Strider headed for their hootch. It was his turn to cook dinner again and he was thinking of something concocted from C rations and whatever else he could find in their larder that would not take much work to throw together, surprise, surprise.

Strider took three cans of the C ration spaghetti and meat sauce from the shelf in the back room, modified it with some canned tomato sauce from their stash, added some hot sauce, heated it up in their electric skillet and dinner for three was ready. For an added touch, he broke out the last three hard bread rolls the Boeing Tech Rep had left two nights before and a can of dried parmesan cheese he had been saving. The rolls were a bit stale, but even stale they were better than the doughy white bread the mess hall served. Last but not least, he opened a bottle of Chianti he had bought the last time he was at the PX. By the time he was finished spreading it all out, Cobb and Steiner were back from the flight line and had changed out of their wet flight suits for dry ones. Modified C ration spaghetti or not, Strider's dinner looked good to both of them.

Dinner was quiet, with little conversation about anything, but then dinner was often quiet. They didn't talk about the weather. What was the point, since they were in it all day? The three warrants did not talk about the war amongst themselves, ever. There was nothing to talk about, really. None of them were outright for the war or against it, though you could make a case that 159th's two Canadian citizen warrant officer pilots, one in Playtex and one in Varsity, who came south to enlist in a war their country wasn't fighting, were pro-war. Not to say the Canadians couldn't be violent—the Playtex Canadian knocked Strider unconscious with a pugil stick in bayonet training when they were in basic training together—they just weren't militaristic people in person.

When you talked to the Canadians you found out that, far from being pro-war, enlisting in the U.S. Army was the only way they could afford to learn to fly. Instead of using money, they were paying for the flight training with four years of their lives and, if things went badly, with their lives, period. If it meant going to war, so be it. There was a lot of demand for experienced helicopter pilots back home and there was no way in Canada to get experience like this. Even if you were rich enough in the first place to pay for basic helicopter training, there was nowhere to learn to fly big aircraft like the Chinook. The experience they gained here would mean good jobs waiting for them when they got back home. Then again, after four years military service, they could easily get U.S. citizenship if they didn't want to go back north, another good reason for being in the U.S. Army in Vietnam.

For the rest of the warrants in Playtex, the war just was and they had been caught up in it. If you told them they could go back to the States tomorrow, they would have started packing their clothes right then. Some would leave their clothes where they were and start walking over to Phu Bai to get on the C-130 for the flight south to Cam Ranh where they would catch the Freedom Bird home. But they weren't being told they could go home tomorrow, so they flew their missions each day and did not tell war stories over dinner. They didn't talk politics or sex either, perhaps unusual for young men, which doesn't mean they didn't think about sex. In the kitchen area of their hootch, the walls were covered in Playmate of the Month pictures, something very typical for young men, given their first dream in life. Maybe the three roommates in this hootch got along so well because they didn't go into deep subjects like war and sex.

It was the first hootch evening meal in a while, because missions had been heavy lately, often running eight or more hours, counting wait times. Every time there was the slightest break in the weather, the Chinooks headed for the mountains, sling loads dangling below them. Division was loading up the FSBs as much as possible in case the weather socked in too much to fly during the monsoon season. The three roommates had been too tired at the end of the day to do anything except go to the mess hall, eat, and go back to the hootch to prepare for the next day's flying. Clean your pistol, polish your boots, write a quick letter home and maybe drink a glass of wine or have a beer before shower and bed. Tonight, in addition to the usual things, getting ready for the next day meant drying off your wet flight suit and boots in the clothes-drying closet so they would be ready early tomorrow morning.

No Glee Club tonight, but after dinner was over and the dishes cleaned,

Jerry broke out his guitar and sang them a tune he was going to introduce at the next meeting. It was called "The Phu Bai Song," the tune following along the lines of "Sweet Betsy from Pike":

The Phu Bai Song
"Oh, Phu Bai Oh, Phu Bai's a hell of a place,
The organization's a fucking disgrace.
There's Captains and Majors and Light Colonels, too,
With thumbs up their assholes and nothing to do.
They stand on the runway, they scream and they shout,
About many things they know nothing about.
For all they accomplish they might as well be,
Shoveling shit in the South China Sea.
Out in the forest a young soldier lies,
All covered with blood and with tears in his eyes.
He's not crying because of the pain,
He's crying because the brass is insane.
Phu Bai! Phu Bai!
Ring-a-dang-a ding dong,
Blow it out your ass,
Better days are coming bye and bye,
Bullshit!
Nuke'um, Nuke'um, Nuke'um!
Ho Chi Minh sucks.

They all agreed that it caught the exact spirit of the war as conducted by Playtex and the 101st and that the Glee Club would love it.

CHAPTER NINE

OCTOBER 26, 1970

KATE MAKES AN ENTRANCE

Super Typhoon Kate arrived at Liftmaster in earnest around 0700 hours. The wind had been building all night and now it was howling, with rain coming down in sideways sheets. The sound of rain and wind on the tin roof had been building all night, too, until it was a constant roar. When they checked later, just as Steiner and Strider figured, some large roof sections came off some of the hootches, while on others the roof didn't completely come off, the wind just pealed back some of the tin panels letting the water gush in. This included several tin panels on the Officers' Club roof.

The wind and rain pounding on their roof and walls made it impossible to sleep after 0500 hours, so they were all up and checking things out early. After checking their spaces, the three could find no leaks in their hootch's roof; the sandbags had worked as planned to keep everything in place. Rather than go out in the rain and wind to get to the mess hall, the three of them prepared a breakfast made mostly of Steiner's extra special care packages. Strider even cleaned out their percolator and made coffee for them. This was not a small thing, since the last time someone used the percolator they did not empty the leftover coffee. When Strider opened it there was half inch of green scum in the bottom. It took him 20 minutes of scrubbing and three perk cycles to get it usable again.

All in all, it was a right homey scene as they sat at the table enjoying breakfast in the warm, dry hootch.

At about 1000, since it was too late to do anything about their own roofs and the club roof was leaking in numerous places, some of the warrants started knocking at the door of the three's hootch. The refurbished sandbags on their roof had not gone unnoticed. The pilots who came knocking might have been wet and bedraggled, but they had booze in their hands and were welcomed by the three. Particularly welcome was the pilot with a cold bottle of French champagne in his hand. There would be no flying today, so drinking heavily at 1000 would not be a problem. Strider, having learned his lesson, did not join them in the early morning drinking. He had decided that watching men doing stupid things while they were drunk was better fun than being drunk yourself. Besides, the next day's pain just wasn't worth it, although, he thought to himself, watching other men's self-induced pain could be quite a lot of fun.

By early afternoon there were around 15 men, including the XO this time, crammed into the main room of the hootch. It was almost a continuation of the "USO Show" party, but without the promise of major entertainment later. Jerry tried to get the Phu Bai Glee Club going, but no one would join in. It just wasn't the same, singing in the middle of the day, hurricane or no hurricane. Instead, most everyone was talking about sports, a subject that did not interest Strider in the slightest.

The exception to the sports talk was a conversation between two warrants who were discussing the young man's first dream, which involved loudly singing the praises of the Australian women they had met on R&R in Sydney. This interested Strider. What was different about Australian women, Strider asked? The two warrants were not drunk enough to go into the juicy details, but they were both vowing to move to Australia as soon as they got out of the Army, a very high recommendation indeed. At that point someone chimed in about the charms of the hookers in Taipei and the conversation degenerated from there into an argument about whether the hookers in Taipei were better than the hookers in Thailand. There is, of course, no answer to this question, since "betterness," like beauty, is all in the eye, or some other body part, of the beholder.

Because the three were always planning ahead, Steiner had broken out some lanterns he had "borrowed" from the S-4 sometime in the past, since with the windows completely sealed, it got very dark immediately in the hootch when the power went out. He went ahead and lit the lanterns in anticipation, but the power did not go off or even flicker, for that matter.

Playtex had its own generator and complete electrical system, so they did not have to depend on a central grid of the main Phu Bai complex, which had indeed gone dead around by 0600 hours. Playtex's maintenance department, in their auxiliary role of Public Works Department, made sure all was well with the power station long before the wind and rain arrived, lest the entire company be pissed off at them.

Fortunately, none of the things flying through the air in the wind, like bits of tin fencing and other debris, took out the wires between the power station and the hootches, so the lights stayed on even when the wind was at its worse. The lanterns did add a certain ambiance to an otherwise crowded room. Steiner was going to keep the lanterns instead of giving them back, because you never know, a mortar round might hit the generator and then they truly would be needed.

2LT Taylor was one of the partiers in Strider's hootch, albeit a non-drinking one, but a partier nonetheless. He voiced no opinion on the merits of hookers, but seemed very interested in the Australian girls. When Strider saw him, he steered him into the back room for a little private conversation. "Jim, what kind of performance of mine did you film at the club during that Philippine show," he demanded.

2LT Taylor laughed, "You'll just have to wait and see when I get the film back."

CAMERAMAN JAMES TAYLOR

2Lt James Taylor was a "Penny Postcard" commissioned officer and at 25, more advanced in years than most of the other pilots. He was also a brand new AC, having just met the minimum Chinook and in-country flight hour requirements, and being designated the CO. Even though he had been there for five months, no one in Playtex knew him very well; he was a quiet man who kept to himself, mostly. Strider couldn't decide if he kept to himself because he felt he couldn't hang out with the warrants after becoming an RLO, or if he was just naturally shy. Nor, apparently, did he feel he could hang out with the other commissioned officers, since they were all much older than he, maybe 30 to his 25.

Also, because he was a devout Mormon, he drank no coffee, alcohol, or soft drinks, as his religion required. He also did not gamble or smoke, so he stayed away from such activities. This meant that 2LT Taylor did not take part in the Phu Bai Glee Club or the poker games running nearly every night in the Officers' Club. These activities usually brought the pilots together, but you have to participate to get the maximum team effect, so he was a bit of an outsider. After 2LT Taylor bought the movie camera, he became more outgoing, sometimes filming the poker games and the Glee Club in action. Since everyone wanted to be in his 8mm movies, they would seek him out to document the goings on in Playtex. They wanted something to show the folks back home what life in Liftmaster was like.

Because 2LT Taylor was a brand new AC, the operations officer usually assigned another AC, or someone very experienced, like Leonard, to him as his copilot. Strider had no opinion on whether he was a good AC or a bad one, having only flown with him once. That day had been a light one: just two missions, both involving 500-gallon fuel bladders, the easiest load of all. Nice and heavy, the fuel bladders, a.k.a. "elephant nuts," were about a perfect load since they had no tendency to swing or oscillate in flight. They might, of course, blowup in flight if they got hit with heavy anti-air-craft fire, but that was just a risk that went with being a Chinook pilot in Vietnam. While he might be a little green right now, the operations officer thought 2LT Taylor would be fine, just as soon as he got another 100 hours or so in the air, just like all new ACs usually needed to be really competent.

Ah, Strider understood. "Get the film back" meant that 2LT Taylor had sent the film to the PX film developing service, instead of having the Gook Shop develop it. The Gook Shop got it back to you the next day, but it cost twice as much as the PX and you never knew if they were passing a copy off to NVA intelligence. Strider was relieved. Everyone in Vietnam knew that the PX would not develop anything pornographic or with dead bodies in it, so whatever film came back would be clean. Of course, if it didn't come back, Strider would never know what kind of "extraordinary performance" he had given that night unless he could talk someone into telling him. Since he had not yet developed symptoms of any vile diseases, he suspected he was just getting a bit of the harassment from the ACs that all copilots get. Then it struck him: 2LT Taylor would not have been there with a movie camera at all if anything untoward was going on, since he did not "go in for that sort of thing." No doubt about it, Strider was just getting harassment because his self-induced drunken condition had made him an easy target.

NO MORE PARTY TODAY

By 1400 hours, Strider had had enough typhoon party for one day, so he put on his rain gear and headed out to see what was still standing after all the wind that came through that morning. All things considered, the visible damage to the company area was slight. Only a couple panels on the tin fence around the officer's area had come loose, so the wind must not have been as strong as expected. The banana trees in the courtyard had bent over in the wind but they would live, stunted things that they were. The sand in the courtyard was now completely covered in water, all the low spots having long ago filled up. Only the stobs marked the horseshoe pit now, with the shoe impact zone completely under water. There were no walking fish out and about today. Do they instinctively take cover in deeper water during typhoons, Strider wondered? Do they need to? Do fish, especially ones that walk, even know it's raining? There were no angry banana vipers visible either, at least none actively chasing pilots up on top of ping pong tables.

Many of the officers not in the party in Strider's hootch had gone instead to the clothes-drying hootch, because its roof remained intact. This was pure luck, since no one had done any maintenance on it, ever. There was a party going there, too, but not at the same intensity since the clothes-drying hootch was unheated and lacked any kind of seating, except for seating on the floor; it was not as welcoming as Strider's hootch. Still, it was dry, more or less, and any port is a good port in a storm, or a typhoon.

As Strider walked toward the Officers' Club, he saw the door to the clothes-drying hootch fly open and one of the warrants stagger shirtless out into the rain. The warrant spun in a complete circle, like a clumsy dancer, yelling defiance at the top of his lungs against the force of the wind and rain as he splashed through the standing water. For a moment he did a little dance, jumping up and down in the puddles. Then, almost like he had been shot, he fell forward into the deepest puddle, hitting face first in the dirty brown water. His head wasn't completely under the water, but his face was, and he wasn't making any effort to turn himself over or get up. He appeared to be out cold.

Strider considered leaving him there, face down in the puddle, but decided against it. The warrant had passed out and would not get up or turn over without help, and if left as is, would probably drown, resulting in unwanted paperwork. Not wanting to see if he remembered how to do cardiopulmonary resuscitation, Strider quickly rolled the unconscious one over and checked to see if he was breathing. He was, but he was a big guy and in his limp condition, Strider could not lift him alone. So instead, Strider dragged him a little way through the mud over to the sidewalk and left him there lying on his back while he went for help. Strider stuck his head in the clothes-drying hootch the warrant had just left and spotted the unconscious one's roommate sitting on the floor, beer in hand, deep in some important conversation with one of the RLOs. Strider told him what had happened and that he needed help to get the unconscious one out of the rain. With some difficulty, the warrant got to his feet and went out to help Strider move his roommate.

Between the two of them, they got the shirtless, dripping wet warrant at least semi-up onto his feet and dragged/carried him back to his hootch. Fortunately, the roof of his hootch was mostly still attached, and while it was leaking in two corners, it was not leaking directly over the unconscious one's bed, not that it mattered since he was completely soaked anyway. Strider and his helper dropped him on his rack and left him there, dressed in wet flight suit trousers and shirtless, snoring, to sleep it off.

By dark, Typhoon Kate must have completely passed or broken up, because the wind had mostly died. But while the wind was gone, the rain had not stopped. It continued to come down as hard as ever, just more vertically now than horizontally, like it had been in the morning. So much water was on the ground that even the sidewalks in the officer's area were covered and it was still rising. Some of the low-lying enlisted hootches might get flooded, while the officer's hootches were on higher ground and would not.

Sticking his head back through the door of his hootch, he could see that the hurricane party continued, so Strider splashed through the standing water down to the operations bunker to take a break from it. There was never a party going on in the operations bunker, so it would be quiet. That is to say, it would be the same as it always was. And it was: the operations officer was at work, as always, sorting through mission sheets from previous days and planning for the time when the missions would resume. With a grin he motioned Strider into one of the gray folding chairs scattered around the office. Strider, after taking off his dripping wet rain jacket and hanging it on a hook by the door, chose a chair that was free of clutter and sat down.

Since the operations officer had a cigarette going, Strider reached into his lower pocket, pulled out his pipe and tobacco pouch, filled the pipe, tamped the tobacco down and lit up with his Zippo. He looked forward to the day when he could get to the PX and get some other kind of tobacco. This cherry flavored stuff was all they had the last time he was there and it tasted awful. That said, like the flat beer had alcohol, the cherry tobacco had nicotine, so he would use it. Besides, his roommates had both told him they liked the smell it left when he smoked, something Strider could not smell himself. Cherry flavored tobacco or not, Strider was glad his tobacco pouch was waterproof, because the legs of his flight suit were soaked. Neither of them said a word as the smoke filled the office with a gray cloud.

"Had enough party, have you?" the operations officer asked after a minute or so, smiling even wider now. "I guess the "USO" show was enough to last you for a while. Has your head quit hurting yet?"

Even though he had not made an appearance, the operations officer knew the party was going on in Strider's hootch. Strider thought it odd, how much the RLOs seemed to know about what was going on, even when they weren't present. He made a mental note to himself to always keep that in mind when dealing with RLOs.

Strider laughed, "Yes, Sir, it has, but I have done learned my lesson on that one. I thought about taking the "no drinking" pledge, but then, I would just break it. What's battalion saying about when we go back on standby?"

"They're not saying much. The weather is about the same as it is here all over I Corps, so we're on standby for now. Didn't you check the mission priority board in the club?" the operations officer replied.

Strider blushed, "No, Sir, I didn't."

"It's just as well that you didn't, because there's nothing on it. I was just messin' with you. You are easy to mess with aren't you? Battalion says we should start flying again tomorrow, but there's nothing from them on what missions division is passing out right now. Seems like everything is just on weather hold until they figure out how much damage this latest typhoon has done," the operations officer said as he leaned back in his chair and exhaled more cigarette smoke into the office. The cigarette smoke mixed with the pipe smoke, leaving the room in an even darker bluish haze than before. Strider thought it gave the office the look of an old black and while World War II flying movie, only in the movies, the offices weren't nearly as cluttered as Playtex's Operations office always was.

After that they sat in silence, smoking and thinking about what would happen over the next few days. Neither of them could imagine anything but weather holds, high tension missions trying to get through to the FSBs in the cloud and fog, and things being shitty in general until the monsoon rains were over. After that, things would just get back to normal, long days of boredom and occasional danger as the Chinooks carried their sling loads of ammo, fuel, and water to the mountains.

Outside the operations bunker, the rain continued to fall on the saturated ground and the water continued to rise.

CHAPTER TEN

ANTICIPATION

The wind was more or less calm when Strider headed over to the mess hall for breakfast at 0730 hours. He knew that the standby was still in effect, because the duty clerk had not stopped by at 0430 hours to wake him or either of his roommates, both of whom were still in bed. Strider would leave the cleanup from the typhoon party to them. The rain, while no longer coming down so hard, still had not stopped, nor had the clouds lifted. Looking out toward the hill between Liftmaster and Camp Eagle, Strider could see only fog, no distinct skyline, meaning the visibility was less than a mile: not good.

Usually the place would be crowded just about now, but only WO1 Barry Fivelson was in the officer's dining area when Strider came in from the rain. As Strider hung up his dripping rain gear on the hooks by the door, he could not help but notice Fivelson looking glum as he ate his runny eggs, cereal, and toast washed down with orange juice, instead of showing his normal, bright-eyed interest in what was coming up for the day. Fivelson glum? It was unheard of and so was worth exploring.

THE CAMERAMAN: BARRY FIVELSON

WO1 Barry Fivelson was a nice Jewish boy from Evanston, Illinois. He did not, unlike Steiner, loudly proclaim his Jewishness, but then neither did he deny it. It was pretty much like everyone else's religion, just not a subject of interest or conversation among the pilots. Fivelson was also the newest of the newbies in Playtex, having arrived just a month before. Strider was vastly "shorter," having been in-country an entire month and a half before Fivelson arrived.

Fivelson was 20 years old but seemed much younger than that, partly because he had a young face without a dark beard popping out daily like most of the men. But he also seemed younger because he had a keen interest in all that was going on around him, not having embraced or even grasped the concept of being "cool." Instead of just accepting events as a matter of course, Fivelson simply marveled at them. He, like Strider, did not yet know when he was supposed to be afraid and when he wasn't, but so far he hadn't shown that he was even aware of this deficiency. Naivety, it seems, can take the place of courage, at least for a little while.

While 2LT Taylor had his 8mm movie camera, Fivelson had his 35mm Nikon. He bought the camera on his first trip to the PX in Vietnam two weeks ago and was apparently now spending most of his pay on film and film development. He shot roll after roll of film on things so commonplace that none of the other pilots had much interest in them: aircraft taking off and landing, the officer's hootches, the enlisted hootches, the aircrews working on their Chinooks, combat volleyball games, horseshoe pitching, even the bunkers between the hootches and the clothes-drying hootch.

When he wasn't scheduled to fly, Fivelson would sometimes climb on-board a Chinook heading out on missions and ride along for the day, helping the crew when he could and taking pictures the rest of the time. He took pictures down through the "hell hole," the hatch in the center of the cabin that opened up so the flight engineer could see the sling load in flight. He took pictures of the FSBs over the door gunner's shoulder as they came in to drop their loads. He took pictures of the Cobra escorts as they flew alongside: pictures, pictures, pictures.

"So, Barry, what's up?" Strider asked.

"Just saw the XO. Over breakfast he tells me I'm the new public affairs officer (PAO)," Fivelson said. He continued, "I have no idea where that came from. I kind of liked being the assistant admin officer. Not much to do because the admin officer doesn't trust me, so I had time to shoot some pictures when I wasn't on the flight schedule. Now I'm PAO and I have no idea what being PAO involves. You know anything about public affairs?"

"Yep, I do, in fact, I know about public affairs, because, you see, I was the PAO until just now, apparently." Strider said. "You're supposed to send news releases to hometown newspapers whenever someone is promoted, gets a medal, rotates home, anytime something happens. That is, anytime something good happens. Someone else higher up reports bad things. If, and when, battalion sends over some press people, you're supposed to escort them around, but as far as I know, that has never happened, at least there's nothing in the files about it. Anyway, I never had to escort anyone anywhere, worse luck. As I see it, PAO's a good job, because it doesn't get in the way of flying. Besides, the way you like to take pictures, it will be perfect for you, since you can send pictures of the hero of the moment attached to the back of the home news release form. They'll love that if any of them get printed. When the XO formally tells me about the job change I'll turn all the files over to you."

At this last point, Fivelson brightened back up to his usual cheerful self. He had not considered that being PAO would give him even more opportunity to take pictures, this time under official cover. Maybe the Army would even buy his film, or at least pay for developing it. The possibilities were endless.

Strider had, in fact, done very well as PAO, though not necessarily through any deliberate actions on his part. Every week after getting the list of promotions and awards from the S-1, he had dutifully filled out and submitted the hometown news releases to the stateside newspapers and wire services, but nothing much happened. Very rarely someone back home would send a hometown newspaper cutout showing that Strider's release had been printed. Then, out of the blue, three weeks into his tenure, a picture of a Playtex Chinook carrying an external load of ammo appeared in *Stars and Stripes,* the worldwide U.S. military newspaper. While the caption under the picture did not specifically mention Playtex, the blue triangle on the forward pylon and the Screaming Eagle on the aft pylon marked the helicopter as a Playtex aircraft. Two weeks later, the AP released another photo of a Playtex Chinook that was picked up by newspapers all across the U.S. Even better, the second picture identified the helicopter as belonging not to "Playtex," but by the company's proper name, "Charlie Company of the 159th Assault Support Helicopter Battalion, 101st Airborne Division (Airmobile)," thereby getting a little glory for both the company and the battalion, good things, particularly for their commanding officers.

After the second picture appeared, Strider received a congratulatory personal phone call from the battalion CO himself, after the battalion CO had received one from the division PAO. In neither case did Strider have anything to do with the pictures appearing in print. He was as surprised, if not more so, as anyone when he saw them. But he was not about to tell that to the battalion CO; no point looking gift horses in the mouth and all that.

After he finished breakfast, Strider left Fivelson contemplating how to be a good PAO and splashed back through the rain and standing water in the officer's area. From there he headed out to the flight line to see how things were going. As he walked by, he could see some of the other officers repairing their roofs, hammering away in the rain, trying to get the tin sheets back in place. Like Fivelson, most of them looked glum. After all, hammering nails in the rain wasn't half as much fun as flying, or sleeping for that matter.

Not that all the hammering did much good, either, since the tin was bent from the wind in many cases and just would not go back down flat. The sergeant major had crews of enlisted men swarming over the enlisted hootches looking for damage. All in all, it looked like they had less damage than the officer hootches, perhaps because the sergeant major kept watch on their condition, while the officers, being theoretically more mature, were on their own. Strider avoided the S-1, trying to put off the moment when the XO would formally name him supply officer, in the vain hope that he would change his mind.

CONGRATULATIONS ON YOUR NEW ASSIGNMENT

Out on the flight line, things were very wet in the continuing rain, but just about back to normal. They were normal, except that every revetment had a Chinook in it. Truly "normal" would mean that at least six of the revetments would have been empty, their aircraft out flying missions. The threat from the two typhoons had passed for now, so all the extra tie downs had been removed from helicopters, and the trucks that had been acting as wind breaks were gone back to wherever the maintenance officer had borrowed them from. Even the tower operator had returned to his post in Liftmaster Tower, ready to clear the helicopters for takeoff when the missions resumed. Given how flimsy the tower looked from below, the air traffic controller was probably just as surprised as Strider was that it was still standing after

Steiner's running landing and all the typhoon wind yesterday.

Rain or no rain, all the regular everyday maintenance activity was well underway all over Liftmaster. Because of the unexpected break in flying, the maintenance department was actually getting caught up on tasks that had been deferred, which would make the maintenance officer happy indeed. He liked nothing better than to report to battalion that all 16 Chinooks were flyable, even when it meant stretching the truth a little bit. Of course, with the broken landing gear on 831, the best he could do today was 15; still, that was something.

Strider could see Playtex 820's rotor blades turning in the revetment where Steiner and he had parked it last night. He assumed this meant that its engine controls had been repaired, and that the helicopter would be back in play as soon as maintenance finished the ground checks, probably before dark today. He was wrong. Playtex 820 was making maintenance crazy because they could find nothing wrong, except that number one engine would not stay at the "Fly" position. It insisted on dropping back to idle when it was not supposed to. The Boeing Tech Rep would get the next crack at fixing it. He could fix anything on a Chinook.

Strider was bored enough with the rain to volunteer to do maintenance ground runs himself, but it seemed that other pilots had the same idea. As he walked in, he could see that three ACs and a copilot were sitting around the maintenance office, drinking coffee and talking, so there seemed to be no further demand for ground turn pilots today. The maintenance warrant who normally did most of the ground turns looked like he was enjoying the company. Usually operational pilots avoided the maintenance office like the plague and vice versa, so it was a nice change for them all.

Since he wasn't needed on the flight line, Strider decided to face the inevitable and track down the XO to get formal word on his assignment to a new job. He walked over to the company office, the S-1, wondering all the while why the XO had pulled him off a job that required no effort at all—yet had been richly rewarding from a career standpoint, given the unexpected pictures in the press back home—for one that guaranteed an increased non-flying workload. Had the XO figured out that he was just skating along, working maybe an hour a day when he wasn't flying? Maybe the XO was smarter than the warrants gave him credit for. All warrants should remember that RLOs were tricky like that. As presumed, the XO was in his office, but for once, he was not working on the pile of papers in front of him. He had propped open the plywood that covered the window so that he could see out, and was just staring through the window screen at the rain, feet propped up on his desk with a cup of coffee in his hand, lost in thought.

The XO was an infantry branch officer by trade, and wound up in a cargo helicopter company as the XO when his survival instincts took over between his first and second Vietnam tours. On his first tour he had flown the Korean War-vintage piston-engine OH-23s and when they were all destroyed in combat or accidents, or at least the brass realized how completely obsolete they were, he transitioned to LOHs, a perfect fit for an infantry type. With an LOH he could "seek out the enemy and engage him with fire and maneuver" and all that. When the Army offered him the choice between Cobras and Chinooks prior to his second tour, he chose the Chinook because he had had enough "seeking out the enemy and finding him" for now. He had way too many close calls in the old OH-23s and LOHs to look for more close calls in a Cobra for a second twelve months. Thing was, as an RLO, he didn't get to do much flying in Playtex, but then someone had to do the paperwork and he was good at it. That made the CO happy and by definition, when the CO is happy, the XO is happy.

Since the war was finally starting to wind down and the first American troop withdrawals started, the XO was pretty sure that this would be his last Vietnam tour. Maybe he could get back to Fort Benning and the infantry after this tour, or maybe be assigned to Europe instead. Infantry officers were always in demand in Germany. Korea wouldn't be bad either. But right now being company XO and putting up with shit from a bunch of snotty-nosed-kid warrant officers was his lot. Not that he minded, really. They did the missions well and did them without complaint. Of all of them, Cobb was the biggest pain in the ass, but he was keeping a close eye on him as the end of his tour neared. The XO knew, as they all did, that the only thing that really mattered was doing the mission and doing it well.

Speaking of warrants, he thought to himself as he saw Strider come into his office. He decided to ignore him for a while.

"Morning, XO. I understand I am no longer PAO. I saw Fivelson at breakfast and he told me you are putting him in the job" Strider said, after standing there at the door for a minute or so, waiting patiently for the XO to look around at him. He probably should have saluted his superior officer, but they tended not to salute in Vietnam. Saluting someone would mark him as a target if the NVA were watching and as such, was discouraged—unless, of course, you *wanted* to mark someone as a target . . .

After a pause, the XO took a sip of his coffee and then said, "Yeah, that's right. PAO just wasn't enough of a challenge for you. You are career indefinite, you're not getting out of the Army when you go home. You could easily stay for 20 years; if you are going to stay in the Army, you need to learn how to do something other than just fly. Pilots are a dime a dozen in peacetime. Besides, you remember the guy who was the S-4 (supply) officer?" The XO was smiling now, never a good sign when the XO is giving you news.

"Was?" Strider thought, not liking the way this conversation was headed.

"Well," the XO continued, "out of the blue he had a lung collapse last night and was medevaced (medical evacuation) this morning. He only had a month left on his tour anyway, so he won't be coming back. In fact, he's probably in Japan by now. I'm going over to his hootch a little later to box up all his stuff, throw away the porn, take back any Army property, all the usual, before I send it back to the States. You, therefore, are my new S-4 supply officer. Congratulations on your new position. Now, I want a complete inventory of all the company property and I mean ALL of it, on my desk no later than ten days from now. I'd do a thorough inventory, if I were you, since you are going to have to sign for all of it. Remember, if you sign for it and it isn't there, it could come out of your paycheck. You might want to go over to the S-4 office and talk to the supply sergeant about how your predecessor left things."

The XO was smiling broadly now, clearly enjoying the look of dismay coming across Strider's face as the realization hit him that, unlike PAO, S-4 actually was a real job and would require him to actually work in an office for the first time in his military career. The XO had long since figured out that PAO was a nothing job. He also suspected that the pictures of the Playtex aircraft that everyone was so proud of were published purely by accident, but he didn't mention this to Strider.

The S-4 job would definitely cut into Strider's flying. It was definitely not something that would make him want to stay in the Army, even if he was "career indefinite." Strider knew that a "real job" was inevitable for everyone, staying in the Army long term or not, so he did not fight it. Besides, this would be the first time he ever had anyone working for him: the supply sergeant and the two supply clerks who made up the S-4. He would have responsibility for something other than a two-seat helicopter for the first time in his life. He became resolute that he could handle it, maybe…

Even so, Strider now regretted not joining the typhoon party yesterday. A hangover might have helped dull the pain of being told he now had a real job, particularly this real job. Strider had known the last supply officer from Fort Campbell, Kentucky, where they both had been stationed before Vietnam. An old paratrooper before he became a pilot, the former S-4 officer was known by all at Fort Campbell for having a very informal way of passing out things at times, a practice apparently continued here in Vietnam. Strider suspected that it would be a difficult "real job," a fact that the supply sergeant soon confirmed.

Leaving the XO's office, Strider walked next door to the S-4 office and introduced himself to the supply sergeant, who, of course, knew who he was and had been expecting after getting a "heads-up" from the XO the day before. The supply sergeant told Strider he simply had no idea what the previous supply officer had done with a lot of the items on the company property books: tents, generators, all manner of things. They were probably around Liftmaster somewhere, or perhaps he had loaned them to the Varsity or the Pachyderms, but since the previous S-4 had not confided in him or written many things down, the supply sergeant had no idea where to tell Strider to look.

The list would, in the supply sergeant's estimation, certainly run into hundreds of thousands of dollars' worth of missing stuff, maybe more than that. If the items couldn't be found, the Army might try to recoup at least some of the cost out of the former supply officer's pay, or maybe even court-martial him. The former supply officer was a friend, of sorts, well, at least their wives were friends back at Fort Campbell, so Strider vowed to find it all if he could, but it was going to be a "real job" indeed. Sigh.

Steeling himself for the coming horror, Strider sat down at the supply officer's desk. Where to start? He supposed he should first look at the property book that listed everything the company owned, but before he could really get started sorting through the books and miscellaneous papers stacked there, the duty clerk came into the S-4 office in a rush. The duty clerk told Strider the XO wanted all the officers in the mess hall ASAP. Leaving the pile of papers untouched, Strider was out the door and back into the rain immediately, leaving all the mess and missing stuff to the supply sergeant and the two clerks for now. They all knew the mess would be there when he got back from flying, so there was no reason to get too spooled up about it right now.

CHAPTER ELEVEN

TYPHOON JOAN ARRIVES AND THE TYPHOON TRUCE BEGINS

THE WARNING ORDER

The CO was not happy. Playtex had survived Typhoon Kate with little real damage, some roofs lost, but nothing that couldn't be readily repaired. Most importantly, no damage had been done to the aircraft. He had anticipated that with Typhoon Kate past, the weather would clear rapidly and they would soon return to normal missions resupplying the FSBs up in the mountains. He was not happy because the phone call he had just received from the battalion CO had put an end to that thought: another typhoon, Typhoon Joan, was on the way toward them—two typhoons in less than ten days! This one was different from Kate, in that it did not have the high winds. It had lost a lot of energy as it passed over the same portion of the Philippines that Kate had just devastated. What Joan had instead was rain, lots and lots of rain. Joan was really big too, nearly covering the entire ocean between the Philippines and Vietnam. Joan was so big that the outer rain bands were arriving already in I Corps, adding misery to the damage already done. To make matters worse, Joan was moving very slowly, giving it time to flood everything that was not already under water.

However, the arrival of Typhoon Joan so soon after Kate didn't mean that Playtex and her sister companies wouldn't be flying missions. They would just be flying missions that none of them had ever done before in a Chinook: search and rescue of Vietnamese civilians. To make it even more interesting they would be flying those missions without helicopter gunship escort.

124

The CO had told the XO to assemble the pilots in the enlisted men's area of the mess hall, the only space Playtex still had with a non-leaking roof big enough to hold them all, so that he could tell them what was going on. After giving the XO 45 minutes to get it done, the CO walked up the wet sidewalk to the mess hall. As the CO entered the room, the XO called everyone to attention. For once they looked very military as they all stood in unison and came to the position of attention with a solid thump that would have made their old tactical officers from Fort Wolters proud. In the silence that followed, the CO motioned for everyone to take a seat.

"We got through Typhoon Kate, but now another one, Typhoon Joan, is on its way. Division says that the war is suspended, an unofficial typhoon truce since no one talked to the NVA about it," the CO began. "Division has, however, given us another mission, suspended war or not. For the next few days your mission is going to be rescuing people, nothing else. We got the mission because our aircraft are the only ones in the division that can do water landings, a critical feature since basically, all of I Corps is under water right now and will stay that way until Typhoon Joan passes and the water goes back down. All three companies in the battalion will be launching six aircraft each to start with. As usual, you will be operating single aircraft. We have too much terrain to cover to send two aircraft at a time. Besides, as poor as the visibility is, you'd probably run into each other anyway. You will not have gunship cover for the same reason. Plus, with visibility as poor as it is they couldn't cover you anyway, since the odds of seeing a target under these conditions is small to non-existent.

"Each aircraft will be assigned a sector to search. The job is simple: search your sector and when you see people trapped by the water who look like they need to be rescued, land your aircraft as close to them as you safely can, load them onboard and move them to the closest high ground. Do not, I say again, *do not* take them to any U.S. or Vietnamese base. If you do, they will just be escorted, at gunpoint, off the base. They will then have one Hell of a time getting back to where they belong, since you dropped them so far away from home. You will also get your ass chewed, just to make sure you understand not to do it again. Just drop them off as close as you safely can to where you picked them up, so that they won't have far to go when the water goes down. Then, go back and look for more people who need help.

"Here's another 'do not': Do not get into the clouds because all the nav aids (radio aids to navigation) and the GCA radar (ground controlled approach using precision radar) at Phu Bai in I Corps are down, except for the Air Force radar down in Da Nang. If you get in the goo (clouds) and can't get back down safely, climb to 10,000 feet and head south. Call the Air Force on your way up and they'll give you a GCA down at Da Nang Air Force Base. Also, get back here or to Camp Eagle or Camp Evans before dark. The weather is way too bad to night fly with no nav aides or radar.

"Check in every hour with the artillery clearance unit on their radio frequency with your position, so you are not flying through any gun-target lines, and more importantly, so that we can keep track of you. No one is shooting, but artillery clearance's radios, being located on a mountaintop, cover all our area of operation, so they can relay your radio calls to us here at Liftmaster. If you do hear someone else calling on Playtex company frequencies, pass it on to us here if you are in radio range, so that all our aircraft are acting as relay backup to the artillery clearance frequency.

"Finally, I say again, understand that this is not an official truce. No one has talked to the North Vietnamese or Viet Cong about this. We are making it a truce because a lot of people are going to die if we don't help them. Even so, DO NOT hang your asses out any more than necessary. Save people where you can, but do not kill yourself and your crew doing so. Any questions?"

MEETING THE LOCALS

There were no questions, at least none asked out loud, but the thought that went through many of the pilots' minds was, "What are the Vietnamese they would be rescuing going to do? How are they going to react to our aircraft landing next to their villages?" No one was sure, but they all knew that helicopters usually did not bring good things to the people who live there; they usually bring soldiers, who often do not treat the villagers well. Sometimes in the past, the soldiers loaded the villagers onto the helicopters for forced resettlement in "pacified hamlets" far from their homes. Although in some ways they might have looked like it, these hamlets were not concentration camps, but neither were they home. The relocated people were not free to leave and therefore hated these places.

In any case, the aircrews' collective contact with the Vietnamese people had been very limited; in fact, it was nearly nonexistent. Playtex's pilots and air crewmen were forbidden by division to go off base, unless they were on an assigned mission. Even when they were on a mission, they were strapped into their aircraft, not walking around interacting with the local people. On their missions they never shut down for lunch among the locals, because they only shut their aircraft down when they were securely behind the wire at a base, not out beside a village somewhere.

Even on the rare occasions when they carried Army of the Republic of Vietnam (ARVN) soldiers in the back of their Chinooks, there was no interaction between them and the Vietnamese. The soldiers got on, sat there until their destination was reached, and got off. Immediately after a lift of Vietnamese soldiers, the flight engineer would search the cabin, since the ARVNs sometimes left grenades or other "presents" behind, supposedly by accident.

Unlike the Americans assigned to Da Nang or Saigon, the Playtex crews never went to a market, a restaurant, or anywhere else Vietnamese people were because Division Headquarters had restricted them to the base unless they were on an assigned mission. The only Vietnamese the pilots had seen up close were the two men who ran the Gook Shop, the kitchen helpers in the mess hall, the barber, the men who burned the shit, and the two women who had worked as barmaids in the Officers' Club for a short while.

It occurred to Strider that he had never had a proper conversation with a Vietnamese person. He had only given the barber direction on how he wanted his hair cut, pointed to the things he wanted to buy in the Gook Shop, said hello to the Vietnamese workers, and ordered drinks from the barmaids. Other than that, he had only spoken to one other Vietnamese person in the two months he had been in county. He supposed he could have tried to have conversations with the barmaids, but their conversations were limited to taking orders for drinks. In any case, the barmaids had not been there long before they both quit. One of the Penny Postcard lieutenants, in a charming gesture, burst through the door to the Officers' Club and, while sliding across the floor on his knees, sang a song to the two young women behind the bar, apparently having learned it during his three semesters in college. While kneeling on the floor with both arms outstretched toward them, he sang, in his best operatic voice:

Leprosy, Ye gads, I've caught leprosy!
There goes my fingernail into your ginger ale.
There goes my eyeball into your highball.
Kiss me quick, never mind, there goes my upper lip . . .

The barmaid's English wasn't that good, but apparently she caught the word "leprosy," and it scared her to death, so she quit. When she left, her friend, the other barmaid, left, too. At the XO's direction, Steiner never replaced them. Strider assumed it was because the presence of women, even Vietnamese barmaids who didn't speak much English, created competition among the men for their attention and Playtex didn't need that!

But then, maybe they did speak English. Maybe they were gathering intelligence for the NVA, so it was better they were gone anyway. Then again, if they were spies, maybe they quit because they found out it was a waste of time to try to gather intelligence in the Playtex Officers' Club, because there wasn't any intelligence to be gathered. Cargo helicopters don't have any classified parts to speak of and the pilots really don't know much, if any, classified stuff. You just don't need to know classified stuff to haul sling loads to mountaintops. Everyone assumed the barber was Viet Cong (VC), but that was OK, because everyone assumed every other Vietnamese who worked at Liftmaster was VC, too: the guys who burned the shit, the cook's helpers, the guys who ran the Gook Shop, all of them. Of course, some you had to trust. The barber, for example, because he got to hold a straight razor to your throat when he shaved the hair on the back of your neck after your haircut, so everyone hoped he was just a guy trying to make a living and wasn't really VC.

Of course, there was one other way to get close contact with a limited number of Vietnamese people, very close contact, in fact. The United States military does not allow prostitution on its facilities, ever, period, well, at least they didn't in 1970. But they did allow steam baths and massage parlors, all staffed by Vietnamese women. The popular name for the massage parlor over on Phu Bai Main, and everywhere else in Vietnam where there was one, was the "Steam and Cream." While straight out sex, conventional or oral, was not generally available, even for a fee, "manual relief" was offered, usually involving Dial shampoo in a way perhaps not envisioned by the manufacturer. But then, that wasn't really *contact* with the Vietnamese people, either. It was the same service available to men who need it virtually everywhere in the world where there are military bases, or anywhere there are men without women, for that matter.

Other than that, the only close-up view of the Vietnamese for the men of Playtex, was when they had to go over to Battalion Headquarters at Phu Bai Airport by jeep, the same ride Strider had taken when he arrived. After leaving Liftmaster they travelled a stretch of QL1, the national north-south highway, for a mile or so. Old Renaults, Honda 50 motorbikes, bicycles, people walking down the side of the road with conical hats and loads of produce or ducks for the market—all of them were there and quite exotic in their own way, but the men of Playtex never talked to them. A lot of the men were in western dress, while the older people were dressed in what appeared to be black pajama bottoms and varying colored shirts, as they went their way. Of most interest were the young women in *ao dai*. This national costume was made of silky material, often white, with long sleeves and a fitted upper body, the straight skirt going all the way down to the ankles, but then slit up the sides all the way to the waist, worn with slim, ankle-length, black trousers—very sexy without showing anything at all. Those young women were so very beautiful and so very far away from the men of Playtex.

Strider was wide-eyed with wonder from the first moment he arrived in Vietnam. It started with the midnight bus ride through the streets of Saigon, with no armed escort and an unarmed driver who was not even in combat gear, taking the newbies from the airfield to the receiving station on the other side of town. The only difference between that Bluebird bus and any other stateside military Bluebird bus was that this one had chicken wire over the windows to prevent a grenade from landing inside. It was the first time, other than a brief visit to Mexico with his parents and five days in Bermuda on his Honeymoon, that Strider had been out of the U.S. Now here he was, a big white guy, living for a year in an Asian country, full of small Asian people, a prospect he had never considered while growing up in the Kentucky hills.

While in-processing, Strider stood inside the chain link fence around the receiving station and looked out at the Vietnamese going about their business there in the heart of the city, so different from anything in his experience. He didn't realize at that moment that he would never know any of them.

Strider's next experience among the Vietnamese came in the ride from Phu Bai Airport to Camp Eagle, 50 miles north, for two weeks at the Screaming Eagle Replacement Training Center (SERTC). All the replacements for the 101st flew from Saigon to Phu Bai, crammed into a C-130. There were no seats in the cabin of the aircraft. Instead, an Air Force crewman directed them to sit down on the aircraft's deck in rows, back-to-back. Once they were settled, the crew put cargo tie-down straps over them to hold them in place, a sort of giant seat belt for 10 people at a time. Had the C-130 crashed, there would have been no way for the passengers to escape the wreckage, but at least all the bodies would be in nice, neat rows, making recovery so much simpler. But the C-130 did not crash, and when it arrived at Phu Bai, they were unstrapped and marched out onto the tarmac for the next leg of their journey.

On the tarmac there at Phu Bai, a convoy of flatbed trailers, pulled by military semis, waited for them. In the front of the convoy was a gun truck: a duce and a half with homemade armor around the cab, and a quad .50 machine gun mounted in the bed. It looked quite fearsome, very war-like. There was a similar gun truck in the middle and another at the end of the line of ten or twelve trailers. The trailers had a single layer of sandbags on the decks and a wall four sandbags high around the sides to provide some protection to the passengers against small arms fire and land mines. The newbies climbed up into the flat bed trailers, were handed an M-16 with a couple of magazines, instructed not to fire at anything unless directed by the grunt truck leader, a bored specialist 4th class infantryman, and off they went up QL1 among all the civilian traffic.

As they traveled up QL1, 40 miles to Camp Evans, the Vietnamese, who were quite used to the military convoys, paid them no attention whatsoever, cutting their motor scooters in and out between the trailers loaded with wide-eyed men. As the trucks drove through Hue City, about halfway through their journey, the newbies could see the battle damage left over from the NVA and VC's Tet Offensive a couple years before. It took the U.S. a week of hard fighting to take the city back, and it was visible in blown up buildings and bullet holes in the walls around some of the compounds. Strider was particularly distressed when the road narrowed and they entered a more densely populated part of the city; he could see people above, hanging out the windows of the old French-built apartment buildings, looking down at them and laughing as they went past. It would have been so easy to drop a grenade in the back of one of the trucks, but no one dropped anything. Four hours after the convoy left Phu Bai, they arrived at Camp Evans without incident. The grunts took back the M-16s and the SERTC people marched them to the barracks where they would live for the next two weeks.

The first Vietnamese person Strider actually spoke to was a kid, maybe an eight- or nine-year-old boy. The 101st wanted everyone to know what it was like to be an infantryman, a grunt, so that everyone would appreciate what the grunts experienced. To get the point across, the SERTC graduation exercise after two weeks of training was a real live helicopter-borne combat assault. Dressed in full combat gear, all the newbies were loaded into the backs of Hueys and flown to the rice paddies about five miles to the west of Camp Evans. Under the tutelage of a couple of experienced grunts, the newbies did a combat sweep back to the base, supposedly looking for bunkers the NVA might be building.

The flight from the PZ to the LZ took all of five minutes. As the Huey touched down, Strider jumped out of the back, and just like in the movies, was instantly knee deep in mud. He was praying that there weren't any "punji stakes" (wooden or bamboo spikes) hidden in the deep mud of that paddy, since he did not have jungle boots with steel-plated soles, but only the plain leather combat boots aviators wore. He kept thinking about how the sharpened bamboo would go right through the sole and right into his foot, but there weren't any punji stakes in the paddy, just knee-deep mud. Strider didn't think that the people at SERTC would actually send them into an area where the enemy was likely to be. All these new guys would just be massacred if they got into a real firefight. Sure enough, they did not see any bunkers, NVA, or VC, just some small boys herding water buffalos.

These small boys were not shy. One of the kids ran up to Strider, shouting "Give me cigarette! Give me cigarette!" and when Strider said no because kids that small should not be smoking, the kid shouted, "Fuck you, GI. You number 10," those two phrases apparently the limit of his English.

Even so, it was more English than Strider knew of Vietnamese. It was not a good first contact with the locals.

That night, to his amazement, Strider watched air strikes go into the area they had swept through that very afternoon. As the jets pounded the area, the thought occurred to him that maybe there wasn't a place in Vietnam to send anyone where there weren't NVA or VC.

Things were no different for Strider on the ride from Battalion Headquarters up QL1 to Liftmaster three days later, after he had completed SERTC. He was still wide-eyed and transparently a newbie, not yet ready to go for "Cool Points" by being blasé about mixing with the locals. He caught a ride from Camp Eagle to Phu Bai and was in base operations looking for a ride over to Liftmaster when someone heard him ask about C Company. Two Playtex pilots, a warrant and one of the Penny Postcard lieutenants, just happened to be over at battalion at that moment. After figuring out that he was joining Playtex, they loaded him and his gear into a jeep for the short ride.

Both officers in the front of the jeep had their pistols on, but paid no attention to the swirl of traffic around them as they pulled out of Phu Bai's gate and onto QL1. Strider was weapons naked, without even a rusty M-16 this time. What if someone tried to throw a grenade into the jeep, or pulled out a pistol as they went by on their motorbike, Strider wondered nervously to himself, but no one did anything except ignore the jeep moving among the other traffic on the highway. By the time they arrived at Liftmaster, 15 minutes later, Strider was trying his damnedest to look blasé, like the other two pilots, by lighting a cigarette and looking bored as they drove along. He was not yet succeeding.

Now, for the first time, the men of Playtex would truly be out among the people of Vietnam. They would be loading them onboard their helicopters, seeing them up close with no barbed wire separating them from the aircrews. Although interaction would still be limited to loading them on and off, this time they would be close enough to be touched. These Vietnamese would be civilians, not ARVN soldiers, another new experience. How would they handle the noise and vibration of the big helicopter?

After the CO sat down, the operations officer took over. He announced that six aircraft would launch within two hours to get started on the rescues that afternoon, then he read off the crews and aircraft assignments. Strider was assigned to fly with CW2 Alex Kelley, popularly known as Alice, in one of the mission aircraft. Strider had no idea why the other pilots called him Alice, but Alice didn't mind, so Strider went along with it too. Strider was excited because this time he would not be just a copilot in one of the backups, but would be actually doing mission stuff other than sling loads, an interesting prospect. They would be flying Playtex 506. The crews were to bring overnight gear with them, in case they could not get back to Liftmaster before it got dark.

After he finished reading off the assignments, the operations officer dismissed everyone else. He then gathered the six ACs around one of the tables and passed out maps showing the area of the lowlands where each was to search, while the copilots watched over the AC's shoulders. Alice was assigned an area northeast of Camp Evans, stretching from QL1 all the way to the sea, 20 miles away. The map showed many villages in the area, but the maps were old, perhaps going back to the French days in the 1940s, so there was really no way of telling if the villages were still there or not, except, of course, to go and look.

When everyone was getting ready to head back to their hootches to pick up their flight gear before going out to their aircraft, the assistant operations officer came running into the mess hall and called a halt, to everyone's confusion. Once he got the pilots settled down, he told them that division had put a hold on the launch, based on weather reports that it was near zero ceiling and zero visibility throughout Northern I Corps. The visibility in the mountains was zero and it was just as bad in the lowlands where they were supposed to be working. They would instead launch at dawn tomorrow, provided the weather improved. Everyone would keep the same aircraft and crew assignments, as well as search area for tomorrow.

Since he wasn't flying today after all, Strider returned to the supply office and did his first official act as the new S-4 officer: he turned in his .38 revolver and issued himself an M1911A1 .45 automatic pistol, a holster, a 50-round box of ammunition, and three magazines. The automatic seemed to him more military somehow than the policeman-like .38. It was cooler, too. He did not start reviewing the property books, though. That could wait until after the flood was over and things were back to normal. Strider told the supply sergeant and the two supply clerks to start looking around for the obvious missing things, like tents and large generators, and they promised they would. Since nothing had happened previously with regard to finding missing items, Strider sincerely doubted anything would happen now, at least until he was there full time to oversee it.

There was no typhoon party that night, or even any heavy drinking by the pilots, at least not by those listed on the flight schedule. There weren't even any card games in the Officers' Club. It was, in fact, the quietest night that Strider had seen in his time in Playtex. Tomorrow promised to be a long, difficult day and all the Playtex crews knew it.

Chinooks landing on water. *Courtesy Tom Smith*

Playtex's generator.
Author photo

Phu Bai's mailbox.
Author photo

Playtex hootches.
Courtesy Jim Morrical

CW2 Dick Steiner walking across the ramp at dawn. *Author photo*

Drinking coffee before chow (known as "Chop Chop" in Vietnam), 1971.
CW2 Marvin Leonard, center, and two Playtex RLOs. *Author photo*

Above: CW2 Robert F. Curtis
by the company sign, 1971.
In the background can be seen
Playtex outdoor movie theater.
Author photo

Left: "Tricky" Dick Steiner
(self-named "Super Jew"),
author's roommate, January
1971. *Author photo*

CW2 Robert F.
Curtis with Jerry
Cobb's crossbow,
Phu Bai, RVN,
1971. *Author photo*

Playtex 831 after it rolled off the Currahee Pad at Camp Evans. *Author photo*

CW2 Robert F. Curtis, Camp Evans, RVN 1971. *Author photo*

CW2 Dick Steiner relaxing in his hootch, Phu Bai, RVN, 1970. *Author photo*

CW2 Robert F. Curtis leaning against prized air conditioner, Phu Bai, RVN, 1971. *Author photo*

CW2 Robert F. Curtis, Playtex Officer's courtyard, 1971. *Author photo*

CHAPTER TWELVE

OCTOBER 28, 1970

LAUNCH! LAUNCH!

Trough the duty clerk worked from 2200 hours until 0800 hours every day, sitting at a field desk in the sand-bagged operations bunker. He liked it that way, working alone in the night after the assistant operations officer left around 0100 hours, reading his paperbacks when nothing else was happening. Because he worked all night, he was excused from the sergeant major's work parties during the day, a very sweet deal for him. The usual routine was that his work really began around midnight, when battalion sent over the mission sheets by courier.

The assistant operations officer, a Penny Postcard RLO, had already given the duty clerk the list of crew priorities, i.e. who would fly the most hours the next day, so that when the mission sheets came in, the two of them could line the missions up with the aircrews. To come up with the priorities, the assistant operations officer looked at flight time running totals to see who had flown the least number of hours lately. He tried to keep the pilots to 90 hours in the last 30 continuous days. At 110 hours, the pilots had to see the flight surgeon for clearance to fly. At 120 hours they were automatically grounded until they had some rest. The AC with the lowest total flight hours would get the most missions, the same for the copilots. It was a good way to even out the load among the pilots and make sure everyone got a break from the daily grind now and then.

Both the operations officer and the assistant operations officer talked to the standardization instructor pilot (SIP) and IPs, as well as the ACs about how the pilots were doing. If they knew someone was weak in certain types of missions, they would take that into account when they assigned copilots, assigning someone more experienced, instead of just the one with the least flight time. If the assistant operations officer was really concerned about a certain AC, he might assign another AC as the weaker one's copilot, but this was rare. Together, the assistant operations officer and the duty clerk would then look at the big map of Northern I Corps pinned up on the wall, comparing the number of sorties each mission had with the distances between the PZ and FSBs, to decide how many aircraft would be assigned to each one. They had done it so many times that it was long since routine.

At around 0030 hours, a runner from maintenance would come in with the aircraft assignments for the morning launch. When all missions and aircraft had been assigned, the duty clerk would then type up the company mission sheets. After he finished typing them, he would individualize them for each AC, highlighting the missions that a particular AC was to execute and the aircraft he was assigned. There were always two more aircrews assigned than there were missions, so that if an aircraft developed a mechanical problem on start-up, there was a spare ready to launch without delay.

Each mission on the sheet either listed a discrete start time or had a simple priority number if it could be done at any time the aircraft was available. The ones where the crews would definitely be shot at always had a time and place where the Chinooks were to rendezvous with their Cobra gunship escorts. Of course, the Chinooks could be shot at on any mission, but that was a given. The primary difference between the "shot at for sure" missions and the "may get shot at missions" was in Air Medal awards. If you were going to be "shot at for sure," the flight time was considered "combat assault" time, and each crew member would be awarded one Air Medal for every 25 hours of flight time. If it was uncertain if you were going to be shot at, it was "assault support" flight time and you got an Air Medal for every 50 hours of flight time. If you were on an "assault support" mission and you did get shot at, the crew would log "combat assault" time for that entire mission. Sorting this all out took a major portion of the assistant operations officer's time, that is, when he did not fob it off on the duty clerk. It was not uncommon for a Playtex Chinook pilot to finish his year-long tour with 20 or more Air Medals.

At around 0415 hours, the duty clerk would head for the officer's area to wake up the aircrews. He woke ACs first, then copilots, unless they shared a room, in which case he would wake up both at the same time. Today was different, though, because there were no missions listed on the sheet, only pilot's names and aircraft assignments. Today, the only mission was to rescue people. Just as the duty clerk started to walk out the door, the field telephone rang—battalion reporting that the weather had improved and all aircraft should takeoff at first light.

When the duty clerk woke the pilots at 0430 hours, he passed the word from battalion that the weather had improved and they would launch at sunrise, around 0630. The ACs acknowledged the information, mostly without enthusiasm. It was all too common for weather reports, particularly ones from battalion operations, to have no bearing on reality. The copilots had no comments one way or another, since their opinions did not matter. Why bother having one? Without waiting for the ACs to tell them what to do, the copilots dressed, walked to the mess hall and ate a hurried breakfast before heading out in the rain and darkness to begin the pre-flight inspections on their aircraft. The ACs had breakfast and then reported to company operations to get final instructions.

The flight engineers had been up since 0330 hours and had already completed their daily inspections, so the work platforms and all the inspection panels were open, ready for the pilot's pre-flight. After this was done the crew would usually stretch out and doze off while waiting for the pilots to arrive. The flight engineers on each Chinook always had stashed away an extra case or two of C-Rations (each containing 12 meals), a 5-gallon can of water and some soft drinks, just in case the aircraft broke down or for some reason couldn't get back to a base for meals. Chinooks, being helicopters—sometimes called "a collection of various loose parts flying in close formation" by fixed wing pilots—routinely broke down and it was always good to be prepared for any eventuality.

The flight engineers had been told they would probably be doing water landings, so they screwed the drain plugs into the aircraft belly tightly. Normally the drain plugs were left down and open to allow condensation to drain out of the belly of the aircraft, but they needed to be tight today to prevent the belly from filling up when they landed in the water. All the crewmen were looking forward to water landings since, not being a routine maneuver, they had never done them.

The door gunners spent a little extra time checking out their machine guns; they had no idea how this day's mission would go, since they would not be landing in secure FSBs like they usually did. How could they know what was going to happen? No one in Playtex had ever done this kind of rescue mission before.

In an hour, the copilots had completed the pre-flight, the flight engineer and crew chief closed all the open panels, the ACs had briefed the crews on what they were going to do, and as the sun came up, invisible though it might be in the heavy cloud and rain, they started the aircraft and taxied out onto Liftmaster's short runway. The helicopters then took off, one Chinook after another, until six Playtex aircraft were airborne and headed out toward their assigned areas to begin their new mission: rescue.

ALICE AND STRIDER GO FLYING IN PLAYTEX 506

Alice and Strider were assigned Playtex 506, the same aircraft Maas had used to follow 831 back from Camp Evans after 831's unplanned trip down the Crash Pad. Having only been in Playtex for a few months, Playtex 506's flat green paint was a little less mottled than most of the other Chinooks, but that would change quickly, as the flight hours flying into sandy landing zones and oil spills down its side built up.

Playtex 506 was a "Baby C" Chinook, meaning it had a less powerful, but more reliable, engine than the "Super C." Truth be known, even though the "Super C" had more horsepower and would therefore lift more payload weight, all the aircrews preferred the "Baby C." "Super C" engines had a tendency to explode, and not just quit, well before they were due to be changed. When they exploded, there was a very real chance the engine pieces, traveling at 20,000 RPM, would slice through the back of the aircraft and maybe destroy it. No, Playtex ACs preferred the "Baby C," weaker engines or not.

Playtex 506 was a good flying helicopter, with nicely tracked rotor blades giving it its smooth ride. Some of the company's Chinooks had a sort of shuffle from side to side as they flew, not disconcerting necessarily, but not completely right either. The pilots liked to be assigned to fly 506, a major point of pride for its enlisted crew. It didn't hurt that the flight engineer had a couple extra seat cushions for the pilot's seats, so he could rotate them allowing the pilots to remain dry, mostly. It was a clean aircraft, too, since its flight engineer directed the crew chief and door gunner to sweep it out after every internal cargo lift that was even slightly dirty, and clean the windshields every morning. They even washed the aircraft when they could arrange a tow over to the wash rack on non-flying days.

As the CO stated when briefing the crews on the mission, Chinooks were the only helicopters in the 101st, or the entire Army for that matter, that could routinely do water landings. Playtex 506, like all Chinooks, would float very nicely, as long as the drain plugs were in. The operator's manual advertised that the CH-47 had demonstrated the ability to remain afloat with no engine power for two hours, even adding a picture of a Chinook floating serenely on a lake with its rotors stopped. To prove that to the pilots during transition training, the students all had to do three landings and takeoffs in Lake Tholocco at Fort Rucker, Alabama.

To land, the student pilot would first bring the aircraft to a high hover, maybe 100 feet above the surface, and then slowly lower it into the water. The trick to landing was to look at something on the edge of the lake, trees maybe, to gauge your height above the water, then bring it down slowly, but keep it moving. The spray from stopping too low pretty well took away visibility. After the third landing, the flight instructors had the students taxi the helicopter around in the water for ten minutes or so, just so that they would know what it was like. When it was his turn to taxi round the lake, Strider thought he could probably get enough speed to tow a water skier, but that was not in the syllabus, so he never got to try it. While he enjoyed the exercise, he never thought he would actually make another water landing after he completed the Chinook transition course.

PLAYTEX 506'S CREW

THE AIRCRAFT COMMANDER (AC)

The second of the three pilots who laughed when Strider came into the Officers' Club with the story about the walking fish was CW2 Alexander Kelley, a.k.a. Alice. Alice was tall and thin like Strider, but had blond hair, instead of dark, like Strider. While Strider had just started his tour, Alice was nearing the end of his, making him one of the senior aircraft commanders (AC). He had a wild streak that was not readily apparent. It only came out when you were flying with him, like it did on one of the first flights Strider had with Alice right after joining Playtex.

A mission everyone dreaded was the "Bus Run," not because it was dangerous, but because it was the opposite of dangerous—it was excruciatingly boring. Every day one of the companies in the 159th ASHB had one aircraft assigned to fly from LZ to LZ, from one end of I Corps to the other, ending back up in Phu Bai at the end of the day. Your Chinook was no longer a combat aircraft flying into danger in the mountains, but instead, it was, in effect, a big, green bus, hauling passengers from stop to stop, exactly like the local buses do in every big city. The Bus Run was a very long, boring 10 or 11 hour day: land, load passengers, takeoff and fly to the next LZ, land, drop off passengers, pick up passengers, takeoff, etc. The longest leg of the Bus Run was the flight from Phu Bai over the South China Sea past the mountains that ran right down to the sea, separating the coastal lowlands to the north from the big natural harbor at Da Nang, a 40-minute flight.

You didn't have to go out over the South China Sea on the Da Nang leg. You could stay over land and take a short cut by flying through the Hai Van Pass, located two miles inland from where the mountains came down to meet the sea. However, wreckage of at least four aircraft around the top of the Hai Van Pass showed that using it as a short cut was probably not a good idea. The NVA liked to set up a machine gun near the top of the Pass and wait patiently for some unsuspecting aircraft to fly through the gap. It was an easy "kill"—just hold down the trigger on the machine gun. Instead of risking it, most helicopters swung out to sea, passing between a small island and the mainland, the so-called "Low Van Pass," thus avoiding the Hai Van Pass. Not too far out to sea, though, because no one onboard any of the aircraft had life jackets, nor did the aircraft carry a life raft, considered useless extra weight when your missions were all over land. Swimming was also difficult—no, impossible—when the swimmer was wearing body armor, like the Playtex pilots did.

Chinooks are set up to drop paratroopers. The jump master controls the drop with a set of troop debark signals mounted on the bulkhead in the front of the cabin. The troop debark signals consist of a square metal box with a red light over a green light and a very loud bell, almost like the ones schools once used to signal class changes. As the paratrooper marching song goes, "Stand up, buckle up, and shuffle to the door. Count to three and out once more." The red light meant that the paratrooper should stand up, hook up their static lines to the wire running the length of the passenger cabin from the bulkhead behind the cockpit to the ramp in the back. Green light and bell both meant that they should shuffle to the back of the aircraft and jump off the ramp into the air.

The flight engineers on the Chinooks also used the troop debark signals to help control the passengers, since none of the passengers had headsets to talk to the crew over the ICS. The flight engineer's pre-flight briefing to them was, "Listen up, when the green light is on, it's OK to smoke. Keep your seatbelts on, but relax and enjoy the flight. When the red light comes on, there will be no smoking, and make sure your seat belt is tight. If the red light and bell come on at the same time, we've got trouble, so tighten your seat belt. Do not exit the aircraft if the blades are still turning unless one of the crew tells you to. The crash position looks like this. Are there any questions?" There were none, but there were looks of concern, since no one had ever actually given them a briefing on what to do in flight before.

Strider was Alice's copilot on the bus run one day in September. Alice was flying as they swung out over the sea for the leg to Da Nang, avoiding the Hai Van Pass. As they always were on long legs, they were at 6,000 feet, above the possibility of small arms fire from the enemy and into the nice cool air, a welcome break from the heat and humidity down near the surface. There were maybe 25 passengers in the back of the Chinook, all looking grateful for the cool air, but bored by the flight. After the aircraft had climbed to cruising altitude over the South China Sea, the flight engineer turned the red light off and lit the green one.

"Everybody ready," Alice asked the crew over the intercom five minutes later.

"Ready for what," Strider asked.

After the flight engineer replied, "All set in back," Alice looked over at Strider and said with a grin, "You'll see." He slammed the power all the way down, starting the Chinook on a very rapid autorotative descent toward the sea, one so rapid that it caused the passengers unexpectedly to rise up against their seatbelts in mild negative "g-force."

At the same time as Alice dropped the power, the flight engineer ran to the front of the aircraft and activated the red light and the bell on the troop debark signal. Simultaneously, both door gunners opened up with their M-60D machine guns, blasting away at the empty ocean below. The flight engineer then ran to the back of the aircraft, pulled out his pistol, and started firing it off the ramp. Up in the cockpit Alice pulled out his .38, and holding the stick in his left hand, began firing it out the open cockpit window with his right.

Strider was perplexed, not excited, but very perplexed. Was this a moment when you were supposed to be afraid? The aircraft was over the sea. All systems were operating normally. There was no threat requiring either dropping from the sky or returning fire. Turning to the left in his seat, he glanced back through the companionway to see how the passengers were taking it. From what he could see, not well, summed it up. One or two of them might have been screaming, but he couldn't tell over the usual Chinook roar and the sounds of the machine guns firing. At a bare minimum, all the passengers were worried, very worried.

After ten seconds or so, his pistol now empty, Alice said over the intercom, "cease fire, cease fire" and the door gunners let go of their triggers. Alice put his .38 back in its holster and pulled the power back on, stopping the descent, positive "gee" forcing the passengers down on their seats. The flight engineer, too, put up his pistol, then came back forward, turned off the bell and switched the red light off and the green light back on. The passengers looked a bit shaken, but relieved that whatever had happened was over and they had survived it. The crewmen in the back kept straight faces. They had done this before and knew it wasn't a good idea to let armed passengers know you had just been "messing with them," but in the cockpit, Alice was laughing his head off.

After they were established back at 6,000 feet, Alice turned the flight controls over to Strider for the remainder of the leg. He re-loaded his pistol as they flew along. Fifteen minutes later they landed at China Beach in Da Nang, very near their sister company, the Hurricanes, who had their parking ramp. Before they could even get the aircraft shut down, about half of the passengers came to the cockpit one by one to shake Alice's hand and thank him for "saving" them. The rest waved to the pilots as they walked away. Without ever knowing what had really happened, they all would have a good war story for the folks back home.

After that, Strider wasn't too sure about flying with Alice, but knew that when he did, the day would not be complete boredom.

THE COPILOT

Technically, Strider was not the "copilot," he was the "pilot." It was never explained to Strider why it was that way, but while other helicopters might have pilots and copilots, Chinooks have aircraft commanders (AC) and pilots. He thought it might be so that both pilots could log first pilot time, perhaps giving some benefit later in their aviation careers, but he wasn't sure. Be that as it may, at this point in his tour he was in the right seat, doing whatever the AC in the left seat wanted him to do, just like all copilots do, whether or not you call them a "pilot."

Strider was 21 years old, married, and the father of a two month-old son. He missed his wife and son terribly, but took to heart the Army training that told him over and over that to think of anything except flying when he was in the air was tantamount to suicide, and put them out of his mind while he was working. Still, he wrote home every day. In his letters he never mentioned bullet holes or mortars going off on the FSBs as they were trying to set down their sling loads. Instead, he just wrote how many hours he had flown that day and what they cooked for dinner in the hootch. When something funny happened, like the walking fish, he put that in, too.

He thought he was keeping the danger from her, but Strider didn't fully appreciate that his wife could track the war and aircraft losses better than he could. She watched the news every night and knew when a Chinook went down in I Corps and what the weekly casualty figures were. Because she lived on Fort Campbell, Kentucky, with the other "Waiting Wives"—women whose husbands were also in Vietnam—she sometimes saw the chaplain come with the casualty assistance officers to other women's doors when the worst had happened. All the waiting wives worried that the chaplain would be coming up their walk next. She read his letters and hoped they were telling the truth, but she doubted it. She knew from the war stories the pilots told among themselves that there was a lot missing from the letters, but she tried not to think about that.

Fourteen months before, as time came to graduate from flight school at Fort Rucker, Alabama, Strider and the other students in his class spent hours debating the merits of the various places in Vietnam where they might be assigned. Some hoped for assignment to the Delta. There were no mountains there and it seemed a little calmer than where the war was, up north in I Corps, while others thought the Central Highlands was the place to be. Oddly, no one mentioned I Corps.

Strider didn't much care one way or another where he would be assigned. His grades had been good enough that he had been offered Cobra transition immediately following flight school, but he turned it down, even though he had gone through gunship training earlier at Fort Rucker. While he was learning to shoot mini-guns and fire rockets in the old "B" and "C" model Hueys the Army used as trainers, it occurred to him that if you shoot at people, those people will definitely shoot back. No, Strider would take his chances with the default helicopter option, Hueys, instead of Cobras. It didn't work out that way, though.

Then, in a bolt out of the blue, everyone in Strider's class was assigned stateside instead of going straight overseas, the first time that had happened, ever, or at least since Vietnam got going strong ten years before. There was dancing in the streets! Strider and his wife had been planning on starting their family after he got back from Vietnam, but with that news, they threw away the birth control pills and started making a baby that very day.

Strider was sent to Fort Campbell for a year, where he became an instructor pilot, transitioning returning Vietnam pilots and brand new warrants straight from Fort Rucker into the OH-13E. The helicopter was an underpowered, two-seat, wooden-bladed, Korean War vet from 1951 and Strider loved it. At the same time, he knew that Fort Campbell wouldn't last forever, so six months into the year he made a deal with the warrant officer branch up in Army Headquarters. In return for agreeing to stay in the Army after his initial three-year commitment as a "Career Indefinite" warrant officer, they would send him to Chinook transition, which sounded like a lot better deal than being a Huey pilot. When he told the assignments officer that his wife was pregnant and that he would like to be home for the birth if he could, the assignments officer sent him to a Chinook class that was over three weeks before the baby's due date. As icing on the cake, the assignments officer also gave Strider six weeks of leave after Chinook school before he had to report to Vietnam. His son was born in the middle of the six-week leave period and three weeks later Strider was on his way to war.

While he was still very new to Playtex, Strider was making good progress toward becoming an AC. That year in the States as an instructor pilot had done him well in his aviation career. His mentor there had also been his boss, a major who had flown in World War II and Korea. He taught him tricks of the flying trade, but mostly he taught Strider how to stay calm when things looked bad. If you were going to survive, you had to be calm, because panic causes you to do the wrong thing and, in the end, kills you. Besides, while you gain major cool points for calm, you lose them all the first time you panic.

Strider loved flying Chinooks. That love started during the Chinook transition course, when his instructor showed him a not-necessarily-approved takeoff method Strider had never seen or even heard of before. On the first flying day of the transition course, the instructor took the flight controls for the final takeoff from the practice airfield where they had been working to head back to Fort Rucker. When the control tower cleared them for takeoff, instead of lowering the nose and starting forward, the instructor lifted the helicopter straight up, climbing vertically. As they climbed, he gave the helicopter right rudder, so that they climbed in a slow rotation around the center of the aircraft. At 1,000 feet, the instructor stopped the climb pedal, turned the aircraft in the direction of Fort Rucker, and lowered the nose, quickly accelerating to 120 knots while holding altitude. It was stately. What power the aircraft had, to do such a maneuver so calmly, so serenely! The Chinook certainly wasn't an underpowered OH-13 or even a Huey, but something in another league all together. It also helped that from a distance, the Chinook looked like a flying castle: the forward and aft pylons, the turrets. To Strider's mind it was what a helicopter should be.

The Chinook's mission suited Strider well, too. Unlike Huey pilots, he was not stuck in the middle of a 12-helicopter formation, flying into hot landing zones day after day. Chinooks did not do combat assaults in the 101st because shooting down one CH-47 load of 30 troops would be the same as shooting down four or more Huey loads or eight troops. It is much easier to shoot down one big aircraft than four much smaller ones.

Strider liked that Chinooks often worked by themselves. If more than one aircraft was involved, they were all on separate legs, spaced far enough apart so that the lead aircraft could drop its load and clear the LZ before the next one arrived. All day long, they would be hauling the food, fuel, and most often, ammunition for the artillery in sling loads hanging under the aircraft. All day long, it was hover low to hook up the load, lift it straight up to 20-foot hover, climb out to cruising altitude, and then shoot a precision approach to a mountaintop, positioning the load exactly right so that the recipient could retrieve it easily. It would get deadly dull boring by 10 months into his tour, but right now, every load was exciting, shooting your approach so that the load was right over the spot where it was supposed to be, setting it down smoothly, and going back for another and another till the mission was completed.

As soon as he got 300 hours in a Chinook, he would take the check ride to become an AC and move over to the left seat. Strider couldn't wait.

THE FLIGHT ENGINEER

As has been established, the individual helicopters belong to their flight engineer, not to the pilots who fly them or to the maintenance officer. The pilots changed every day, but the flight engineer stayed with his aircraft and was responsible for it being always ready for action. Playtex 506 belonged to Specialist 4th Class (Spec 4) John Powers, he of the dark wavy hair and a commanding, but friendly, attitude. In addition to owning the helicopter, the flight engineer also ran the aircrew, consisting of himself, the crew chief, and the door gunner. Not only was he in charge of the aircraft and the enlisted crew, he was in charge of decorating it. Nose art, like in World War II, was not allowed in Playtex, but the armor at the front of the cabin, just behind the pilots, was his to paint as he saw fit. Even so, Playtex 506 was not decorated, not necessarily because Powers was conservative, but because he was more interested in having his aircraft ready for missions than he was in decorations, sexy or otherwise.

Since the flight engineer owned the aircraft, he and the crew chief would often sleep in the helicopter's cabin after the day's work was done instead of going back to their hootch. It was quicker to get ready in the morning for missions if you were already in place. Also, there were no sergeants giving them orders out there on the flight line and best of all, there were no drunks or druggies creating hate and discontent.

While the majority of the men were clean, there were plenty of both drunks and druggies to keep things stirred up. It was easy to tell them apart. All you had to do was just look into their hootches. If there was no alcohol visible, they were druggies. Oddly, to Strider, it seemed that the druggies were less trouble than the drinkers. The druggies just kind of nodded off on their heroine or mellowed out on their marijuana, generally smiling a lot more than most people do.

Heroine came in little clear plastic vials, about half the size of a 35mm film tube. It was so cheap and so available that sometimes in the morning, before the sergeant major's cleanup detail picked them all up, there were so many of the plastic tubes on the ground in the enlisted area, it looked like it had hailed. It was a wonder that there weren't more overdoses. Marijuana was cheap, too. It could be bought ready rolled in waterproof packets of 10 for $1 or loose, if you preferred to roll your own.

The drunks, on the other hand, did not nod off quietly. They were often loud and belligerent, always worrying since everyone was armed. Of course, the major difference between the two types of high was duration. Drunks might be hung over, but they usually sobered up the next day. A good drug high might require several days to end, or it might never end if you took drugs again the next night or took too much of the pure heroin one time. Neither sort of high was desirable in people maintaining aircraft.

To Strider, it seemed that the enlisted men got into drugs or drink through boredom and ready availability, not as a reaction to constant danger. Unless you were aircrew, there was probably less danger for the young men at Liftmaster than they would find back home in the States, since the men in Vietnam didn't have cars or motorcycles to drive too fast while drunk. Violence between the men was rare. Even with all the readily available weapons, intramural shootings were nearly unheard of. Perhaps they were rare because everyone knew everyone else also had an automatic weapon and even grenades, if they wanted them.

Availability of the high of your choice was never an issue, since the Army issued the same booze ration card to everyone and drugs were readily available everywhere. The official feeling seemed to be if you were old enough to die for your country, you were old enough to drink. Each booze ration card allowed a man to buy more than most people could drink. Since most of the men were either just under 21 or barely over it, they had limited experience with alcohol and it hit them hard when they drank too much. It was easy to drink too much because if you wanted more booze than your ration card would allow, you could always borrow one from a non-drinker or one of the druggies to get more.

Drugs, of course, required no ration card, making them even easier to get than alcohol. For hard alcohol, you had to go to the Army's Class VI store, a government liquor outlet, or the PX for beer. For drugs, no PX or liquor store was required, since any user would sell you some, or, if you preferred cutting out the middleman, you could buy them from the Vietnamese men who "helped out" at the Gook Shop, or the hangers-on who lingered just outside the barbed wire in front of the guard bunkers. Not even men who used drugs back home had ever seen them so cheap or so readily available as they were in Vietnam. Add in the fact that the heroine wasn't cut, so a high came easily, often in the form of a heroine-laced joint. Few people injected heroine; it was so pure that it was too easy to overdose.

Either way, drugs or alcohol, many of the users were going to have trouble when they went back home after a year's nearly constant high. Some were alcoholics or addicts by the time they were 21 and would never recover from it.

The aircrews were neither druggies nor drunks. Make a mistake because you are high or hung over and die right now, taking a lot of other people with you. Drunks and druggies were not tolerated by the other aircrews or the maintenance officer. While their fellow crewmen might not report them to the officers, anyone suspected of excessive drinking or drug use might be warned by their peers to quit being an air crewman. If they did not do so voluntarily, they might well be given a "blanket party," i.e. a blanket thrown over their head, so they could not see who was doing it, followed by an anonymous severe beating. It only took one blanket party to get the point across.

So, as noted, to avoid sergeants, druggies and drunks, the flight engineers and crew chiefs often slept in their aircraft. Besides, takeoff was always at dawn and being on the aircraft already let them sleep a bit longer before they had to get the "bird" ready for the pilot's pre-flight inspection. The flight engineer always had a stretcher stashed under the troop seats. During the day when on missions, he would lay on it while looking down through the "hell hole," the hatch in the floor that opened to allow the crew to look down at an external load. At night, it made a passably comfortable bed, particularly when covered by an inflatable air mattress, a "rubber lady" in Army slang. The crew chief and door gunner didn't have the privilege of a stretcher, but they might have a hammock they could hang from the tie down rings in the cabin ceiling if they didn't want to sleep on the troops seats.

No matter what the flight engineer's rank was, the pilots always called him "Chief" when they were talking to him on the ICS, even though he was neither a chief warrant officer, like most of the pilots, nor a Navy chief petty officer, nor even the crew chief of the aircraft. Being called "Chief" was a job description that marked him as the flight engineer and one that all flight engineers took with pride. In the air, as well as on the ground, the flight engineer's job was all encompassing. After he had completed the aircraft's daily inspection, before the pilots arrived to pre-flight, he made sure the area around the small jet engine auxiliary power plant's exhaust was clear before the pilots started it. Standing outside, first on one side and then the other, he cleared the pilots to start the engines, which started the rotors spinning. He checked the aircraft clear for taxi and directed it when it moved forward out of the revetment. Before takeoff, he checked the area around the aft transmission for leaks and ensured everything in the cabin was ready. On sling load missions he lay on his stretcher on the cabin deck and directed the pilots over the load. He made sure internal loads were tied down properly. He supervised the crew chief and gunner when they were refueling the aircraft. He directed passengers where to sit and when to exit. He kept C-Rations hidden away for when the crew missed lunch. When bullets came through the thin aluminum skin, he checked for critical damage. When the day's missions were done, he and the crew chief inspected the aircraft and "turned it around" for the next day's missions. He washed the aircraft's outside and cleaned the aircraft's inside. When his helicopter went into scheduled maintenance, he helped with all that was required. Flight engineer was a full time job.

John Powers, owner of Playtex 506, was very good at his job. It was, in all respects, his Chinook; any flaw in it was a direct reflection on him, and he did not like that. His days often ran 14 to 18 hours, but Powers didn't mind. His aircraft was one that pilots looked forward to being assigned to and he was unabashedly proud of that.

THE CREW CHIEF

The crew chief wasn't really the "chief" of the crew; that was the flight engineer's job. He wasn't called "Crew Chief" by the pilots either, but usually by his last name, just as the pilots did among themselves. Like a copilot under training to become an AC, the crew chief was actually a mechanic in training to become a flight engineer. The job was so coveted that this usually only occurred when one of the flight engineers finished his one-year tour.

The crew chief on Playtex 506 was Specialist 4 Don Crone. He had blond hair and thick glasses above his green, fireproof Nomex flight suit shirt. He didn't say much, because he was self-conscious about his broken front tooth, but he was good soldier. He worked hard for the flight engineer, looking for the recommendation from him that would help him move up when an opening came. They made such a good team, Powers and Crone, putting in 12–18 hours a day, day after day without complaint, and Powers let Crone store his own sleeping stretcher onboard, no small honor.

Crone watched the other Chinooks carefully, mentally deciding he would like this or that one when his turn to be a flight engineer came, even though the decision was not up to him. Playtex 506 would be nicest, he thought, but he would take any one of them if it were offered. In flight, he manned the right door gun when not helping out with whatever Powers wanted him to do. Just like manning the right door gun, when they refueled, he would always take the right side tanks. In his heart, Crone knew he would be a better flight engineer than anyone else in the company. He would never say it out loud, but he knew it.

THE DOOR GUNNER

The Chinooks all mounted a 7.62mm, M-60D machine gun on each side of the cabin, right at the front of the aircraft, just aft of the cockpit. The door gunner always manned the one on the left, the port side, of the cabin. The left gun was mounted on a bar in the space where the removable window went. The one on the starboard, or right side, the one that was mounted in the crew door, was manned by the crew chief; he could help the flight engineer by moving the machine gun out of the way, if required, so that they could use the crew door. The right gun was mounted on a bar that was pinned so that it could be swung back into the cabin to allow the crew door to be used; even so, it still got in the way at times. Since there were never enough door gunners in Playtex to man all 16 aircraft, they were often rotated between aircraft. This was not really a problem, because all 16 Chinooks were never in the air at the same time due to maintenance schedules.

The door gunner would check the two M-60D machine guns out of the armory every morning, well before daylight, and carry them in the dark out to the flight line. While the flight engineer and crew chief were doing the morning pre-flight inspection, the door gunner would mount the guns on their pintles (upright pivot pins on which other parts turn) and check their operation, stopping just short of loading them. The machine guns would be locked and loaded, i.e. ready for action, as soon as the aircraft cleared the wire at Liftmaster on the first takeoff of the day. Once the guns were ready, they would stay that way until their final landing.

Because Chinooks hadn't really been designed for door guns, the door gunner sometimes had to improvise a bit to get the ammunition to feed. For example, if he didn't have the proper mount, he would take a C-Ration can and wire it into place on the side of the machine gun to make the ammo feed smoother from the ammo can on the aircraft's deck. The door gunner would bring at least two cans of ammo for each gun, even though the flight engineer usually had more stashed away somewhere in the cabin. After his guns were ready, he would help out the flight engineer or crew chief as much as he could.

Even though they usually only mounted two, Chinooks could carry three M-60Ds, one on each side and the third one mounted on the rear cargo ramp as a "Stinger" for the flight engineer to man if a second door gunner was not available. Playtex almost never mounted the third gun, because it got in the way of loading and unloading internal cargo, particularly palletized cargo. For pallets, the gun would have to be removed so that the pallets could be dragged onboard using the aircraft's winch. The gun would have to be stored somewhere until the mission was completed and then reinstalled, adding time to what always was a long day. Another reason Playtex aircraft didn't use the stinger was that at least twice, the machine gun had somehow become loose and had fallen away, disappearing into the jungle below, bringing wrath down on the entire crew.

Unlike in Huey companies or gunship companies, Chinook door gunners rarely got to fire their weapons. This was because they seldom went into hot LZs, operating instead out of secure PZs and depositing their loads on secure FSBs in the mountains. Sometimes, if they were lucky, the AC would take the aircraft out to a "free fire" area between missions. In free fire areas, everyone and everything was considered hostile and therefore, could be shot. Even the trees and dirt were considered the enemy. When the AC OK'ed it, the gunner and crew chief could blaze away at objects, both animate and inanimate, in the free fire zone. That was rare, though, because free fire areas were free fire areas for a reason: they were full of NVA and the NVA shot back, especially at big, slow Chinooks. ACs usually avoided free fire areas unless they were working missions there anyway and feeling their oats. It was better to go out over the sea to fire the guns, even if there was nothing there to shoot at.

Many door gunners had been grunts before they joined Playtex. Often they volunteered to be door gunners because they were tired of walking, day after day, through the jungle. Other grunts considered the volunteer gunners crazy, feeling that flying into combat was far more dangerous than walking. When the helicopter was completing its approach you were just hanging out there in space, coming into an LZ, a big fat target for anyone with a weapon. Some of the grunts disliked it so much that they would start jumping out of the Huey before it actually was on the ground. While acknowledging that might be true, the grunts who volunteered to be door gunners figured that if you were going to die in combat, it was better to fly to where it was going to happen than it was to walk there. Why die tired?

Today, Spec 4 Willis Crear was 506's door gunner, but he wasn't a former grunt looking to get out of walking. He was a crew chief looking to move up to flight engineer. He just loved flying, so when his aircraft, Playtex 107, was down for maintenance, or not on the flight schedule, he was only too happy to volunteer to fly as door gunner on someone else's crew. After all, better to be cool in the air than sweating while working on a helicopter back on Liftmaster Pad. Flight engineers liked to have Crear as the door gunner; he could help with many maintenance requirements on the aircraft instead of just sitting behind an M-60D machine gun like the former grunts did.

Like Crone, Crear was looking to move up to flight engineer as soon as he could. He figured he had a better chance than most to move up soon, because he volunteered to fly in whatever capacity was needed to show he was a team player. That didn't really make any difference, though, because as always, it was up to the maintenance chief and maintenance officer who was a flight engineer and who wasn't, and no one really knew what their selection criteria was. Crear, too, had picked out the Chinook he wanted when he did make flight engineer: Playtex 820 was the bird for him.

THE WAR IS SUSPENDED, DAY ONE

Pre-flighting an aircraft, especially one where you have to climb 18 feet off the ground to see the rear rotor system, is never a lot of fun when it's wet. To get up there, you have to learn a complicated dance of which foot to move to which foothold (the steps built into the side of the aircraft), before you can get to where you need to be. It's a different dance step coming down, but it becomes routine after a while. Pre-flighting in the dark, with a flashlight in one hand while holding on to the aircraft with the other, and the rain is making the inevitable spilled fluids and grease even slicker than they normally are, is even less fun.

Strider was philosophical about pre-flights. After all, the crew was out there doing their own inspections an hour before he got there, no matter what time that was. When the day was over, they would be there for at least an hour after he left, doing a turnaround inspection. Still, when he slipped and nearly slid off the top of the fuselage halfway between the forward and aft rotors, which would have resulted in a 13-foot fall to the PSP, he longed for the day when he would be an AC and could send his own copilot out to do the dirty work.

When Strider had finished pre-flighting the top of the Chinook, he noticed that Alice had not yet arrived, so he continued with the bottom of the aircraft. In ten minutes he was finished with it, too. He found nothing wrong with the aircraft worthy of note, so the crew buttoned it up, i.e. closed and locked all the panels they had opened for pre-flight. When Alice arrived, they would be ready to go, provided there wasn't something he particularly wanted to look at.

Copilots didn't normally stop at operations on their way to the flight line, but this morning Strider had stopped by for two reasons: one, to find out if he and Alice still had 820 today; and two, to sign for the KY-28, the scrambler for the radios. The KY-28, weighing 10 pounds, was an armored box with a plug in the back that attached to the aircraft's communications radio. With the KY-28, they could talk to Playtex Operations or other aircraft without the NVA understanding what they were saying. The KY-28 had a big, red covered switch at the top marked "Zero." Every day, the intelligence officer would use a big punch to load the day's code into the boxes. If you went down, you were supposed to hit the zero switch, which would erase the code, making the box unusable to the enemy. Strider doubted anyone ever did that. If you were in the process of going down in a hostile area, you usually had other, higher priorities.

The KY-28 may have let you talk without the NVA being able to understand you, but they often did not work well, if at all. To use them, one aircraft would call another, the pilot saying, "Switch covered." When you flipped the switch on the KY-28 to "Secure" and then keyed your radio to transmit, you would hear a tone that sounded like "Be Bonk, Be Bonk," which let you know you were, indeed, transmitting in the secure mode. Because getting the aircraft's KY-28 working properly was difficult, in frustration, the pilots would sometimes say, "Switching simulated covered," followed by transmitting "Be Bonk, Be Bonk." Operations was not amused when the pilots did this, but the pilots figured that it didn't really matter that the NVA could hear them, since they could clearly see the big, fat, slow Chinooks approaching the FSBs with their sling loads anyway.

The AC normally picked up the KY-28, but with it, the survival gear, and the ACs own personal flight gear, it was quite a load for him to drag out to the flight line. Strider really wasn't "sucking up" to Alice when he saved him the trouble. Warrants rarely, if ever, sucked up to anyone, especially fellow warrants, since no warrant would ever make general, or wanted to do anything but fly until their three year Army commitment was up. The saying was "the only way you can hurt a warrant officer with a fitness report is roll it up and stick it in his eye." While that may or may not have been true, Strider wanted to help out this morning, so he picked them up hoping Alice would speed things along.

Alice was later than usual in getting to the aircraft, not because he wanted Strider to do the entire pre-flight, but because all the ACs had to go by operations for a briefing prior to flying. That day's visit to operations went more slowly than usual because the operations officer held him there until all ACs for the day's launch had arrived, so that he could give them an extra caution about their mission. They had already heard it from the

CO, but he wanted to say it again. The basic message was, do the mission, but don't take stupid chances.

When the briefing was over, Alice signed for their survival gear, the blood chit and the maps. The blood chit offered a gold reward in several languages for the locals' assist in returning the downed crew to U.S. control. This was a handy thing, should they go down in hostile territory, i.e. anywhere outside the wire of the U.S. bases. Alice was pleased to see that Strider had already picked up the KY-28, one less thing for him to carry. When he finally got out to the aircraft, Alice was not in the mood to be silly or to play practical jokes. He got all the crew inside the cabin and quickly passed on what information he knew.

"We are supposed to rescue people," he began, "But as the operations officer reminded me once again, we all need to keep in mind that some of those people would gladly kill us, given half a chance. So, let's not give them half a chance. I want everyone to be especially on the lookout for any kind of threat as we do this, people pointing guns and things like that. Unless you actually see someone shooting directly at us, do NOT open fire, but do let me know immediately if you even see anyone with a weapon. Chief, clearance underneath us is going to be critical since we are not landing at prepared LZs, so be double careful today. Questions? OK, let's get over to Camp Eagle and top the aircraft off before we start."

The duty clerk's pronouncement notwithstanding, weather had not improved according to Strider's observation from the right sight in 506. If anything, it had deteriorated since the day before. Alice made the first takeoff of the day, as ACs always do, to make sure everything in the aircraft is working properly. He was looking for little things wrong that a less experienced copilot might miss. Actually, Playtex 506's takeoff was more a slow climb to 200 feet than a normal takeoff would have been, as the clouds prevented them from going any higher. Ordinarily they would have climbed to at least 500 feet between Liftmaster and Camp Eagle, but the visibility was less than a mile in the fog and mist, as tears of rain ran down the windshield. Back in the States, flying in this weather was prohibited, except in very specific locations and situations, but here the stateside rules didn't apply. The mission was to rescue people, so they were flying. The mission must be done. But then, they weren't flying as much as moving along at a fast, high hover. The weather did not improve as they got further away from Liftmaster and closer to Camp Eagle.

The flight from Liftmaster to Camp Eagle took them over the firing ranges used by South Vietnam's Army of the Republic of Vietnam (ARVN). Everyone in Playtex 506's crew was particularly watchful as they passed over the ranges, because the ARVNs sometimes took pot shots at passing helicopters. It was called "friendly fire" when your allies took a shot at you. The radio call joke went, "Am taking friendly fire, am returning same." Nothing happened this time, though, since the ranges were empty. All the ARVNs were staying in out of the rain, it seemed.

Strider liked the rifle ranges. Soon after he arrived in Playtex, he had been occasionally assigned as rifle range officer. As rifle range officer, once a week, his job was to take groups of ten or fifteen men out for familiarization firing of their M-16s and pistols. Even though they were helicopter mechanics and office clerks, they were still soldiers and needed to be reminded of how to shoot every now and then. After going to the part of the range that had proper targets for a single magazine's worth of firing, Strider would take them to a deserted section that faced a barren hillside. It was normally used as a range for machine guns and M79 grenade launchers. There was a low hill between the long-range targets and the firing line that was a bit short for the trajectory of the M-79 grenades, so lots of unexploded 40mm rounds were laying down range. Since the shooters usually had two 30-round magazines each for their M-16s, they would have one left, which they would expend trying to shoot the grenades and make them explode. The grenades almost never did explode, since the shooters rarely actually hit them. It was good fun when one finally did go off, a small red flash followed by a puff of black smoke.

On one trip to the range a few weeks earlier, a duce and a half with a tarp over the bed pulled up to where they were firing at the hillside. The grunt driving it approached Strider, actually saluted, a rarity, and said, "Sir, could you guys help me fire off these magazines? They're old and the CO told me to get rid of them, but there are just too many for me to handle." When Strider asked how many magazines there were, the grunt didn't reply, but instead walked to the back of the truck, climbed up and pulled back the tarp. There were hundreds of loaded 30-round M-16 magazines, loose in the bed of the truck. Strider smiled and called the men over and told them to help themselves. Strider had always wondered how many magazines you could fire on full automatic through an M-16 before it jammed from the heat. The answer was six. After six magazines his M-16 was nearly glowing. The barrel was too hot to touch and the weapon was frozen solid. It took 15 minutes before the metal on the rifle cooled down enough to start firing it again.

But that was a few weeks back, now it was raining and the ranges were cold as Strider flew over in Playtex 506 headed out to rescue people.

The trip to the fuel pits over at Camp Eagle was short, only about five miles from Liftmaster. Instead of taking on only the fuel they normally needed, around 3,600 pounds, Alice told Powers he wanted him to completely fill all six fuel cells for a total of around 6,800 pounds of jet fuel. This would give them enough fuel for about five hours of time in the air instead of the usual two and a half hours. They could take the extra fuel because they were not hauling typical loads today. Normally, they were hauling an 8,000-pound load of fuel or ammunition and had to keep a relatively light fuel load to do so; but people, specifically Vietnamese people, were light. A combat loaded American grunt would be at least 250 pounds, sometimes 300 with full equipment, but a Vietnamese civilian would be 100 lbs., at the most. The limit would be cube, not weight, i.e. how many people could physically fit in the aircraft's cabin. There were seats, the red troop seat-type, along both sides of the cabin for over 33, but Alice told Powers to fold them up, leaving an empty cabin. They would not be taking the people they were going to pick up far enough to bother getting them seated.

HOVERING PRACTICE

Camp Eagle's fuel pits had four spots for Chinooks. Since no other aircraft were there when they arrived, Alice took the forward one on the left, spot one. After he landed the Chinook and turned off the stability system, as is always done when the helicopter is on the ground, Powers lowered the rear ramp and the three enlisted crewmen walked out to begin the hot refueling (refueling with the engines running). Alice decided he needed to take a piss before they took off again, so he gave the flight controls to Strider, unplugged his helmet from the ICS, and unstrapped his shoulder harness and seatbelt. He carefully climbed out of the left seat, making sure he didn't bang into any of the switches or flight controls, climbed through the companionway, walked down the cabin, and out the ramp into the rain.

Every experienced pilot and air crewman knows that magic spot on the outside of your helicopter where you can take a piss with the blades turning without the rotor wash blowing it back all over you. On the Chinook the magic spot is on the left side, right where the forward sponson, the bulge on the lower fuselage that holds the fuel cells, ends. Alice went straight to the magic spot. He had just finished when another Chinook, this one from Playtex's sister company, the Varsity, came in to land at another of the refueling points, the one directly behind Playtex 506.

The Varsity aircraft was coming in a little too fast, so the pilot did a slight flare right at the bottom of his approach to break his speed, which sent a blast of 100+ MPH rotor wash forward onto spot one. When his rotor wash hit Playtex 506, it lifted the helicopter up off the ground involuntarily, tail first. As the rear end lifted, Strider could see the forward rotor blades getting perilously close to the ground in the front, so he added power and took the Chinook up into a hover. As Playtex 506 broke ground the stability system was off; Strider was alone in the cockpit, and the rest of the crew, including the AC, were outside.

As the Chinook rose wobbling into the air, Crear, refueling on the left side, jerked his refueling hose out of the tank and jumped back, well clear of the aircraft. Crone, for some reason known only to him, dropped the refueling hose but held on to the aircraft by jamming his hands into the opening of the fuel cell. Suddenly he was 10 feet or more in the air, dangling by his hands as the aircraft gyrated above the refueling pad. Alice ran clear to the left side, mouth open and momentarily in shock, as his aircraft rose above him. Powers, being the flight engineer, had a very long microphone cord that connected him to the aircraft's ICS, allowing him to talk to the pilots while standing outside the aircraft. Fortunately, Power's cord was long enough to remain connected to the ICS when the Chinook inadvertently lifted off and hung there, wobbling 20 feet above him. After a couple seconds of open-mouthed wonder, Alice reacted. He ran back to where Powers stood, rooted, staring up at the Chinook now directly above him, and unplugged Power's long cord, then plugged it into his own helmet.

"Strider," Alice said as calmly as he could, "You OK up there?"

Strider wasn't sure he was OK, but he said he was anyway. The lessons from his mentor at Fort Campbell came back then and he forced himself to be calm. Anything else would only make a bad situation worse: if he lost control of the Chinook in the fuel pits, things would become worse right now for all concerned. He was controlling the Chinook, but it was very difficult for him because the stability system, the computer that helps the aircraft stay steady, was off, like it always was when the aircraft was on the ground. The problem was, of course, that the Chinook was not now on the ground. To reach the switch that turned the stability system back on, Strider would have to look away from the outside references he was using to try to steady his hover and look left and down at the center console. Then he would have to let go of the thrust lever, the control that makes the helicopter go up and down, to reach over and turn the switch back on. He decided it was too much to attempt and concentrated as hard as he could on keeping the aircraft steady without the stability system's help.

"Strider, bring it down slowly. The ramp is not all the way down, thank God, but it is down far enough that you are going to have to touch down as gently as possible," Alice told him, his voice very calm. "Try not to drift backwards as you come down. I've got everyone clear, so start down now. I'll talk to you if you need me to, but you can do this, so I'm going to shut up and watch. By the way, not to put any more pressure on you, but Crone is hanging on the left main fuel cell, so try not to shake him off."

If the ramp had been all the way down, it would have been virtually impossible for Strider, or anyone else, to land the helicopter without doing major damage to it, bending the ramp up at best and bending the fuselage at worst. Where the ramp was now, a few degrees above all the way down, there was a good chance Strider could do it. Strider forced himself to be as calm as he possibly could as he hovered the Chinook unsteadily over the refueling pad. He lowered the thrust level slightly and the helicopter started down slowly from its 20 feet. "No backward drift, no backward drift," he kept saying to himself.

As the helicopter began to descend, Crone managed to let go of the fuel tank opening. He fell the last ten feet to the ground and after he hit, he picked himself up, scrambled to his feet and ran away from the descending Chinook, joining Powers and Crear a safe distance, or at least a safer distance away. Alice, still calm, stayed right behind the aircraft, ready to talk Strider down if he needed it.

Just before the rear wheels touched, Strider wobbled the aircraft a little, bobbling in ground effect (the most efficient portion of hovering when the aircraft is just a few feet off the surface). He lowered the power a little more, and when he felt the right rear wheel touch the ground, pushed the thrust lever full down removing all power and held it there. Moments later the left rear wheel and the front wheels hit with a forceful bump, but that didn't matter. The aircraft was safely on the ground, and in one piece. Strider realized that his right hand was hurting from squeezing the flight controls so tightly, so he took a deep breath and relaxed his grip. The whole incident from lift off until landing had taken less than a minute.

Before Alice went back inside and joined Strider in the cockpit, he checked to make sure Crone was OK, which he was. Crone was laughing a little from nervousness, but was not hurt in any way. His flight gloves had protected his hand from being cut on the fuel cell opening and even though it had been quite a drop, the fall had done him no damage. He would later say that he had no idea why he had held on to the fuel tank lip instead of letting go, but right now he was just glad it was over.

Alice had a big smile on his face as he climbed into the left seat. Strider had done the job perfectly, just like an AC would have, not that the situation had occurred before, that Alice knew of. Alice would put in a good word for him with the operations officer when they finished up rescuing people. Maybe they would give him his AC check a little sooner. Outside the helicopter, Powers was doing a quick check to make sure all was well before they began refueling again. All was well, no damage to be found. Ten minutes later, with everyone's heart back to beating at a normal rate and the refueling complete, they were ready to launch again—time to get on with the mission.

THE NEW MISSION BEGINS

Alice took the flight controls back from Strider and lifted the Chinook into the air. He did not stop in the hover like they usually did, but instead, transitioned straight to forward flight. He was not going to blow anyone around with his rotor wash if he could help it. As they left the fuel pits, he turned the aircraft to the northeast, to where their assigned search sector was. It would be difficult to find, mainly because they didn't normally work much over the coastal lowlands. Their missions normally took them to the mountains, so they weren't very familiar with the terrain in the lowlands.

Their map wouldn't be much help either: all the terrain features it showed were under water by now and therefore, would be no help in orienting them. Add in the fact that the visibility couldn't have been much more than a mile, and it was clear that they would have no idea exactly where they were at any given time.

Before they had been in the air for 20 minutes, they discovered that it really didn't matter if they found the exact area they had been assigned—the entire countryside from Da Nang to the DMZ, a strip of at least 100 miles long by 30 miles wide, was under water. By this time, anyone who lived there was in dire need of help. The reality of this came to them after they saw that the first three villages they flew past were completely covered with muddy yellow-brown water, with only the tops of the hootches visible.

Alice turned the aircraft around after they passed the third semi-submerged village and headed back to the first one they had flown over. As Playtex 506 came close, the crew could see villagers huddled on what little high ground remained, while others had taken to their wooden fishing boats, all trying to stay out of the foul-looking water. There was no apparent hostility from the people below, at least no one in the crew reported seeing any guns, so Alice looked carefully for what appeared to be a clear enough spot to put the big helicopter down. He found one, and after a couple of low circles to make sure it was clear of obstacles, such as power lines and antennas, began an approach into it.

Without knowing how deep the water was, Alice gingerly set the helicopter down, holding a little power on in case he had to lift off again quickly. Fortunately, in the spot he picked, the water was shallow enough that it only covered the bottom half of the wheels, meaning that with its belly mostly clear, the Chinook was not floating but was actually on the ground. He lowered the cargo ramp enough for the people to climb onboard through the rear ramp; that way, they could wade to the helicopter instead of having to paddle up to the crew door on the starboard side.

As the helicopter settled down on that first landing, no signals passed between the Vietnamese villagers and the crew of Playtex 506. The villagers sat there in the rain at some distance back, and looked at the Chinook, seemingly expressionless, not moving even when Powers stood in the crew door and signaled them to come to the helicopter. He used the Vietnamese hand gesture for "come here"—right arm extended, fingers down, with hand sweeping back and forth. The people still did not move, they just sat there in the rain looking at the big helicopter. Who could blame them, Strider thought. It was doubtful any of them had ever been up in any kind of aircraft. Where was this helicopter going to take them? Would there be a re-settlement camp waiting when they landed? Would they be able to come back to the homes when the water went down?

After what seemed like ten minutes, but was probably only one, from the right seat of the cockpit, Strider could see a young woman finally start to move toward them. She was wearing the typical peasant black pajamas and conical straw hat, as were all the villagers. They were the picture of rural Vietnam. When the woman made up her mind, she stood up quickly and with her right hand, picked up her small child and put it on her hip. Then, she slung a bundle over her shoulder with her left hand. With that, she started to wade through the water and rotor wash toward the back of the aircraft. Since she did not raise her feet as she walked, Strider could see that as she moved she left a slight wake behind her. After a moment's pause, the others huddled there also stood up and started to follow her.

Strider twisted in his seat so that he could see a little ways back into the cabin, and watched them board. No one had been screened for weapons—the crew would be wide open if there were Viet Cong (VC) with them and they chose to attack. Both Crone and Crear were near their guns, but not touching them, letting the barrels point down at the water. At some point, human beings just have to trust each other; in the rain and the misery of the rising water, that point was now. Not to help these people would have been a crime, not war. They came and came, Powers helping them up onto the ramp, Crone and Crear moving them toward the front of the cabin, until at last, Powers signaled to those waiting to board that they could take no more this trip.

"Sir, we're full. Ramp's coming up. Looks like at least one more load in this village," Powers called over the ICS. "All set in the back."

"OK, Chief, coming up," Alice replied as he added power.

Alice lifted the aircraft out of the water while Strider called out the pre-takeoff checklist. Strider was very curious to know how much power it would take to lift this load. Very little, it turned out, since they were not pulling much more power than it took to takeoff with a full fuel load 25 minutes ago. The fuel they had burned and the weight of the passengers just about evened out. Adding a little more power as he eased the control stick forward, Alice climbed the Chinook to just below the clouds at 200 feet and headed toward a high patch of land they had passed on the landing approach to the village.

In a few minutes, they landed on the spit of land still clear of the water. When Powers lowered the ramp, the villagers filed out into the rain, carrying the few things they had brought with them. It wasn't home or even out of the weather, but at least it was not under water. The refugees didn't appear to have any food, so the flight engineer threw a case of our C-Rations out to them before he raised the ramp. It wasn't much, but at least it was something. He regretted he had no water to give them.

"Your turn," Alice said to Strider over the ICS.

"I have the controls," Strider said as he took the controls and after another ". . . all set in back" from Powers, and he lifted the Chinook back into the air. He couldn't see the people they had just dropped off, but knew they were getting blasted by the big helicopter's rotor wash, so he added more power as he lowered the nose and climbed out without hovering first.

In a few seconds, the Chinook was on approach to the village again. Strider landed in just about the same spot as Alice had on the first run. He was a little slower on landing than Alice was, and the spray completely covered their windshield before he got Playtex 506 settled in its landing spot. It also further soaked the crew, not that it mattered. They wouldn't be dry again until they were back at Liftmaster. Again, the wheels were on the ground with the water not quite high enough for the aircraft to float, but it was getting close now.

Powers started to lower the ramp, but changed his mind when it became apparent that the water was too high at this spot to keep it from filling the inside of the ramp structure. Strider was in a slightly different place from where Alice had landed, and the water was about six inches deeper. Instead of lowering the ramp, Powers told Crone to demount the right-hand door gun so that the villagers could come in through the crew door. With help from Crear, Crone got the M-60D machinegun out of the way and stowed under the left door gun, where they could get it back in place quickly if they needed to.

Alice had briefed all three crew members to stay in the aircraft as much as possible in case they had to do a quick takeoff. Crone lowered the crew door hatch that then became two steps and helped lift the villagers up into the cabin. Crear stood just inside the cabin door to help them with the top step and to pass them on to Powers. If any of the crewmen were concerned that the aircraft was now defenseless on the right side, they didn't say it out loud. Their mission now was rescue, not combat, and if the mission required being partly defenseless, so be it.

The mission must always be done.

Again, looking back through the passageway into the aft cabin, Strider could see that the people did not fill the entire aircraft this time, but he did notice that several of them were carrying piglets. Dinner or the last of the things they owned? It didn't matter on this load; there was lots of room in 506's cabin. Strider also noticed there were more men in the back this time. He suspected it was because they did not know what was going to happen on the first load and did not want to get caught up in something bad. Then again, they could have been VC and needed time to stash their weapons before evacuating their village. Right now, the war was off and they wouldn't be needing their weapons just yet; later, they might. The flight crew and the Vietnamese alike knew the war would start again soon, but not right now.

Looking out through the windshield at the flooded village, Strider thought back to when he was in the sixth grade. He went to school in Dayton, Kentucky, a small town on the Ohio River, right across from Cincinnati, Ohio. Dayton didn't have a floodwall around it, so when the Ohio flooded, it always flooded Dayton, too. When the flood came that year, he walked down to look at the houses standing in the water. As he got close, he could see a fire engine and firemen standing beside it, looking out on the flooded streets. A house was on fire there in the water. How it started, Strider never found out, but it was burning brightly, standing completely surrounded by the water, and the firemen could do nothing but watch it burn. The floodwater was too deep for them to drive their fire engine into and, even if they did, they couldn't plug their hoses into the hydrants, because they were invisible under the brown flood. Some people wrapped in blankets stood with the firemen, apparently the occupants of the burning house, watching everything they had disappear.

There was no fire here. It was too wet for anything to burn, but for the people who lived in this village, the feeling must have been the same as it was for the people who lived in that house in Dayton. Everything they had was being taken and there was nothing they could do about it, nothing except survive and build again; that's what people do.

When everyone looking to evacuate the village was onboard, Powers called ready to lift, and Strider picked up the aircraft again and flew toward the same drop-off point as last time. Five minutes later, the helicopter was on the ground and the second load of passengers was joining their fellow villagers. They had carried 83 people in their first two evacuations of the day, nearly the same number of people they usually carried in three loads. Alice wrote the number down so that at the end of the day, he could report to operations what they had done.

The Playtex 506 crew knew where they were geographically at that point, but unfortunately, they also knew it wasn't their assigned area. Alice took the flight controls back from Strider and climbed back up as high as he could go without getting into the clouds, and as he turned the aircraft to the northeast, headed out deeper into lowlands east of Hue City where they were supposed to be working. The other villages near there would just have to count on the possibility of being seen by the Chinook assigned to this area, a slim prospect, but the only one there was for them.

Alice wasn't concerned about getting lost today—fly east far enough, east in the coastal lowlands, and you will reach the South China Sea. From there, turn south and follow the shore until you reach a large inlet, then fly west until you see the railroad tracks or QL1, the main road north to south in South Vietnam, on its western shore. Follow either north until you came to Phu Bai, and you were home. They just had to be mindful of their fuel state, and if necessary, be able to make it back to the refueling points at Phu Bai, Camp Evans, or Camp Eagle.

After a few minutes, Alice gave the flight controls to Strider, instructing him to continue northeast, still toward their assigned area. Even though they couldn't get lost, Alice unfolded the map and studied it, a not very helpful exercise since most of the landmarks were already under water. Even so, within minutes Alice reckoned they were on the western edge of their assigned area. At that moment they arrived over the top of another village, this one in worse shape than the first one they had evacuated.

This village was almost completely under water. The crew could see that the people of this village didn't have the luxury of higher ground to shelter on, as the first one did. Some of them were already in boats, tethered to the poles of their houses. Others were huddled on top of the bigger, more solid buildings, the ones with tin roofs, along with their chickens and an occasional small pig. Their flocks of ducks, it seemed, had been let loose to fend for themselves. Since their wings were clipped, they couldn't fly away, but they could be rounded up later when the water went down. Strider circled the village twice, looking for a place to land where the wheels might be on the ground, but couldn't find one. To complicate things for the people they were going to pick up, palm trees and small buildings that might interfere with the rotor blades would prevent him from landing too close to where the people were waiting.

But then, the people who lived in this village weren't waiting for the Chinook at all. Strider was sure they had no idea the helicopter's mission was to rescue them. No one could have told them since there were no telephones in villages like this one, and all the roads were long since under water. They were trying to do what they always do in situations like this one—wait it out and survive somehow. No help had ever been given to them by anyone before when the rains came, not their own government, not the Japanese in their day, not the French in their day, and not the Americans now, so why should this time be any different? Besides, helicopters usually brought soldiers and that was never good news.

Strider finally saw an area fairly close, maybe 100 yards away from where most of the people were, that was apparently clear of obstacles, or at least clear of anything visible above the water. It looked to be a rice paddy, with an outline of dykes barely visible in the muddy, brown water. Strider told Alice that he was going to land the Chinook there and after he nodded OK, started the approach. Instead of landing directly on the spot like they had done at the last village, he brought the aircraft to a high hover and, with directions from Powers, brought it as straight down as he could. The spray increased rapidly as they got lower, but with the windshield wipers going full blast, he could still see out well enough to fly.

This time there was no solid touchdown, because this time Playtex 506 was floating—the water was too deep for their wheels to touch ground. Strider gingerly lowered the power until it was all the way down, but the aircraft started to move a little, so he had to add some back to keep it in place. It seemed like he was "flying" the aircraft in place as he held it there. The muddy brown water was just below the chin window as he looked down between the rudder petals, just like the lake water had been back at Fort Rucker.

Playtex 506 floated in the brown water quite nicely, just as advertised by Boeing, just as it did back at Fort Rucker. The aircraft presented no problems to keep Strider from holding it in place once he got the feel for how much power was required. Then he felt the floating movement stop. In their very slight drift, their wheels must have lightly touched something, maybe one wheel was up against the rice paddy dyke, but Strider couldn't tell. All he knew was that they were safely down and everything was stable.

Looking over toward the village, Strider could see the people watching them, but none of villagers moved toward the Chinook, until, once again Powers gave them the Vietnamese hand signal version of the "come here" wave. One small wooden boat with four people in it was the first this time. After some initial hesitation, it started toward the helicopter, two of the people propelling it forward with poles in a graceful motion. In a repeat of their first lift, the rest of the boats soon followed after one made a move.

Strider kept the power as low as he could as the boats glided slowly toward the helicopter. He knew the rotor wash would easily knock them over or blow them back away from the aircraft if he did not. Because they had moved behind him as they came forward, he couldn't see the boats come under the rotor disk, but Alice was looking intently toward the back of the aircraft. From the left seat, he could see the people coming onboard through the crew door, like they had done on their second lift of the day.

"Sir, we've got a full load. Door's closed, ready to lift," Powers called over the ICS after about ten minutes had passed. At the signal from the Alice, Strider added power and Playtex 506 lifted up from the water into a 20-foot hover. Looking over at the gauges, Strider could see that it was taking a lot more power this time than it did on the first two loads, which could only mean that the aircraft had taken on water.

With the belly of the Chinook full of water, they were very heavy, but they made it into a hover without using all the power they had, a good thing. Strider lowered the aircraft's nose to start moving forward as he added a little bit more power to begin takeoff. Soon they had climbed to 200 feet, still just below the clouds. In a few minutes, Strider was landing the Chinook at the nearest high spot, on the road to their village, maybe a mile and a half from where he took off, to allow their passengers to disembark. When the water went down, they would have to walk back, so, as Playtex's CO had directed, he placed them at a point where the return trip to their village wouldn't be any harder on them than necessary.

Once Strider had landed the helicopter, he told Powers to count the people as they left the aircraft. After a few minutes, Powers said, "98, we had 98 onboard." Most of them were women and children, but, 98 is still over three times the number of passengers a Chinook normally carried, provided they all had a seat. The entire crew was stunned by that number. Who would have thought it possible to get that many people in the back of a Chinook at one time? It had taken twenty minutes to get all the villagers onboard, but it only took five minutes for all of them to debark. They might have been grateful for the lift, but if the speed with which they moved away from the aircraft was any indicator, they were simply glad to be out of the roaring helicopter and back on solid, if damp, ground.

After the villagers were all out of the cabin, Powers and Crone crawled under the aircraft to check that the plastic drain plugs were screwed in tight. Sure enough, two of the six had worked their way partly open, probably from vibration, letting water into the belly. They fully opened all of the drain plugs to let any water out before completely screwing them all back in again, a process that took about ten minutes. Powers would have to check them regularly throughout the day from now on to see if any of them had worked their way loose again. The good news was that on their first real water landing, nothing had poked a hole in the bottom of the aircraft.

WEATHER HOLD

The weather continued to deteriorate as the morning progressed. Sometimes it got to the point that Alice would have to bring the helicopter into a hover to prevent going into the clouds, fog really, since it touched the ground. The rain got worse too, falling in sheets again, but at least the wind stayed nearly calm. By 1000 hours, it was not just near zero visibility and zero ceiling where Playtex 506 was operating, it was the same throughout Northern I Corps. Other aircraft were reporting how terrible the conditions were when they tried getting back to Liftmaster, so Playtex Operations sent out a call over the artillery clearance radio net that all aircraft should shut down at the closest U.S. base and wait it out. They would begin rescues again as soon as they could, as soon as the weather lifted a little.

Since Camp Evans was closer to their search area than Phu Bai, Alice took Playtex 506 there to wait. It took some hovering along to find it, but after crossing QL1 they quickly recognized where they were and 20 minutes later they were crossing the wire around the base. After a stop at the fuel pits to top off, he shut the aircraft down on a large, mostly empty helicopter staging area, a small airfield really, with parking lanes reserved for the "Skid kids"— Hueys, LOHs, and Cobras that used skids as landing gear instead of wheels. The saying among Chinook crews was, "Skids is for kids—wheels is where it's at." There were also four Chinook pads at the landing field, but only one other Chinook was there when they arrived. All the landing lanes were empty today, since the Hueys and LOHs were at their home bases, waiting out the weather, a good plan in Strider's estimation.

Playtex 506 had picked up and moved three loads of people, 181 in all. The crew all felt good about what they were doing, but were glad they were through hovering around in the rain and fog, even if it was only for a short while. They broke out their bag lunches and started in on the sandwiches and fruit the mess hall had packed. It was nice to have something other than C rations for once. Strider swapped the orange he had brought from the mess hall for an apple, savoring the crunch as he bit into it. It would have been nice, too, to have a heated building to go to so they could start drying off their clothes, but that would have been too much to ask. Still, at least the cabin of the helicopter was out of the rain and it was quiet without the APU or engines running, so that was something. The sound of the rain hitting the skin of the aircraft reminded Strider of rain on a tin roof, like at his grandparent's house in the hills of Kentucky long ago.

CW2 Steve Maas and CW2 Marvin Leonard were the pilots of the other Chinook, Playtex 820, which was already shut down when Playtex 506 landed. Alice and Strider would get together with them shortly and maybe swap a war story or two about water landings.

PLAYTEX 820'S CREW

THE AC

The man who brought the actual walking fish into the Officers' Club when

Strider ran in to tell his story was CW2 Steve Maas. Maas was a little guy, with a shy grin and a gleam in his eye. He hadn't been an AC very long when Strider joined Playtex, but was doing well in spite of a few personality quirks.

One of his quirks was that Maas didn't like to do maintenance ground runs of the aircraft. Everyday an AC and copilot who were not on the flight schedule for that day would be tasked with starting up the aircraft that the maintenance department had been working on, so that they could do checks of repaired systems. From a pilot's standpoint it was hot, boring work, holding no possibility of going flying, and was therefore to be avoided, if at all possible. Maas' way of avoiding maintenance runs was to grab a couple of soft drinks and hide in an abandoned refrigerator that had been dumped behind the Officers' Club. It was a good plan, since no one would suspect Maas was hiding in the old fridge, but it stopped working after someone saw him close the door behind him one day. That someone, probably an RLO, told the operations officer where he was, but busted or not, that did not keep him from trying that same trick again. In fact, he kept trying it until someone decided to roll the refrigerator over on its side with him in it. It took him ten minutes to kick his way out and he was not happy, not happy at all, when he finally did. But, at least he did give up on that particular trick after that.

Maas was quirky in other ways, too. Strider went with him to the dispensary once. Both men had minor colds and wanted to see if the doc could do anything for them. When they walked in, they saw about 15 men lined up ahead of them. Steve took a look at the line and then stuck his arm in the ceiling fan overhead. The fan was barely turning, just stirring the air a little. When the blade contacted his arm, it bounced right off, but Maas fell to the floor, holding his arm and screaming in apparent agony. The doctor came running from the back room where he had been seeing patients to deal with the "emergency" in the waiting room. He skidded to a stop when he saw Steve and said, "Mister Maas, you are going to have to wait your turn like everybody else, so knock it the hell off!" With that, Maas promptly stopped screaming, got up, and without comment, took a seat. He and the doctor had been through this routine before.

Maas didn't really like to hang out with the other pilots, or anyone else, for that matter. Instead, in dry weather when he wasn't flying, he could be found sunbathing on the deck of the Officers' Club and in wet weather, reading in his room. Odd twitches notwithstanding, Maas was a good pilot and always got his missions done. Strider liked to fly with him because his twitches were all on the ground and not in the air.

THE COPILOT

CW2 Marvin Leonard was the third pilot in the Officers' Club when the walking fish arrived. He was also the other second Vietnam tour warrant officer in Playtex at that time, but he had not flown Hueys like Jerry Cobb had. Marvin had flown LOHs, finishing his first tour with many Air Medals, a Purple Heart, and a Distinguished Flying Cross.

The LOH mission was either the first or second most dangerous one in Vietnam. It was a toss-up between LOH and Medevac, also known as "Dustoff," with losses in aircraft and aircrews consistently high in both missions. To Strider, Medevac was the most dangerous because they always went where the landing zones (LZ) were hot to pick up the wounded. The VC and NVA did not respect the Red Cross painted on their doors, so the Dustoff Hueys had M-60 machine guns mounted just ahead of the Red Cross to return the favor if needed. Mostly the door guns were psychological protection for the crew, since it was rare to see who was shooting at you and where the rounds were coming from. Still, everyone liked to have door guns, psychological protection or not. Everyone also knew that Dustoff always came, no matter how hot the LZ. Their pilots and crewmen were held in great regard by all.

Other pilots thought the LOH mission was just as dangerous, or even more so than Medevac, but for a different reason. Medevac went to hot zones to rescue people. LOH went to zones to make them hot. In fact, LOH pilots were, at least in Strider's mind, just plain insane. Strider once sat next to a LOH pilot on an international flight who proclaimed the OH-6 was the greatest helicopter ever made. "Why, I've crashed five of them and never got a scratch!" he declared. And that was why their pilots loved the OH-6: its egg-shaped fuselage protected the crew when it went in. Sometimes there would be nothing left of the aircraft after a crash but the cockpit and cabin—the rotor blades, tail boom, and skids would all be gone, and yet the crew would walk away, shaken, but alive. Strider did not mention to his LOH pilot seatmate that he had never crashed anything and considered not crashing a far better survival strategy than depending on a flying egg to protect you.

Once, when the clouds were too low and the visibility too limited to fly resupply missions out in the mountains, Strider went over to the Pachyderms area at Phu Bai airport to visit a friend. As they sat on the porch of his friend's hootch, talking about life, the universe, and all that, they heard the sound of a LOH from over near the runway. They heard the LOH, but couldn't see it because the low clouds and poor visibility had nearly hidden the runway. Jokingly, Strider said the pilot was probably getting some instrument time. They both laughed, because the LOH was a visual flight rules (VFR)-only aircraft; they had only the most basic of instrument flight rules (IFR) equipment needed to fly in the clouds and often even what they had was not operational.

Then, out of the low clouds came a LOH, flying almost sideways and in a rapid descent.

The LOH hit the concrete aircraft parking ramp on its left side, sending pieces of rotor blade flying everywhere as the rotor disk hit the concrete. The aircraft slid up against the left side of one of the Pachyderm Chinooks, rocking it slightly in its chalks, before the larger aircraft stopped the wreck of the LOH moving. Moments later, the LOH's engine stopped and so did the rapidly spinning stumps of what remained of the rotor blades. From the wreckage of the LOH, the pilot emerged, shaky, but walking. No one ran to help him, because everyone was momentarily in shock, but then it turned out he really didn't need help. The LOH had protected him. Though the crash had destroyed the helicopter, it left the pilot with only bruises to his body and ego. He had been doing a maintenance check flight on the LOH, but got in the clouds without intending to and shortly thereafter, lost control of the aircraft.

The LOH may have protected the pilot in the crash, but it couldn't protect him from the wrath of the battalion commander, who also saw the little helicopter hit the ramp, destroying it and damaging one of his Chinooks. So much for the battalion CO's theory that the OH-6s were too dangerous to leave in the hands of the Chinook companies and so should be held at Battalion HQ.

Administrative flights were one thing, but the LOH's real mission was quite another. Flying a light observation helicopter as a scout meant your mission was to look for the enemy, sometimes scouting for the Cobra gunships and sometimes for artillery. If you were part of a "Pink Team" you went looking for the enemy with a second LOH instead of with a Cobra. The Pink Team mission often consisted of one aircraft hovering around, looking into the top canopy of the jungle for the enemy, making that helicopter an easy target, a very, very tempting easy target. After a while, the enemy just couldn't stand it anymore—such an easy target right there in front of them—and would open fire on the target LOH. At this point the wingman LOH was supposed to pop into view, open up with his mini-gun, and wipe out the enemy. This worked about as well as it sounds it would, explaining in a nutshell why the Army went through so many OH-6s and OH-6 pilots so quickly.

After many such adventures on his first tour, Leonard decided that, having made it to 35 years of age, being married with three kids and all, he would like to survive his second year-long tour, so he requested Chinook transition, the same decision the XO had reached. Chinooks might get shot at, but at least they didn't go looking for the enemy every day, so were inherently safer. That was Leonard's theory, anyway . . .

Like Strider, Leonard was still a copilot, since he too had only recently arrived in Playtex. Company Standard Operating Procedures (SOP) dictated that you had to have at least 100 flight hours in Chinooks and 300 hours in Vietnam before you could take your AC check ride, but that was a formality for second-tour pilots like Leonard. He had over a thousand hours in Vietnam the day he arrived in Playtex. He was considered so steady that the operations officer often assigned him as copilot to new ACs. He gave the operations officer confidence that with Leonard's calm steadying influence, the new AC would get the job done and bring the aircraft back in one piece. In another month he would have the required 100 hours in Chinooks and would be an AC himself.

WAR STORIES AND LUNCH

Maas and Leonard walked over in the rain to 506, bringing their C rations with them, as soon as Alice and Strider completed the shut down and the rotor blades had stopped turning. They were both bored and wanted to talk to someone other than each other.

Playtex 506's enlisted crew went the other direction. After making sure

506 was ready to go again, Powers led Crone and Crear over to 820 to visit with that crew, so that the officers could talk officer stuff and the enlisted men could talk enlisted stuff openly. Besides, officer stories, even warrant officer stories, were all exaggerated and usually boring, too, particularly after you had heard them ten times.

As the four pilots settled down in 506's cabin to eat, Maas started a story about their trip from their search area back to Camp Eagle, a "no shitter" story, as in one that starts, "Now this is no shit . . ."

Now this is no shit. Leonard was flying in the right seat, just below the clouds at about 200 feet above the water as they headed back toward Camp Evans from their assigned rescue area. They were cruising at 130 knots, fat, dumb, and happy, when both pilots simultaneously saw a flock of wild ducks taking off from the water directly in front of them. Before Leonard could turn or take any evasive action, the Chinook was blasting through the middle of the rising flock.

They hit one or more of the ducks, whereupon their Chinook tried to swap ends in flight at 130 knots, tail whipping around to the right and nose to the left, the aircraft way out of trim and very nearly out of control. The out of trim condition was so bad that the wind coming through the left window nearly blew Maas out of his seat, with only his harness stopping him from going into the cyclic stick and the aircraft's dashboard. Leonard, in the right seat, was fighting hard to get the aircraft under control with both stability systems off-line and the aircraft severely out of trim.

The master caution light, the big red one on the dashboard directly in front of both pilots, the one that tells you something is wrong in general, was glaring in their faces. All the smaller capsule lights on the master caution panel in the center of the dash, the ones that tell you specifically which system is having a problem, were nearly all on. Something major was wrong with the aircraft, but what?

Concentrating on the master caution panel, Maas noticed that the capsule lights showed both generators were off-line, even though the control switches were both in the "On" position. He reached up to the overhead panel and turned #1 generator to "Off," then back to "On." Instantly, the generator came back on line and instantly both stability systems also came back on, while all the capsule lights on the master caution panel, save one, went out. Stability system restored, Leonard was able to bring the wild, nearly uncontrolled yaw quickly under control and straighten the aircraft out back into level flight. Only the #2 generator light was still lit on the master caution panel and it went off when Maas re-cycled it.

By the grace of God, no one in the cabin of Playtex 820 was injured. By some strange coincidence, the flight engineer, crew chief, and door gunner had all been sitting down and were strapped in when the Chinook hit the ducks. Had any of them been standing up, it would have been a different story, whether or not they were wearing their gunner's belts. They would not have fallen out of the aircraft, but they would certainly have been whipped around inside, bouncing off the cabin sides and deck. As soon as Leonard had the aircraft back under control, the flight engineer was up and running toward the aft pylon area to see if he could find any damage back there. There was none.

It took a few minutes for all five of the crew members to get their heart rates back under control, even though they would never say anything about being scared out loud, can't lose your cool, ever, and to their minds, that would have definitely been uncool. Because at this point everything was back to normal, they continued on back to Camp Evans to await further instruction from Playtex Operations.

After landing at the helicopter pad, the aircraft was shut down immediately. After the rotor blades had stopped turning, the flight engineer called Maas up to the nose of the aircraft. There, on the portion of the nose hatch that was painted black to reduce sun glare back into the cockpit, was a good-sized dent and smear of blood, no feathers. Opening the hatch and looking inside, it was apparent that nothing important was behind the place where the duck hit, only empty space, really. It must have been the impact of the several-pound fowl, hitting the Chinook straight on at 130 knots, that provided enough shock to the aircraft's electrical system to drop both generators off-line. The impact took the stability system, and every other electrical system except those powered directly by the battery, with them when they went. When Maas turned the generator back on, everything came back. Good thing the duck had not hit a few feet higher, because if it had hit the windshield, the glass would probably have shattered at the impact, and the duck would have hit one of the pilots directly in the face.

When Maas had finished, Alice shared the story of Playtex 506 getting blown into the air with only Strider onboard. Everyone had a good laugh at both stories, a particularly good laugh, because "copilots in peril" always make for good stories. Best of all, what could have been disaster in both cases was not—no one was hurt, both aircraft still airworthy—making them perfect war story material.

Pilots tell war stories for entertainment, but also as a way of passing on oral history of situations that aren't covered in the aircraft manuals. "This happened. I did this. It worked. It didn't work." That said, war stories are still mostly for entertainment, often mostly for the teller . . .

DAY ONE ENDS

After a while, Powers and the other two crewmen came back to Playtex 506 and Maas and Leonard went back to Playtex 820, leaving Alice, Strider, and the three crewmen sitting in the damp cabin to wait out the rain. Alice would fire up the auxiliary power plant every now and then, so that he could turn on the radios and check in with Playtex Operations through the artillery clearance unit, but all missions remained "on hold" all day. Operations told Alice to check in one last time at 1600.

Finally, at 1600, as darkness approached, Playtex Operations directed all aircraft to return to Liftmaster; they would try again tomorrow. On the way back down from Camp Evans, Alice took 506 into Camp Eagle for fuel one more time before he returned the aircraft to Liftmaster for the night. No risk of being blown back into the air this time; their Chinook was the only aircraft in the fuel pits. By the time they landed at Liftmaster a half hour later, the entire crew was as exhausted as if they'd done their normal ammo, water, and fuel re-supply missions to the fire support bases out in the mountains. They were beat even though they had only flown three hours that day, far less than their normal six to eight. It must have been the tension of almost losing the aircraft in the fuel pits, flying in really bad weather, and then landing in the water that did it to them. After their final landing, Liftmaster pad looked good to them all, like home, almost. Of course, for their time in Vietnam, it was their home.

The first thing the crew did after Alice shut down the Chinook in its revetment was to check the aircraft one more time for damage, combat and/or inadvertent, as in landing on top of something hidden in the brown water. There was none. If anything had been lurking to poke a hole in the Chinook's belly, it missed them. There were no bullet holes either. If anyone had shot at them during the day, they too had missed. Tomorrow there would be plenty of chances for both to happen again, but they had made it through this day, and that was all that was important at that point in time. The last thing Powers did before he crawled out from under the aircraft, was to open the drain plugs to let any water trapped there out of the aircraft's belly.

The belly damage check the flight engineers always did reminded Strider of a radio call from one of Playtex's ACs he overheard while hanging around in the operations bunker soon after he arrived in Playtex.

"Operations, Playtex XXX (aircraft number redacted to prevent embarrassment); I just landed on top of something in a zone."

"Playtex XXX, Operations; Did you put a hole in the belly?"

"Operations, Playtex XXX; Affirmative."

"Playtex XXX, Operations; How big is the hole?"

After a long moment of radio silence: "Operations, Playtex XXX; How big is a water trailer?"

Instead of leaving Powers and Crone to do all the turnaround to get the aircraft ready for the next day, Strider stayed to help them with the rotor blade tie downs and anything else they might need. After he had done all he could, Strider helped Crear carry the M-60s and the ammo back to the armory. Crear would have to pick them up again in a few hours, but the guns were never left mounted overnight when the aircraft was back at Liftmaster. Besides, after being out in the rain all day they needed to be cleaned and oiled to keep the rust away. That was Crear's mission and the mission must be done.

While Strider was working with Powers, Alice checked in at company operations to report what they had done, how many people they had rescued, and where they had dropped them, at least as close as he could guess to where they dropped them. The operations officer told Alice that the crews and aircraft assignments would remain the same for the duration of the rescue operation, provided the aircraft didn't require maintenance. That was fine with Alice; all had gone very well today, the aircraft performed fine and so did the crew. Alice gave his sheet with the number of Vietnamese they had lifted to the operations officer, who then added it to the report he would later send over to battalion operations.

Before he left, Alice told the operations officer the story of Strider getting blown into the air on the refueling pad and how well he had handled it. The operations officer was glad Strider had done well, but made a note to himself to bitch to division about how close those refueling pads were to each other. They were lucky this time, but the next . . . Strider would be up for AC just as soon as he had the hours. He needed to be able to handle whatever came at him, so this event had been a good test.

Out on the flight line, as Alice was talking with the operations officer, Powers was conferring with the maintenance chief about what came next. Normally after a water landing, all six sets of wheel bearings had to be repacked, but they just didn't have the manpower. The maintenance chief decided to let 506 slide right now and do two of the other aircraft instead, much to 506's crew's relief. Powers and his crew would do their repacking the next time they were at Liftmaster overnight.

After leaving Crear to clean his machine guns, Strider stopped by the Officers' Club to check the assignments board and his mailbox before he went to his hootch. As the operations officer had told Alice, the board showed that all the crews and aircraft were the same for the next day and would stay the same until further notice. Playtex would again be launching six Chinooks the next morning, with another two firing up as spares in case one of the primary aircraft had a mechanical problem.

DOMESTIC MATTERS, PART TWO

There was no letter from home today in Strider's mailbox, but that was not a surprise, given how bad the weather was. The C-130s that brought the mail up from Saigon wouldn't be flying routine missions, like mail delivery, in this weather. No letter today just meant he would get two or more letters the next time the mail came. Strider and his wife wrote each other every day, even if the letters often didn't say much. He didn't want to worry her with combat stories and she didn't want to burden him with domestic problems he could do nothing about, so the letters were really just to let each other know they weren't forgotten. Sometimes the letters would come in a bunch and he would have to check the date on each one so that he could read them in the right order; again, not that it made much difference, since little happened from day to day back at Fort Campbell. The Army told them to destroy their letters after reading them to keep the enemy from stealing them and mailing propaganda to the families back home.

Strider wasn't sure this was a real threat, but each day after he read them, he burned the letters anyway. The pictures of his son and wife that she sent did not get burned. Instead, they went under the plexiglas panel covering his desk top, where they remained until new ones arrived.

It was after 1800 hours when he finally got to the Officers' Club, but there was no one there. Strider found that odd, since not everyone had flown that day and therefore could not be as tired as he was. Usually there would be at least four or five pilots trading lies and war stories at the bar. Wait, the card table was set up for play, meaning there would be a game later for those not flying rescue missions. For those who were, maybe there was a movie in the mess hall tonight, or maybe the rain had everyone too depressed to socialize at all. It was still dinner time so he could have gone to the mess hall, but he decided instead to just go back to the hootch and open a can of something for dinner. He had his daily letter to write and if he was lucky, Steiner or Cobb would have cooked something.

When he came into the hootch, he saw that he was indeed in luck. Half of something one of them had cooked was still warm in the electric skillet there on the dining room table. After he dumped his flight gear on his bed and hung up his pistol on the hook next to his desk, Strider took a paper plate from the stack on the table and opened one of the plastic flatware and sundries packets they had scrounged along with some Air Force In-Flight rations—a fancier version of C rations that only the Air Force used, prized for their little juice cans that came with each ration—before he helped himself.

Steiner was at his desk, reading something, soft music coming from his speakers. Cobb was cleaning his pistol at the other end of the dining table. Strider's little electric heater had kept the room dry and comfortable against the rain and chill outside. It was almost a domestic scene.

"So, how shitty was it out there," Cobb asked no one in particular. He had not flown that day, instead he had been doing the hated ground runs and helping out the maintenance officer all day, things that never improved his mood. That said, he seemed almost jovial tonight after cooking dinner. Maybe he wasn't upset about missing flying missions when they involved wandering around unfamiliar terrain, in shitty weather, doing water land-ings to pick up Vietnamese who might be enemies.

Steiner immediately launched into a long tale of woe: low clouds, bad visibility, a leaky aircraft cockpit that allowed his seat cushion to get wet making his butt cold all day, an aircraft that had a "beat," a vibration that made the pilots bounce a little in their seats as they flew—very annoying, and, yes, cold C rats for lunch. Cobb, having had the same experiences many times, added in comments about that particular aircraft and how the flight engineer must have deliberately cut the windshield sealing tape so that the rain leaked directly onto the AC's flight bag, no matter if it was stuffed down by the left-hand emergency door or to the right next to the center console. Also, why didn't maintenance get off their collective dead asses and track the goddamn aircraft instead of just letting them fly with a beat. Strider, the copilot, just listened. ACs get to tell the stories when talking with other ACs. Copilots must save their own war stories for when they're with other copilots.

The three roommates didn't usually tell too many war stories over dinner, since they all worked on the same missions all day; they already knew what had gone well and what had not. When they did tell a typical war story, it did not usually involve anyone getting shot at, but rather it was about something silly or stupid someone had done. There was never a shortage of those. Strider did not mention Maas' story about hitting the duck, nor did he mention getting blown into the air on the refueling pad. He was sure his roommates would make the latter somehow his fault, because that's what pilots do—pick on each other, always. Maybe it's a male thing, look for weaknesses to gain an advantage, but then maybe it's a way to show acceptance as a peer. Either way, it is something all pilots must do if they want to be accepted as a member of the company. But while accepting it, you have to be able to give it back, too. You just had to keep a sense of humor to avoid it getting to you in the wrong way.

Dinner conversation was much more likely to be about "The World," as in the United States: the land of the Big PX, the all-night generator, and round-eyed women, rather than about flying or the war. They talked about what they had done before the military, what they would do after the military, where they wanted to be assigned next. Steiner and Strider didn't have too many stories about where they were stationed before because they had been in training, mostly, before Vietnam, not at regular duty stations doing regular jobs. Strider didn't talk about flying OH-13Es at Fort Campbell. No one wanted to hear about flying old bubble helicopters. They had all done it in flight school anyway. Cobb never told war stories from his first tour or about being a flight instructor at Fort Rucker.

Funny, Strider thought, how their conversations were almost never personal—never about loves, parents, kids, fears, hopes. Maybe merely talking about such things showed too much weakness for men to safely discuss them.

Fifteen minutes after he sat down, Strider was done eating and had cleaned up the table, his contribution to domesticity for the day. Not much left of the dish du jour, so he scraped the remainder into the trash before he washed the electric skillet in the sink. Before he left the back room, he started running hot water into the washer tub. Coming back into the hootch's main room, he picked up his flight gear off his bed and put it on its hooks next to the bed. As always, the water pressure was low, so the tub filled slowly. He used the time to prepare for the rest of the evening. A letter home first, "Hi, Honey, I only flew three hours today, but did spend a long time waiting for the next mission, so it was a long day anyway. I didn't see any walking fish today. Ha, etc., etc." He had to stop in the middle of the letter or let the tub overflow.

After turning off the water, Strider took out the boots he had put in the clothes-drying closet the night before and replaced them with today's wet boots. The warm dry pair went into his closet and the pair in the closet went under his bed for tomorrow's wear. Strider felt it very important to rotate his boots, given his big feet and the potential difficulty of getting another pair that actually fit. He checked the tub again and decided it was full enough for a shower. He stripped down, wrapped himself in a towel, and turned the washer to the "Drain" cycle. As the hot water started coming out of the shower head, he climbed into the tub and stood there with it pouring down on his head: luxury, pure luxury. After he dried off, he shaved to speed things up in the morning and the day was nearly done.

All that was left was to finish the letter and sleep. As he addressed the envelope, he drew a stamp on the upper right-hand corner, a little personal touch, since stamps weren't required for letters to the States from Vietnam. Sleep now, tomorrow would be a long day, with more rain, fog, clouds, and people trapped by the water. For a few minutes before he turned in, he lit his pipe and leaned back in the leather desk chair he had scrounged on a mission down south of Da Nang. He let the smoke from his pipe float up around his head as he sat there contemplating the day's events. He didn't really know what he expected Vietnam would be, but this was far better than he thought it would be. Take away the possibility of being killed every day, and it would have been right pleasant. Only ten and a half months to go.

He put his pipe into the ash tray on his desk, turned the rotating fan over his bed on "low" to keep the mosquitoes off, pulled back the camouflage poncho liner that served as a bed spread and climbed in. He turned off the gooseneck desk lamp and was probably asleep before his head hit the pillow.

CHAPTER THIRTEEN

OCTOBER 29, 1970

DAY TWO: PLAYTEX 506 LAUNCHES AGAIN

This morning was a replay of the morning before. Once again, the duty clerk woke the pilots at around 0430. Once again, he told them that the weather was better and, once again, they did not believe him. Once again, Strider splashed through the rain and the mud in the dark to the mess hall for a breakfast of runny eggs and semi-raw bacon, as usual. Once again, it was pre-flight the top of the aircraft in the rain; once again, he was wet when he climbed into the cockpit, but then once again, the entire crew was wet before they even got off the ground. Still, it wasn't all that different from a normal day of flying missions, except, of course, for the seemingly eternal rain. And, except for the fact they weren't going to be hauling ammunition to mountaintops.

This morning, Cobb had the job of running up one of the backup Chinooks, Playtex 502, that would take the place of any primary aircraft that might break on run up. He bitched about it over breakfast, but Strider suspected Cobb was not flying today because he was getting short and the company IP and operations officer were concerned that he had been under stress for too long now. He was correct. They were both very concerned about him and felt it would be better to give him "supporting cast" roles, than to push him into "leading man" roles at this point. Cobb, while bitching about having to get up so early, never gave any indication he minded not doing mission flying any more.

Supporting or lead role, Cobb did all the things that the launch ACs did, even signing for the KY-28 and survival package in operations, but he didn't have his pistol or bullet bouncer with him. He knew he wasn't flying, so why bother? He pre-flighted the Chinook, strapped into the left seat, and when his copilot was ready, started the checklist. When it got to the place in the sequence where they start the auxiliary power unit, the APU, Cobb called, "Ready APU, Chief?" to the flight engineer. "All set," the flight engineer replied, and Cobb activated the switches to start the small jet engine located at the bottom of the aft pylon at the rear of the aircraft, right above the ramp. The APU powers the utility and flight boost hydraulic systems and generators until the rotors are turning fast enough for the aft transmission to take over the job. Without an APU the aircraft cannot be started.

The flight engineer sometimes stands on the ramp directly under the APU as it starts up so that he can see that everything is alright. Today, for some reason he could not articulate afterwards, Playtex 502's flight engineer moved back away from the ramp to one side of the aircraft as Cobb activated the APU start sequence. In the cockpit, Cobb held two switches to allow the utility hydraulic system pressure accumulator to open, releasing its pressure and spinning the small jet engine up to the speed where it lights off and becomes self-sustaining. This time the APU spun up normally until just before it reached full speed.

Then it exploded.

Bits of the turbine wheels, turning at 20,000 RPM before the explosion, became shrapnel, just like that produced by an exploding mortar round. While some of the APU parts went upward into the aft pylon, others blasted downward, hitting the ramp exactly where the flight engineer normally stood. They were traveling at such speed that the sharp pieces of metal punched shrapnel holes all the way though the helicopter's ramp, hitting the PSP underneath and bouncing off somewhere onto the planking. Somehow all of the flying pieces missed the flight engineer and the other two crewmen.

In the cockpit, when he heard it blow, Cobb immediately turned the APU switch "Off" to stop the fuel flow, followed by turning the aircraft battery off to remove electrical power in case there was a short circuit anywhere.

When he was over his shock at the explosion of the APU, the crew chief, who had been in the front of the cabin, grabbed one of the aircraft's fire extinguishers and ran to the rear of the Chinook. The door gunner had been standing by with one of the flight line fire extinguishers for engine start, so he was already in position if there was a fire. Fortunately, neither of the fire extinguishers was needed, since the blast did not sever the APU's fuel line or any of the hydraulic lines snaking through the aft pylon.

No one else came running at the sound of the explosion because amid the noise of seven Chinooks starting up in the rainy darkness, no one other than the crew of 502 had any idea anything unusual had happened. Cobb climbed out of the left cockpit seat, walked through the companionway to the rear of the aircraft, and with the rest of the crew looked at the damage to the ramp. Because it was still dark, he couldn't tell if any of the shrapnel that had gone upwards had damaged the transmission, or if any that had gone outwards had damaged either of the engines. One thing that was certain was that this aircraft needed major repairs before it was going anywhere. Leaving the copilot to finish up with the shutdown, Cobb gathered up his flight gear and with the flight engineer, walked over to the maintenance office to tell them what happened.

The maintenance officer and the maintenance chief were drinking coffee and looking out at the lights of the aircraft starting to move on the ramp when they saw Cobb and the flight engineer walk in. The mere fact that a pilot and a flight engineer were walking into maintenance this early was a clear indicator of a problem. When they heard the story of the exploding APU, they looked at each other and simultaneously said, "Shit." They were now down to 14 operational Chinooks and their two broken ones were going to take a while to get back into the air. Take away three undergoing scheduled maintenance and they were down to 11.

After he told the story, Cobb shrugged at the news of only 11 operational aircraft left. Since he was not on the schedule and did not work for maintenance, it was no longer his problem. He remembered he had forgotten the KY-28, so he headed back to the aircraft to get it before going to operations to turn it back in. After all that, it's back to bed for me, he thought.

Alice and Strider, oblivious of the drama that had just happened on Playtex 502, were ready to launch. They taxied Playtex 506 out onto Liftmaster's small runway behind two other Chinooks, Playtex 107 and Playtex 542, both of which had been a little quicker getting started up and completing their checklists. Behind Alice's aircraft, Playtex 540 and Playtex Balls Niner waited their turns to take the runway.

From Liftmaster Tower, the air traffic controller had quite a light show below him, with six aircraft ready to lift and one more turning in its revetment, all of their red anti-collision lights spinning in the fading darkness. As daylight came, the controller cleared each of them in turn for takeoff, and soon, they were off again, one after another, headed back out in the rain to their assigned areas for more evacuations.

As the Playtex aircraft headed northeast, the weather still did not let them climb above 500 feet. This time they were each carrying 15 cases of C rations, the ones made especially for the Vietnamese, with lots of pork and rice in the meals. A duce and a half with a pallet load of them had arrived at Liftmaster an hour before sunrise. After the maintenance department broke the pallet down, they spread its load out among the launching helicopters. Each aircraft also carried 15 five-gallon water cans to pass out to the people they were picking up, since the floodwater was undrinkable. All the crews knew that this was probably not half enough food and water to provide for everyone they were likely to pick up that day, but at least they had something to give them, some little bit of hope.

Everyone in Playtex knew today's flights were different from normal missions and everyone wanted to contribute more than they usually did, to do their part to make it work. The mess hall did its part to support the mission by sending two of the cooks around to each of the launching aircraft, where they dropped off five bag lunches, one for each of the aircrews, and a big thermos of coffee. The S-4 also added in an additional two standard cases of C rats for the crew, figuring that while the bag lunches the mess hall sent around would take them through mid-day, they would probably not be able to get to a base for evening chow.

THE RESCUES BEGIN AGAIN

As Playtex 506 headed northeast, Alice tried to go back to the first group of villagers they had lifted yesterday, to give them some food and water, but he couldn't find them in the rain and gloom. It was like they had disappeared, more like the entire area had disappeared, actually. The rain had been a light mist when they departed from Liftmaster, but had turned heavy again up here, 40 miles north. It also seemed like there was more fog to go with the higher water this time, removing even the few visual references they had used to find the village the day before. After 15 minutes of criss-crossing the general vicinity of where they thought they had dropped the first of the villagers they had rescued yesterday, Alice gave up. He turned the aircraft toward the northeast and their assigned search area.

Within minutes of finally reaching what they thought was the right location, they found another group of people isolated by the floodwaters, waiting in their boats for something—the water to go down again, or maybe just waiting to see what fate would bring on this round. Strider thought it would be easy to characterize these people as stoic, but that implied they had a choice about how to look at things, when they really didn't have a choice at all. Panic, hysteria, or both, these would make no difference in the eventual outcome for these people. The rain would continue to fall and they would continue to be on their own, just like they always had been.

There was no obvious landing zone this time, so Alice picked a clear spot in the water far enough away from the boats to keep from blowing them over, and set the aircraft up for an approach to landing. Since he wasn't sure how deep the water was, he brought the aircraft to a high hover, as per standard water landing procedures, and then brought it straight down with Powers guiding him. When he landed the helicopter, Playtex 506 was once again well and truly floating in the muddy water. As always, it was an odd feeling to Strider, a different motion as when they were in the air or on the ground. Not uncomfortable, but not quite normal, as the helicopter moved slightly in a small back and forth motion. The water did not quite come up to the helicopter's chin window, but it was an odd sensation to see it so close.

The crew had not trained on how to lower the ramp on a Chinook when you are in water. It can be done, but the pilots have to keep a moderate amount of power on the aircraft to keep it just barely in the water. This would produce strong rotor wash, which would make it difficult for the Vietnamese to row or pole a boat up to the helicopter. So, when the aircraft was settled and in a stable position, Powers lowered the crew door after Crear and Crone had again removed the door gun. He stepped out on the upper portion of the door and as he had done yesterday, signaled the people to come to the helicopter. Again, the people hesitated before deciding that boarding the helicopter for the unknown was better than staying wet and cold for some indefinite period in an open boat. Still, it was a hard decision, even if their village was under water. Where would the helicopter take them? How would they get back? What would happen to their remaining possessions here in the village while they were gone? Eventually, they apparently decided the unknown was better than an extended period in an open boat in the rain, wet, cold, and hungry.

When the people finally started to move toward the aircraft, it seemed to Strider that this time they were having much more difficulty getting their boats up close to the helicopter than the people had yesterday. The men poling the boats looked like they were working so hard to move forward, hard enough that it seemed they were fighting an unseen current, or maybe fighting some wind that had combined with the rotor wash that was working to keep them away. It was almost like their mostly underwater village was tugging at them, telling them not to go, trying hard to hold on to them.

It took a good ten minutes for the first boat to make it to the crew door and begin transferring the seven or eight people onboard the boat to the aircraft. The transfer itself was a slow process. Crone stepped down and stood on the lower step to help them from the boat to the aircraft cabin. First, they sent up the children, lifted one at a time from the boat to Crone, who lifted them on up and then passed them on to Crear. Crear gently moved them on to Powers, who guided them to a place to stand in the rear cabin.

It was obvious from their faces that the little children were very scared of the extremely loud helicopter's interior, its deafening roar hurting their ears, but there was nothing Powers could do about it until their mother or father got onboard and he could pass the children back to them. Their parents tried to comfort them as best they could, but even they could do nothing about the deafening roar of the helicopter's engines and transmissions. No doubt it was louder inside the helicopter's cabin than anything the children (and most of the adults, too) had experienced in their entire lives. Powers made a mental note to pick up some foam ear plugs the next time he was back at Liftmaster, but he doubted they would use them—too foreign to their normal experience.

After the children boarded the helicopter, the old people came. The procedure for getting them onboard the helicopter was the same as it was for the children, only it was more difficult since they were heavier. The boats rocked back and forth and the motion contributed to the small boat's inherent instability. The young men and women would lift them up from the boat as much as they could, then Crone would pull them, with the younger people pushing them from behind. Once they were on the step, Crear would help them up the second step and into the aircraft's cabin.

The younger adults made it into the helicopter without difficulty, although some of the women seemed uncomfortable being touched by the crew, even with a helping hand. Perhaps they had reason to be afraid, based on past experience with soldiers. Still, in the end, they all, women and men alike, took Crone's offered hand to make that transfer from the boat to the aircraft's step. In fifteen minutes the entire group was onboard Playtex 506, all except one young man.

This young man remained in one of the boats instead of boarding the helicopter. He had apparently been elected by the village headman to stay behind and look after things as best he could while the others evacuated. He took the lines of the other boats in hand as they emptied, tying each of them in turn to the stern of his own boat, so they would not be blown away and lost when the helicopter lifted off. The villagers used those boats to fish for their living and could not afford to lose them.

When all the people were onboard the Chinook, the young man poled his boat off to a stand of palm trees about a hundred yards away with the other boats in tow, well away from the aircraft. He was working hard, but his efforts seemed much less compared with what it took to get everyone onboard the helicopter. Was it because the empty boats were easier to tow, or was it because the village helped, knowing that if their boats were there, they would return?

"Sir, we've got 28 onboard. All set in the back," Powers called over the ICS.

Alice held Playtex 506 in place in the water until the young man was far enough away that the rotor wash was not likely to blow him over when the Chinook was lifted up into a hover for takeoff. When Alice cleared him, Strider made a takeoff and headed west, toward higher ground. From the right seat, Strider could see the young boatman looking up after them as the helicopter climbed away. VC or just a farmer/fisherman, Strider wondered? VC or not, he would be alone with the boats for some time, a solitary guard of what little remained of their possessions. The young man had no expression on his face that Strider could detect, as he disappeared in the mist below them.

THE NEWEST PLAYTEX PILOT

This time, Alice could not easily find an even semi-dry place to land close to where they could easily get back to their homes. It seemed like everything within two miles of the village was completely under water, so he reduced the helicopter's bank angle to make a wider circle, looking for someplace, any place even remotely safe from the floodwaters, to drop them. As Alice circled, Strider looked back into the cabin and noticed a boy, probably ten or 12 years old, staring wide-eyed into the cockpit from the companionway. He was a small boy, short enough that he didn't even have to stoop to stand there without touching the top.

"Alice," Strider asked, "How about we put the kid in the jump seat for a few minutes?"

Alice grinned and nodded yes, so Strider motioned the kid forward a little and after he was nearly in the cockpit, Strider reached around behind him and folded down the jump seat so the kid could sit in the companionway between the two pilots. The boy's eyes were shinning in delight at the view of the dash and out the front windows of the Chinook—not that he had much of a view, since he was too short to see over the dash. Catching Alice's eye, Strider pointed at the big knob on the back of the center console marked "Power Steering" and Alice, still grinning, nodded "yes" again.

The power steering is just for ground taxi and does nothing in flight, but it is a big important looking knob right at the back of the center control console and within easy reach from the jump seat. Strider took the boy's right hand and put it on the knob while making a big show of turning the control switch from "Off" to "On." As the boy's hand touched the knob, Alice too made a big show of releasing the flight controls by holding his right hand up and off the cyclic control stick. Of course, the automatic stability system, a semi-autopilot, was really flying the aircraft at that point, keeping it headed where Alice had last pointed it, but only a pilot would know that. As far as this small boy was concerned, that knob controlled the entire aircraft.

Strider made a motion with his left hand, indicating that they should turn right and the kid turned the knob to the right. As he did so, Alice gave the aircraft a little right rudder, so that the Chinook began a slight turn to the right. A huge smile lit up the kid's face, the smile of a boy overcome by joy at the totally unexpected pleasure of getting to "fly" this big helicopter. He turned the knob to the left and Alice added a little left rudder to get it moving that way. After about 30 seconds Strider gave the boy a "thumbs up" and turned the power steering back to "Off," as Alice put his hand back on the control stick. The boy's smile remained bright as Strider motioned for him to go back into the cabin.

TWO WHEELER

After ten minutes of searching, Alice finally saw a stretch of muddy dirt road that was out of the water enough to be a drop-off point. Unfortunately, there were trees close on one side, too close to land the entire aircraft on the road surface. The other side appeared to have a drop off several feet down to a paddy or field. Still, it was the only place within five miles of the village that could provide respite, and at the same time was within reasonable walking distance of where their village was, or at least, had been. Alice did a low pass to make sure there weren't any unseen wires or other obstacles that could endanger the aircraft when they landed. There weren't, so he began to set up for a landing.

"OK, we're going to do a two-wheeler across that road," Alice told the crew over the aircraft's intercom.

Strider and Powers knew exactly what he meant: he would put the two rear wheels down on the dry portion of the road and hover the nose of the helicopter so that the two sets of front wheels would be in the air over the water, without touching them down at all. It is a maneuver that looks difficult to non-pilots, but is actually easier than an ordinary hover. Holding the helicopter that way would allow Powers to lower the rear ramp, and let passengers walk out of the cabin directly onto dry land, much easier than for them to jump down from the crew door. Alice brought the big helicopter around, lined it up with his intended landing spot, and smoothly brought it to a 20-foot hover.

Powers directed Alice over the landing spot as he brought the aircraft straight down, but he didn't require much direction. It was all absolutely routine, if you count landing half on land and hovering the other half, routine. Three minutes after the rear wheels had touched down on the road, all the passengers were off the aircraft and had moved far enough away to keep from being blasted by the rotor wash when the Chinook took off again. The little boy "pilot" ran around the side of the aircraft to where he could see the pilots and waved at Alice and Strider, the big grin still in place. They, too, were grinning when they waved back at him. Maybe they had made a friend this time. Or maybe not, but in any case the kid would never forget the trip. In the end that was the only sign of appreciation they received from any of the people they rescued.

After the last of the villagers had cleared the cabin and before he raised the ramp, Powers had Crear and Crone put two cases of Vietnamese C rations and two jugs of water out behind the aircraft for the villagers. Playtex 506 was ready to go again. Powers knew full well that he would have to carefully allocate the C rations and water. If he left too much at one spot that would mean he would run out quickly, leaving none for the last groups of people they would rescue that day. Even a little might make a lot of difference, compared with nothing at all, and Powers wanted everyone to at least have something.

Up in the cockpit, everything was stable as they sat there on two wheels, so Alice gave the flight controls to Strider. Alice instructed him to make a from-the-ground takeoff instead of hovering, not wanting the people they had just dropped off to be blown around too much. Strider did so, moving the aircraft up and forward with as little power as possible. He began the takeoff and within seconds they were at 200 feet and headed back to the area where they had found that day's first village that needed evacuation. Finding the next one wasn't as easy as they thought it would be.

Instead of the short time they anticipated, it took 20 minutes to find another village that needed help and that also had a spot close enough to serve as an LZ. It seemed that the water just kept getting deeper, covering more of the farmland until nothing was left except water. Whatever life there had been was hidden in the inland sea or great lake that was now Northern I Corps. Now and then as they searched, they would see a grove of trees that might once have marked a village, but now any village that might have been there was completely submerged. The people were either already gone or had drowned. Strider doubted they had drowned, they had lived here since times long past and knew how to deal with floods, even with water this high. Even so, they had lost everything to the flood and it would take them a long time to recover.

Or maybe not, maybe it was easier to recover when you had less to start with. It seemed that way to Strider. The people of the Kentucky mountains, where he had grown up, appeared to recover from disaster quickly, be they floods, fires, or divorces. People with less seemed hardier than people with more. They also seemed to be less daunted by calamity.

SURPRISES

When they finally found a village that needed help, they got a bit of a surprise. They had seen the grove of trees that often marked a village, so they headed over for a closer look. When they got there, they saw what appeared to be a correctly laid out helicopter landing pad marker, a big "H" within a circle, in the middle of the only bit of dry ground anywhere close to the huts. Of course, part of the circle was now covered by the rising water, but someone who knew what they were doing had laid this helipad out quite nicely. It appeared to have been painted on the grass or on the ground, it was difficult to tell, but in any case, it was more than big enough for a Chinook or a couple of Hueys to land on. There was even a windsock, albeit one made of rags, tied to a pole, but it worked, or would have worked if the wind was stronger and it wasn't weighed down with rain.

As Playtex 506 flew over, the crew could see that the people of the village were assembled under a thatched roofed building not far from the helipad. The building had no walls, but was of a big enough size to provide cover for all the villagers, or at least all the ones who wanted to be seen. The other buildings in the village had not fared as well. They were mostly gone, but from the look of things, it wouldn't take too much to rebuild them. The thatched roof on the open building showed that these people were not completely dependent on tin roofing material, as so many other villages were now. Besides the proper helipad, another unusual thing about this village was that it had a yellow and red South Vietnamese flag flying from a pole in front of the big thatched building, the first one they had seen since they started the rescue mission. These people weren't afraid of the helicopter about to land next to their village, because apparently it was, or had been in the recent past, a routine event.

As Strider circled the village, one of the men came out from under the thatched roof and assumed the position of "ground guide" on the helipad, standing at the edge with his back to the wind. Unlike everyone else they could see, this man had removed his traditional black shirt and was wearing only a white, sleeveless t-shirt above his black trousers. By his actions, it was clear that he understood that helicopters prefer to land into the wind, since he had positioned himself accordingly. He began making the standard signals that Ground Guides use, motioning Playtex 506 to come on in for landing, using both hands and arms to motion them down. Since this was a new phenomenon on this mission, Strider looked over at Alice questioningly.

"Go ahead and land" Alice said over the ICS. "I'm betting this is, or was, an Air America Operations Base and these people are well used to helicopters landing. At least our ground guide is."

Strider called for the landing checklist and after an "All set in back" from Powers, began his approach to the helipad, nominally at least, under the guidance of their new Ground Guide. Strider did a normal approach and, seeing no obstacles or loose items that might blow up into the rotor system, took the helicopter directly to the ground instead of hovering before landing. As Playtex 506 approached, the Ground Guide braced himself so that the rotor wash would not knock him down as he gave the crossed arm "land" signal. When Strider had the aircraft firmly on deck, the ground guide straightened back up and made the signal indicating that he wanted permission to come aboard the helicopter.

Alice gave him a "thumbs up" out the left cockpit window, but at the same time said over the ICS, "Everyone be particularly alert. This guy is just a little too pat."

In the cabin, Crone and Crear did not make any overt moves toward their machine guns. In fact, both guns were pointed straight down at the ground. Even so, both men had their hands on grips and could bring them up and into action in about one second, should they need to.

It was obvious that the Ground Guide knew how to act around helicopters and was completely comfortable with them. Staying where the pilots could see him, he moved to the 2 o'clock position on the forward rotor disk, ducked down to remain well clear of the rotor blades, and came up to the aircraft. It was also obvious that he knew the crew was suspicious of him since he held his hands in plain view the whole time to reassure the crew he had no weapons, probably the same reason he had taken off his shirt before assuming the role of Ground Guide. Powers motioned him to the rear of the helicopter since the crew door was blocked by the re-mounted right machine gun.

Powers escorted the Vietnamese man up to the cockpit. He looked to be in his thirties, thin, but in better physical condition than most Viet-namese they had seen over the last few days. He was all smiles as he tried to yell to the pilots over the noise of the aircraft. No way could they hear him, so Alice told Powers to give him a headset. Powers dug the only one he had out of his spares box and after plugging it into a spare ICS jack, gave it to the Vietnamese man. He obviously knew how to use it because he put the headset on correctly and adjusted the microphone so that he could talk.

"How do you hear?" he asked over the ICS. His English had only the slightest Vietnamese accent, in fact, his accent had more of a faint Texas twang to it than most American non-Texans have.

"Got you loud and clear," Alice replied. "We're here to move anyone who wants to go to higher ground. Where did you learn all this, helicopter signals and English and all?"

The man who was their Ground Guide laughed and said with a smile, "I went to language school in Texas with the Air Force and then to Wolters and Rucker for helicopter training. I graduated, too, and was assigned to fly Huey's down south. Unfortunately, I went blind in my right eye about a year later, some infection or another, so they "retired" me, threw me out, actually, and here I am, back in my home village."

Looking closely at him now, Alice could see that his right eye was clouded, almost white. Alice, Strider, and every other Army pilot had gone through the same schools as this man. Strider knew there were Vietnamese undergoing flight training at the same time he was, but they were kept en-tirely separate from the Americans. No one was quite sure who was going to contaminate whom, should they mix, so the Army kept them apart. Probably not the best idea, since they were going to be fighting together, but that was the way it was. Stories circulated among the warrant officer candidates about the Vietnamese students cooking meals on the floor of their BOQ rooms, and other behavior considered bizarre by the Americans. Every now and then, here in Vietnam, the men of Playtex would see a flight of Vietnamese helicopters passing by, heading to who knows where, but they always gave them a wide berth, just in case they did something strange.

Their Ground Guide continued, "After I left the Air Force, I worked with Air America a bit, in fact I helped them when they set up the LZ here a year and a half ago. I saw you go past a couple of times and figured you were rescuing people. Why else would a Chinook be flying so low out here? Anyway, I've got them all organized in groups of 12 whenever you are ready for them. I've got 48 people total, 30 of them women and kids, a few men, and the rest old people. I think there is a pretty good spot about four miles west to drop them. It should be easy to find, just follow the road, if you can still see it. There's a little hill there, not much, but it will probably be dry. You probably noticed there are not a lot of men here. That's because most of them are RUFF/PUFFs (RUFF/PUFFs were the Regional Forces/Popular Forces, a South Vietnamese and U.S.-sponsored, lightly armed militia, a sort of home-grown National Guard) and are armed. I told them to stay out of sight and to keep their weapons in the armory until we had made contact with you. Guys out of uniform with guns, especially Vietnamese guys, always make people nervous, especially you Americans."

They were supposed to provide protection to their own villages against the NVA and VC, but Strider didn't think they did much of anything except provide additional weapons for the VC. Sometimes they were in uniforms of sorts, but more often just a uniform shirt, if that. Their weapons were M-1s, M-1 carbines, and similar rifles left over from WWII and Korea, though Strider had occasionally seen some carrying M-16s. Whatever weapons they carried, they were no real match for the hardcore NVA regulars. As Strider heard it, when the NVA attacked or even were seen in their area, the RUFF/PUFFs would just melt away, stashing their arms and rejoining the other villagers. That is, of course, if they weren't VC in the first place, in which case they would welcome the NVA and provide whatever intelligence they could.

Before he left, the man told Alice and Strider that the RUFF/PUFFS would not be evacuating with the rest of the people. They had enough food to see them through a week or two and would keep an eye on the village until the people got back. Alice looked over at Strider knowingly, feeling there was more going on here than met the eye. Air America must still be active at this site and "other agencies" like the CIA, might also be using this as a base. It wasn't Playtex 506's business, their mission was to rescue people and if the RUFF/PUFFs didn't want to be rescued, that was just fine with Alice.

When Powers signaled clearance, the people of the village began approaching the helicopter in orderly lines, nothing like the crew of Playtex 506 had seen to this point. The old people, women, and children looked like military squads as they waited to be waved into the helicopter. As their Ground Guide had said, there were only a few men among them, and to Strider, they looked more like guards than farmers. Strider hoped that they were sent along to make sure the people were protected, not to keep them in line. These people had more goods with them than most of the other people they had picked up, so even if they didn't weigh any more, they still took up more space. Powers only had two groups board before he told Alice the cabin was full and raised the ramp in preparation for takeoff.

Strider took off and headed west. In short order, the "hill," a spot maybe 15 feet higher than the surrounding terrain, appeared exactly where their Ground Guide said it would be, an island in a brown sea of floodwater. There was a nice clear spot to land on one side, but Alice was still suspicious and had Strider circle the area twice, looking for anything not right. Crear and Powers were looking too, looking over the barrels of their M-60D machine guns, but there was nothing unusual to be seen. It was just an empty little hill in the middle of nowhere, a hill that had the advantage of being above the floodwaters. Now, if there were no land mines or booby traps in the clear area that made up the only real LZ. . . .

There were no land mines or booby traps. Strider landed, the people exited, Alice took the flight controls, took off, and headed back to the village for their second load. The next two groups boarded in the same orderly way as the first and, as with the first, they were well equipped with food, water, and other essentials. Both groups of 12 had two young men in them, guards, presumably. They had no visible weapons, but the crew of Playtex 506 knew they were probably there among the goods the people were carrying.

As Alice lifted off with the second and final load, he could see the Ground Guide apparently giving orders to the RUFF/PUFFs. They had been out of sight on the far side of the thatched building while the villagers were loading into the helicopter. Now they fell into formation, looking far more like regular soldiers than farmers organized into a militia, confirming in Alice's mind that there was far more going on here than just another flooded out village. In short order, Playtex 506 landed back at the hill and dropped the second load off next to the first. Before they continued their search, trapped by the floodwater, they were going to need fuel, so it was time for the helicopter to visit the fuel pits at Camp Evans again.

THE NEXT ROUND

Alice passed the flight controls to Strider and told him to turn west. They could probably get to 500 feet now, because the clouds had lifted somewhat, but that would put them right in range for anyone who had a gun. The war might be suspended from the American viewpoint, but the NVA had been silent on the issue, so far at least. Alice had Strider remain at 200 feet and 100 knots as they headed toward QL1. In ten minutes they came to QL1, but could not really tell if they were south or north of Camp Evans. Alice decided they were north and had Strider turn left to follow the road. In about another ten minutes, they crossed over a bridge that Powers recognized. They were actually south of Camp Evans instead of north, so Strider turned around and headed back up the highway. In short order they found the base, landed in the fuel pits, topped off the tanks up to the full 8,000 pounds of jet fuel, and were off again to rescue more people.

They must have been in a different portion of their search area when they started again. With the low visibility, it was difficult to impossible to say exactly where they were, but this area was definitely more populated than where they had first searched that morning. They found villages in need of assistance everywhere they looked now. These people seemed more desperate than the ones they had picked up earlier: colder, hungrier, more exhausted after another day of being cold, wet, and hungry.

Because there were so many villages in need here, Playtex 506 did not shut down for lunch. Instead, between pickups, the crew ate the bag lunches the mess hall had passed out that morning. The mess hall had done a good job, since the lunch sandwiches and apples beat the hell out of C ration canned pork. The crewmen, though wet, stayed fairly warm from all the exercise they got loading and unloading their passengers, but the pilots, stuck, strapped into their seats during all the lifts, wished they had brought their flight jackets. To get a little break, Strider and Alice took alternating turns getting out of the cockpit on every drop-off landing to stretch their legs, do a few jumping jacks to get their blood circulating, and to take a discrete piss after the people had exited the aircraft.

As they picked the people up from location after location, Strider marveled at how calm the people they were lifting seemed, accepting of whatever came their way, good or bad. All except one time . . .

PANIC

About six flight hours into the day, Alice made a routine water landing near a group of people stranded on a tiny bit of dry land. Playtex 506's crew had done so many of them by now, that they had the drill down to a science. Since there had been no hostilities, the right door gun was more or less permanently demounted to speed up the loading through the crew door. The only clear spot Alice could find to land the aircraft this time was at least 100 yards from where the people were, but like most of the villages they had seen, these people had several small boats that they could use to ferry people from the last of the land out to the Chinook.

After Alice landed the helicopter, and Powers had gone through the now familiar ritual of waving them over, the first group climbed into three boats and started toward the aircraft, one man at the bow and another at the stern, slowly poling their way through the three or four feet of water.

As the first evacuees of this village started to board through the cabin door, Strider, looking back through the companionway into the aircraft's cabin, saw Crear jump up from his post at the left door gun and run to the right side of the cabin, apparently to help Crone on the step with something. Whatever was happening that made him move so quickly was over in a moment. Crear returned to his door gun and once again the Vietnamese began loading into the back as they had done for the last two days. After a routine takeoff, Alice found a drier spot for them about a mile away from their village and landed. Powers lowered the ramp and they started out of the aircraft. There were only about 20 of them this time, so Powers only left one case of C rats and one jug of water. After the Vietnamese had off loaded, Powers came up to the cockpit and, standing in the companionway between the pilots, told them what happened.

Everything on this last run seemed to be normal at first. Powers waved them over, then the narrow wooden fishing boats approached and the people began handing up the children out of the first boat into the Chinook's cabin. At that moment, a woman in the second boat apparently panicked. With a burst of strength that belied her size, she began to shove people out of the way as she began to fight her way onto the aircraft, apparently intent on boarding first instead of waiting her turn. She climbed from the second boat into the first and as she fought her way forward, she pushed a young mother and baby right out of the boat and into the water. She did not try to help them or even look back, but kept on fighting to get to the front of the first boat, shoving people out of her way as she went.

Powers said it looked at first like the people were too shocked to do anything, so Crear started to jump into the water after the mother and child. Powers saw what was happening and held him back, since he could see that a couple of men from the second boat had already jumped into the water after the woman and baby. In a few seconds, the two men lifted the two of them out of the water and back into the first boat. The baby seemed to be screaming, but Powers couldn't tell for sure, since nothing could be heard over the roar of the aircraft. Both mother and child seemed no worse for wear, particularly since everyone was soaked to the skin from the rain anyway and a little swim really made no difference in comfort levels.

The woman who had knocked the woman and baby into the water had by this time pushed and clawed her way to the front of the first boat. As she started to mount the step into the aircraft, Crear, in a red hot fury at what she had done, kicked her squarely in the middle of the chest, sending her backwards off the step and into the boat below. She fell from the crew door step into the waiting people. They apparently approved of what Crear had done, because two of the men promptly picked her up and threw her out of the boat into the water. Powers watched as she came up sputtering, standing in chest-deep water by herself next to the boat. No one in the remaining boats offered her any help or even looked at her; instead they just went past her, leaving her standing alone. Even so, she did not look defeated, just angry. Maybe she was angry at herself, or maybe she was just angry at the world.

As the Chinook lifted off, Powers said he could see her wading slowly toward the soggy remains of the village. Perhaps they would forgive her when this was all over, perhaps not. Strider didn't think the people from his native mountains of Kentucky would have. Babies must survive, because they are the future and anyone who endangers them is an enemy to everyone in the family.

GETTING TIRED NOW

As the day wore on, the rain continued to fall, even heavier now, and the fog got thicker, bringing the visibility down to less than a mile again. Another Chinook, Playtex 542, flown by Steiner and Fivelson, called on the company UHF radio frequency to tell 506 that they were hovering along, trying to get back to Camp Eagle or Phu Bai, because visibility had gone to near zero where they were operating. Alice acknowledged their call and told them the weather wasn't much better where 506 was flying. He would have to make a decision soon as to what they were going to do. In Strider's mind, calling it a day would be the best idea; they would need to start heading toward Camp Evans, the closest base, as it would take too long to get to Liftmaster in the little daylight left now. Attempting night flight would be suicidal in this weather.

Climbing into the clouds was still impossible, because as far as Alice knew, all the radar stations in I Corps were still inoperative, as per the CO's brief on the first day. The Air Force radar at Da Nang might well be too far away to count on, particularly if you didn't have lots of fuel to fly the 70 plus miles down there. So, get into the clouds without radar, and there was no way back down, or at least no safe way. You could put yourself in the hands of God, like the weather check Huey pilot had done, but that was really tempting fate. Maybe you could go out over the sea and descend slowly, hoping you would break out of the clouds before you hit the water. This would truly be a last ditch resort, since Playtex's Chinooks did not have radar altimeters and their barometric altimeters were just not that accurate.

PLAYTEX 107 CALLS IT A DAY

While Alice was deciding what he was going to do, 2LT James Taylor, AC of Playtex 107, had already decided. His aircraft was going back to Liftmaster before it got too dark to find it. Since his navigation plan was the same as everyone else's, 2LT Taylor told his copilot to head west until they got to QL1 and, on crossing it, turn south.

CW2 Marvin Leonard had been moved over to fly with 2LT Taylor as copilot at the last minute. The operations officer felt he might need some steadying as the weather continued to deteriorate. They also had been given an easier search area, one just east of Hue City, unlike Alice and Strider in 506, who was truly searching the boondocks out near the seacoast. There were far more familiar landmarks around Hue than in the lowlands. Like all the other Playtex helicopters, 107 had been out looking for people to rescue for three days now. They were lucky in one sense, having had to make water landing in only one case; all the rest of their landings were just "muddy" landings in semi-solid sand and dirt. Their area seemed to be a little bit more above sea level than the lowlands farther east, so they didn't have to move quite so many people away from the flooding.

The villages that were seriously flooded were mostly next to rivers or streams and many of the people had self-evacuated as the water rose. When they did do a pickup, it was easy to find a nice, relatively dry spot to drop the people off without too much searching. By the afternoon, 2LT Taylor determined that they had lifted 204 people to safety, or at least they had moved them to higher ground. The total would have been higher except for the oddest experience of the entire mission that took place at one village.

This village looked much like all the others, a few thatched-roof huts, along with many more tin-roofed ones, pig pens and gardens for food. The water was lapping at their doors and still coming up, so they looked like they could use some help. As 2LT Taylor brought the helicopter in for a landing, instead of gathering to watch as all the other villagers had done, they all ran away. Watching them disappear into the woods behind the village greatly disconcerted the door gunner, a former grunt, who immediately swung his machine gun in their direction. In his experience, when Vietnamese acted like that, they were on the other side. The flight engineer saw him as he started to charge his weapon and made a motion for him to knock it off, which he did, though only reluctantly.

2LT Taylor found this to be a new experience, too, and wasn't sure what to do. From where they had landed, none of the crew could see a soul. After the helicopter had been sitting there for a few minutes, an older woman came out from the woods and stood about 100 feet in front of the helicopter where she was sure the pilots could clearly see her. She started making motions that seemed to indicate she wanted them to go away. After watching her for a few moments, 2LT Taylor told Leonard to takeoff. If they didn't want to be rescued they certainly weren't going to insist.

As Leonard climbed the helicopter out to look for a more receptive village he thought to himself, "VC. That was a VC village." He held his breath until they were clear, expecting incoming fire at any moment, but there was none. Leonard was pretty sure that there would be if they came back again, since the villagers were probably digging out their weapons right now.

They flew on to the next village, where the people readily climbed aboard to move to a better spot until the water went back down. Leonard wondered how these folks got along with their neighbors five miles away.

While Playtex 107 may have had a better area to search than those ACs assigned to the farther out lowlands, that did not mean that the weather was any better in their area, because it wasn't. The same low clouds, fog, and poor-to-non-existent visibility that was hindering their sister aircraft was bothering them too. In one way, their area was more dangerous than it was in the real lowlands: antennas were far more numerous around the Hue City area than they were out in the hinterlands.

As a new AC, 2LT Taylor had not yet fully developed the confidence in his own ability that the more experienced ACs had, but he was very confident in Leonard's ability to fly the Chinook. He knew Leonard had easily four times the flight time he had, so he left most of the flying to him and as AC, decided to concentrate on navigation. As with the rest of Playtex's crews wandering around in the rain and fog, the usual visual navigation aids were of little use. The bridges, bends in streams, roads, etc., that they normally used to find the FSBs, were very different when seen from 200 feet instead of 3,000; that is, if you could see them at all in the rain and fog. And because of the conditions, 2LT Taylor, like the other ACs flying today, found his map utterly useless for this mission, since many of the points he needed for navigation just could not be found. Experienced pilot that he was, Leonard could not help with the navigation, because as a new guy to I Corps, he was completely unfamiliar with this area. Besides, it took his full concentration to keep the Chinook out of the clouds and from hitting any stray wires or antennas that might cross their path, so he spent his time staring hard ahead into their flight path.

When it got to the point where they were basically hovering along and not finding anyone to rescue, 2LT Taylor decided to call it a day. They were reasonably close to Phu Bai, closer anyway than they were to Camp Evans, so they would just go home to Liftmaster after refueling at Camp Eagle, get some rest and try it again tomorrow. 2LT Taylor decided that the best way to do this would be to do what everyone else planned to do, find QL1 and follow it back home. He told Leonard to turn west, figuring they would be back in the fuel pits at Camp Eagle in less than 30 minutes. Twenty minutes later, still headed west, they had not yet seen QL1.

NOT LOST, MERELY DISORIENTED

Looking at his altimeter, 2LT Taylor noticed that the terrain was higher than it should have been in their assigned search area. Leonard was still keeping them clear of the clouds at 300 feet above the ground, but the ground was now a couple hundred feet above sea level, not 20–40 feet like it had been a short while ago. Had they crossed QL1 without realizing it? How was that possible? They should have seen the road and all the traffic on it, but apparently they had not. Another clue that they were now too far west was that the flooding had not covered everything here, there were entire groves of trees visible now, not just scattered stands in the muddy water. Some of the villages they passed seemed to be completely normal— wet, but normal and not in need of rescue.

The visibility dropped until it was too low to safely continue flying without going into the clouds. Leonard brought Playtex 107 to a hover above the forest and held it there waiting for things to clear a little. The thought went through his mind that this was the sort of thing he used to do in LOHs, but then he was a small target, not a huge one like a Chinook. In a short while, the rain slacked off some and the visibility improved enough to continue moving forward, but it was a temporary condition and soon he had to bring the aircraft to a stop again. Leonard was not happy with this—visions of men with AK-47s aiming in kept coming to his mind.

As he sat in a high hover for the second time, waiting for Taylor to decide what to do next, the mist cleared a little, cleared enough for Leonard to see a full grown elephant standing about 50 yards in front of the aircraft. Leonard had seen elephants in the jungle on his first tour, but he was astonished to see one here. The elephant was studiously ignoring the noisy helicopter hovering nearby.

"Does anyone else see the elephant at 12 o'clock?" Leonard asked calmly over the intercom. Both the door gunner and the crew chief immediately leaned forward over their machine guns to see what Leonard was talking about, rain or no rain. The flight engineer hurriedly came up through the companionway and looked out the windshield between the pilots. 2LT Taylor, in the left seat, stared open mouthed through the windshield at the gray beast so close to their aircraft.

The elephant did not move. It appeared to be standing in a garden, peacefully enjoying the rain as it looked off into the distance. 2LT Taylor suddenly gave a start and knew in an instant exactly where they were. They had, in fact, missed QL1. They had flown over it and were now looking at the life-size stone elephant in the garden of the old Vietnamese Imperial Summer Palace, about ten miles west of Hue. Early in his tour, one of the ACs brought him here so he could get an aerial view of how the last Emperor lived, and particularly his garden of life-sized stone tigers and an elephant. The rain made the stone elephant a darker gray than it was when he first saw it, and it looked more life-like than it had been before. With the mist rising from the garden, it was easy to mistake it for the real animal, at least from a distance.

If they had flown a few miles further west, they would have reached the foot hills, just before the mountains begin to rise up to their full 6,000 feet. As it was, they were already in NVA country. Out here there weren't any VC, just the regular North Vietnamese soldiers with all their Soviet weapons, including heavy anti-aircraft guns. Hovering around here wasn't healthy for big helicopters. 2LT Taylor told Leonard to reverse course, so he immediately pedal turned the aircraft to the southeast. Lowering the nose, he rapidly accelerated the Chinook up to 130 knots. Once again they were headed the right way, with not too much farther to go before they got to Camp Eagle. As they left the beginnings of the foothills a few minutes later, the clouds seemed to lift a little and the visibility increased to more than a mile, just about the best weather they had seen all day.

In a few minutes, QL1 came into view and shortly after that, the old imperial capital, Hue City, with its walled Citadel. Playtex 107 passed just to the west of the city, crossing the Perfume River just above the railroad bridge, with the old walls of the Citadel barely visible in the distance. Ten minutes later, 2LT Taylor called Camp Eagle control for clearance into the fuel pits, which was immediately granted. Twenty minutes after they landed, they had refueled and were airborne again for the short flight back over to Liftmaster Pad. It was a real relief to the entire crew to be back home.

2LT Taylor was worried as they taxied back in. Leonard had not said one word about their less than ideal navigation, but Taylor knew he was thinking about it. Getting a little disoriented in bad weather was one thing, every pilot had done it now and then, but getting flat out lost and heading out into bad guy country at what was essentially a high hover was quite something else. 2LT Taylor knew he would have to work harder on keeping track of his location so that it did not happen again. He would work on that over his next flights as AC, but he wasn't going to ask anyone for help. To his mind, ACs just didn't do that.

PLAYTEX 542 RETURNS TO LIFTMASTER

Like Steiner told Alice he intended to, they did make it back to Liftmaster Pad in Playtex 542, but it took a long time and was not an easy flight. Twice the visibility got so low that, like Leonard had done in Playtex 107, Steiner just brought the aircraft to a hover and held it there until the rain slowed down and the fog lifted a bit. This was desperation, since there was no guarantee that the rain would slow down or the fog would lift before he ran out of fuel, or alternatively, some passing NVA unit or local VC fired on them. It hadn't happened in three days, but that did not mean it would not start again right now. In a few minutes, the low cloud did lift and he continued, sweating the load the entire way.

By the time he reached QL1 and recognized exactly where they were, the aircraft was down to 40 minutes of fuel. By the time he reached the fuel pits at Camp Eagle a few miles away, 542 was down to 20 minutes of fuel remaining, past the point where you could trust the fuel gauges. Pulses went back to normal when they touched down at the fuel pits. Refueling was routine and fifteen minutes later, they took off one final time in the rain and fog to fly back to Liftmaster and to call it a day.

The crew of Playtex 542 all breathed much easier when their wheels finally touched down on Liftmaster's short PSP runway. It had been a very long, very tiring day on top of many other long, tiring days. The rain and low visibility put a real strain on the pilots, as did the uncertainty of landing in villages outside the wire, waiting for the NVA to open fire on their big, fat Chinooks. But the NVA had not opened fire. The crews had made it home safely in spite of the terrible weather, and being semi-lost on the way back. All they wanted right now was dry clothes, food, and sleep.

Steiner was probably more tired than most of the pilots in Playtex. It had worked out that he had flown more than eight hours three days in a row, all of it with one of the newest copilots, WO1 Barry Fivelson. Because Fivelson was so new, Steiner had had to give him far more help with flying than he would have had to do with someone getting ready for his AC check. It was very tiring to have to constantly watch everything your co-pilot did and to be ready to do every difficult procedure yourself while explaining what you were doing and why you were doing it. Fivelson would be fine in time, but right now he was a lot of work for the AC. Even so, Steiner would not ask for another copilot. That might be considered un-cool, that is, to admit you couldn't train a copilot and fly in extremely bad weather at the same time. The 24 hours he had flown in the last three days were on top of the other 26 hours he had flown in the four days before the rescue mission started. He was very tired and ready to get back to his hootch for dinner, a shower, and bed.

Safe on the ground at Liftmaster, Steiner and Fivelson started to taxi 542 to the revetment they had left from this morning. The flight engineer unplugged his long cord, climbed out through the crew door, and walked out in front of the Chinook. Acting as ground guide, he gave Steiner the signal for a left turn toward the second row of revetments. As Steiner started the maneuver, the Chinook's rear end began to slide to the right on the wet PSP. The runway seemed to be much slicker than normal, perhaps from spilled oil or hydraulic fluid from another aircraft, mixed with con-stant rain.

"Power off!" Steiner yelled at Fivelson over the intercom, as he applied the brakes. Fivelson responded immediately and moved the thrust lever to the full down position, stopping the helicopter's movement forward and stopping the slide at the same time.

Now that they were no longer sliding, Steiner considered what to do next. If he shut it down on the runway and called for a tow, the helicopter would block other aircraft from landing. This would add at least an hour to the crew's work day, given that it would take time to find a driver for the tow tractor, get the helicopter coupled up to the tractor and moved.

Steiner decided that he would taxi it into its revetment using an alternative taxi method the maintenance department had briefed the pilots on a few weeks ago.

A month before the rains started in earnest, the maintenance department gave a short plug for an alternative way to taxi the helicopters when the PSP was slick, the exact situation Steiner faced now. Playtex's CH-47C Chinooks really only had two ways to taxi: two-wheel taxi, with the nose of aircraft off the ground and rear wheels on the ground; and power steering taxi, with all six wheels, a set of two on each side forward and a single wheel on each side aft, on the ground.

With the two-wheel taxi, the pilot lifts the front end of the helicopter off the ground, while holding the rear two wheels on the ground. The CH-47A did not have power steering, so two-wheel taxi was the only way for the pilot to move one around without hovering and severely blowing everything around with his rotor wash. The CH-47A could do a two-wheel taxi very well, and while the CH-47C could also do one, it didn't do it well. The pilots joked that it felt like it had square wheels when you tried a two-wheel taxi, the aircraft wobbling all over the place no matter how precise you were on the controls. Add in the fact that the nose was off the ground in a two-wheel taxi, creating a lot more rotor wash—up to 80 knots of wind or more. Having a lot more things blowing around meant that the power steering taxi was definitely the preferred method for Playtex's "C" model Chinooks.

The power steering taxi is a two-man operation. It requires that the pilot in the right seat pull two inches of back control stick and block the rudders with his feet, so that they don't move. Using the rudders while the helicopter is on the ground runs a very real risk of damaging the rotor system. The right seat pilot also works the power in response to commands from the pilot in the left seat, adding power by pulling the thrust lever up to get the helicopter moving and removing power by putting the thrust lever down when they are ready to stop. The left seat pilot works the power steering, that big, important looking wheel on the back of the center console mentioned earlier, to turn the aircraft in the desired direction. He also works the brakes.

Strider had long ago found that, while it sounds cumbersome, power steering taxi is not difficult in practice, unless, of course, the surface upon which the crew is trying to taxi on is slick. Then it becomes quite interesting, with the aircraft refusing to do what the crew wants it to do and going places they do not want it to go—never good things.

What maintenance proposed to alleviate this situation was simple: the AC was to manually adjust the speed trims so that the forward one was all the way forward, bringing the forward rotor disk closer to the ground, thereby generating more force to better hold the aircraft on the ground. This would, according to the maintenance department, make it easier to taxi when it was slick. Speed trims are devices that only tandem rotor aircraft, like the Chinook, have. All helicopters must lower their nose to move forward in flight. The airflow in powered flight is down through the rotor—the faster you go, the lower the nose. This results in high drag, requiring more and more power as speed increases. Tandem rotor helicopters can use speed trims, electric motors mounted on the upper flight controls, to lower both of the rotors independent of the fuselage, thereby allowing the fuselage to remain more level as the aircraft gains forward speed. This reduces the aerodynamic drag and thus reduces the power required for high-speed flight. Normally, the speed trims deploy automatically based on airspeed, but the pilots can manually control them using two toggle switches, one for the forward and one for the aft.

As he sat there considering his next move, Steiner remembered maintenance's pitch for better control on slick surfaces using the speed trims. As they recommended, he selected the "manual" position on the forward speed trim control panel and, using the toggle switch, moved the forward speed trim as far forward as it would go. As he did so, he could see the forward rotor disk move downward on the front of the aircraft from its normal taxi position to a position much closer to the ground, close enough to present a risk of getting hit by the rotor disk if you tried to walk under it without ducking down.

To get the aircraft moving again, over the ICS Steiner told Fivelson to add a little power. After Fivelson checked, he still had the required two inches of aft cyclic control stick applied, and he pulled up slightly on the thrust level, while simultaneously, Steiner released the aircraft's brakes. The helicopter began to move forward again and, as he turned the power steering wheel to try the left turn again, Steiner found that the aircraft was not sliding any more, just as maintenance described. Steiner was happy; now he could get Playtex 542 parked and they all could start to end their long day.

Steiner made the final turn toward the interior of the revetment and under the flight engineer's direction, moved toward the point where he would stop the aircraft and the flying day would be done. At this moment, he discovered the flaw in the maintenance department's pitch for using the forward speed trim all the way forward for taxiing: with the forward speed trim full down, the forward rotor disk was now two feet lower than the top of the revetment in which he was trying to park the aircraft.

As the helicopter entered the revetment the forward rotor blades struck the steel walls and Playtex 542 immediately began tearing itself apart.

By a few milliseconds, the flight engineer was the first man in the crew to realize something was terribly wrong. His 20-year-old survival instincts were all that kept him alive in that moment. He saw a flash of light that should not have been there and without knowing exactly what it was or why it was happening, threw himself flat on the PSP and covered the back of his neck with his hands. Within half a second, pieces of rotor blade were hitting all around him, some hitting hard enough to dent the steel of the PSP. Through the grace of God, none of the big pieces actually hit him, although he was covered with small bits of rotor blade.

In the cockpit of Playtex 542, things had instantly gone from normal to complete and utter destruction. The force of the impact of the forward rotor blades on the steel revetment wall ripped the forward transmission out of its mounts and sent it smashing into the left side of the cockpit. As the transmission pulled away, the shaft that connects the two rotor systems broke, leaving the aft rotor system to freely spin on its own, no longer controlled from the cockpit.

At the rear of the aircraft, the now free aft rotor blades flexed down and hit the fuselage just behind the cockpit, not quite cutting the aircraft in half, but breaking pieces of metal off the forward area and sending them flying through the air. The engines, however, continued to run just fine, since there was no damage to them at all. The aft transmission was not destroyed by the impact of its rotor blades on the fuselage, so the power from the engines continued to turn the damaged aft rotor blades at their normal speed. The engines would continue doing so until someone shut them down or they ran out of fuel. Since 542 had just been refueled, that would take hours. The forward rotor blades were not turning anymore because they were no longer connected to the drive train. The remaining stumps had stopped turning as soon as the transmission was ripped out and sent into the cockpit.

Steiner later told Cobb and Strider that he had always wondered if he would really be able to evacuate the aircraft in a crash wearing his survival vest and chicken plate, or if he would get hung up and be trapped in the wreckage. The answer was a simple yes; yes, he could do an emergency egress in a crash wearing full combat gear and he did one right then. He said he wasn't really conscious of what had happened, but somehow within seconds of the first blade contact with the steel revetment wall he found himself standing in the rain, some distance away from the revetment, with his arms crossed, watching in a very detached manner as the Chinook beat itself to death on the revetment wall. He said he felt detached because the dying Chinook seemed to have no relationship to him. He had no memory of how he got there, but looking at it after all had calmed down, it appeared that the cockpit frame had twisted enough to allow the emergency door to jettison itself. Steiner had somehow released his seatbelt and shoulder harness and leaped from the left seat just as the transmission came into the cockpit, missing him entirely. Somehow he did not see the flight engineer shielding himself among the pieces of rotor blade as he ran past him.

Fivelson escaped the right seat without getting injured either, although he did not get out nearly as quickly as Steiner had done. The transmission cleanly missed him, having gone to the left side. The front rotor blades were gone, with the stumps no longer revolving after the shaft that connected the two rotor systems sheared, so he did not have to worry about getting hit by them as he exited. He calmly unstrapped, and since the companionway was blocked by the transmission, he jettisoned the right door and jumped down to the PSP. He didn't see the flight engineer lying on the PSP in front of the aircraft either. After he was a safe distance away, Fivelson remembered his beloved camera and started back toward the aircraft at a run to retrieve it. One of the maintenance men who had been working nearby on the ramp grabbed him to keep him from going back into the wreckage and with a start, like he just woke from a deep sleep, Fivelson realized he had just survived his first helicopter crash. He also realized he wasn't going to get any pictures of it, not right away anyway.

Both the crew chief and door gunner were at their posts on the left and right door guns when the blades hit the steel revetment wall. In half a second, they could see the aft blades slamming into the top of the fuselage just above where they were sitting, so they did not try to go out the back of the helicopter; instead, when the slamming stopped, they ducked under the door gun and went out the forward crew door on the right-hand side. They, too, seeing that the front rotor system was not turning, ran to the front of the helicopter where they joined Steiner and Fivelson in looking back at the wrecked helicopter.

The flight engineer realized, after the bits of rotor blade stopped hitting around him, that he was not injured, so he jumped up off the PSP and ran to join the other four aircrew 100 feet away. Since the aft transmission and engines were still working, Playtex 542's aft rotor blades continued to spin merrily, no longer hitting the fuselage but not creating any lift either.

Everything on Liftmaster Pad had come to a sudden halt at the sound of the crash. For a few moments, everyone seemed frozen in place with the same questions running through their minds. What the hell was that? Was that incoming rockets? What happens now? Was anyone dead or injured? Was 542 going to burn? If it did, would it take other aircraft with it? Had the flying pieces of rotor blades damaged any of the other aircraft?

In less than a minute, one of the maintenance warrants came running from the maintenance office where he had been doing paperwork to see what had happened. Surveying the scene from behind the aircraft, it was apparent to him that 542's engines would continue to run until they were out of fuel, unless the manual shutoffs in the back of the helicopter were activated. The ones in the cockpit were now useless since the transmission had come crashing down, ripping all the wiring out and smashing everything else. He could see the crew standing in front of the aircraft, doing nothing, so he decided it was up to him to get it shut down.

The aircraft showed no signs of catching fire, so he ran quickly to its rear, climbed through the partially open ramp, and activated the manual fuel shutoffs, first on number one engine and then on number two engine. Both manual fuel shutoffs worked as designed and stopped the fuel flow to their respective engines. The engines, no longer getting fuel, spun down to a stop, sounding exactly like they do when a complete, non-damaged aircraft is shut down normally. As they stopped, the aft rotor blades spun down to a stop, too.

When everything was still, the maintenance warrant stepped calmly off the helicopter's ramp, already mentally congratulating himself on a job well done and already mentally awarding himself a medal. He had not decided which one it should be, but he had stopped this aircraft from causing further damage to other aircraft, as it would probably have done if the engines had continued to run and it had caught fire, so it should be a good one, a Bronze Star, maybe. He was a hero.

The maintenance warrant then slipped in some spilled transmission fluid, or perhaps some spilled oil, fell heavily onto the PSP and broke his right leg cleanly, just above the ankle. His was the only injury incurred during the loss of Playtex 542.

As 542's engines stopped, the flight engineer came out of his shock. He ran to the front of the aircraft's left sponson and disconnected the battery to prevent even the possibility of an electrical fire. Other maintenance personnel had gathered, some dragging the big, wheeled, flight line fire extinguishers into position behind the wreck, but they weren't needed.

The only sounds on the flight line now were the ticking of cooling metal in 542's engines and the rain falling on everything.

Someone, probably the air traffic controller in Liftmaster tower, had called the crash crew over at Phu Bai Airport and ten minutes after that call, two fire engines and an ambulance came roaring up to Liftmaster Pad, prepared for action. The firemen deployed around the destroyed Chinook and stood ready to do whatever was necessary, until about ten minutes later when the maintenance officer told them they would not be needed. The spilled fluids would be cleaned up by Playtex maintenance and since no fuel had leaked from 542, there was no danger of a fire. The firemen packed up their gear and returned to their firehouse, probably secretly disappointed that they had not gotten to actually fight a fire. All that training and no one ever crashed where they could put it to use.

After the firemen left, Steiner, Fivelson, the flight engineer, crew chief, and door gunner were all loaded into the ambulance along with the maintenance warrant. They were transported to the field hospital over at Phu Bai for a post-crash physical check out. This routine procedure was not so routine for Playtex. It was the first time an aircraft had crashed at Liftmaster Pad in the two years it had been operating. As the ambulance pulled away, they could see that most everyone in the company had turned out to view the wreck. That wouldn't last long, because the sergeant major and the maintenance chief would soon chase everyone away, back to their regular jobs, and the cleanup would begin.

The maintenance warrant, strapped on the stretcher in the back of the ambulance, was loudly cursing his bad luck to anyone who would listen and to those who weren't paying attention, too. How could he have fallen after all the excitement was over? He knew full well he had fallen because he was not paying attention to where he was walking, mentally giving himself a medal for shutting the aircraft down and all. He also knew his future was grim, at least from a pilot's viewpoint. It now held nothing but paperwork for at least the next month, since you can't fly or even do maintenance ground runs with a broken leg. Sadly, a broken leg is not enough to get you medevaced home, so you are really stuck at a desk. How the hell was he going to get around? A wheel chair was no use on PSP. It was way too far from his hootch to use crutches to get to his office. Maybe he could get Savick to have the driver chauffer him in one of the company jeeps. Or maybe he could use one of the aircraft tugs as a motorized wheelchair. Or . . . Sigh . . .

The crew of Playtex 542 was not cursing their bad luck; in fact, they were all very quiet on the ride over to Phu Bai. Even though they had survived an accident that destroyed an aircraft with no injuries, no one had anything to say.

Steiner was quiet because he was deep in thought, already bordering on depression, about losing an aircraft under his command in an accident. It was the first time he had even damaged an aircraft in anyway, but it was obvious this one was not just damaged: it was totaled. To completely destroy a Chinook when it was only 50 feet from being safely parked made the feeling of depression even worse. He was quite sure that it would probably cost him his AC rating.

Fivelson was happy about being alive, excited, as always, at yet another new experience, but at the same time pissed off that he had not brought his camera with him when he jumped out of the cockpit. He missed some good pictures there, but then his tour had just started and he was sure there would be many more opportunities. Maybe someday he could get pictures of the Ho Chi Minh Trail.

The enlisted air crewmen were just happy to be alive, especially the flight engineer. He was still marveling at how he had escaped being injured or even killed by the disintegrating forward rotor blades. Even though he was happy at being alive and uninjured, a part of him was already angry with himself for not noticing how low the blades were. He should have looked at the blade clearance, but he was concentrating on getting 542 lined up just right in the revetment, not on how low the rotor blades were. He was also glum at the thought of being just an ordinary maintenance man again until they assigned him another aircraft. That is, of course, if he got another aircraft at all. There were a couple of men in training to be flight engineers, men who had more time left on their tour than he did. Giving one of them the new aircraft might make more sense to the maintenance officer than giving another one to him. He would just have to see, but from the back of the ambulance, the prospects did not look good.

The crew chief and door gunner, far from being glum, were just looking at each other and grinning. What a wonderful war story they had now, watching as those aft blades hit the top of the cabin! The crew chief knew that he would be assigned to another aircraft almost immediately; there were too many missions and not enough trained crew chiefs to go around. The door gunner was also happy because he knew that someone else would be cleaning the two machine guns today. The armory officer would not leave them in the aircraft and he was otherwise detained for the next few hours.

BITS AND PIECES

Back at Liftmaster Pad, the maintenance officer was looking ruefully at the wreckage of Playtex 542. It was rare that the cause of a mishap was so obvious. He could clearly see where the front rotor blades had smashed into the revetment wall. He quickly figured out why that happened: the forward speed trim was all the way down, and he remembered that his own maintenance department had told the pilots to do that when the PSP was slick, not cautioning about how close the rotor blades would be to the revetment walls when they did. Someone's head was going to roll, he just had not yet decided whose it would be. In a few minutes he would walk over to the company area and talk to the operations officer about making sure the pilots got the word never to do that again. Now he was down to 13 poten-

tially operational aircraft, ten really, since three were still undergoing scheduled maintenance.

Playtex's CO came out for a look at the remains of 542, too, but not
until things had settled down. Unlike most of the company, he did not
run for the flight line at the sound of the crash. Within two minutes of it
happening, one of the men came running into his office to tell him what
had happened, but he didn't jump then, either. He knew that younger,
stronger men were there on scene and would do what they needed to do
to get the situation under control without his help. Finally, he finished the
last of the immediate action paperwork on his desk, put on his rain gear
and headed across the road to see the damage. When he got there, he
looked at the wreck and had a quick word with the maintenance officer.
The gash in the revetment wall provided all the information he needed
for his phone call to the battalion CO. The battalion CO would not be
pleased, but it was too late to do anything about that now.

The maintenance chief, however, was far more practical than most people about aviation accidents, especially ones that happened on his flight
line, ones where the aircraft did not burn and no one (if you don't count
a broken leg) was hurt. While not pleased that Playtex had lost an aircraft,
he already had the quality assurance people looking over 542 for parts they
could salvage. "Parts is parts" no matter the source, as far as he was concerned, and these parts would keep the other aircraft in the air. For example, that left rear wheel on 542 just might work on 820, if he could get the
maintenance officer to allow him to remove it. Since it was obvious that
542 was a total loss, it wouldn't matter if 820's broken wheel was substi-
tuted for the good one still on 542, and that would mean another Chinook,
ready to fly!

Within an hour of the crash, the maintenance chief had talked to the
head of the newly-appointed Accident Investigation Board, a school-
trained safety officer warrant from Battalion HQ, about getting the remains of 542 removed. The warrant had been assigned to Playtex before
they moved him over to battalion, so he knew everyone at Liftmaster well.
After talking to the maintenance chief for a bit, he readily agreed that there
really wasn't any reason for the Board to look at the wreckage more than
once. No more examination would be required, because everyone would
readily agree on what happened—a perfectly good aircraft stuck its blades

into a steel revetment wall because the AC ran the forward speed trim to its lowest position as he taxied. Never mind that maintenance had recommended it as a way to handle slick PSP. He was the AC, and like the captain of a ship, whatever happened to the aircraft under his command was automatically his fault. The Accident Investigation Board would be there first thing in the morning and as soon as they had their look, the maintenance chief would be free to start stripping it of anything useable.

After the powers-that-be and all the gawkers left the wreckage and went back to their normal jobs, two of the flight engineers from other aircraft went onboard 542 and gathered up the personal things left by its last crew. Somehow Fivelson's camera had been protected from the rain and spilled hydraulic fluid up in the smashed cockpit and so was in fine shape. They carried the two pilot's soaking wet helmet bags and the KY-28s to operations. Since the door gunner was off at the hospital, the armory officer, WO1 Savick, picked up the two machine guns and took them back for cleaning. After a while, a fuel truck came and sucked all the fuel out of the tanks to reduce the risk of fire. At last, all was quiet; 542 had completed all its missions.

The rain continued to fall, oblivious to the remains of Playtex 542 and the men who had flown her. That evening the maintenance chief had a crew out with buckets of hot soapy water and degreaser to clean the PSP where the helicopter started to slide.

First thing the next morning, and after the Accident Board had their look, all the pieces of 542's rotor blades were cleaned up from where they fell.

Within three days, all the useable parts, engines, and generators, were stripped from the wreckage. Playtex 820's broken left wheel did indeed replace the wrecked aircraft's good one and vice versa.

Within five days, the hulk was lifted by a CH-54 from the Hurricanes and taken to the disposal yard at Camp Eagle. While it was being lifted, the battalion CO watched from above in one of the LOHs. He took off and followed the CH-54 until it set the load down and then flew on back over to Battalion Headquarters in Phu Bai.

Within seven days a new Chinook would arrive from the depot down south and take 542's place on Playtex's flight line.

The mission must be done.

IN PLAYTEX 506, THE AC MAKES A DECISION

As Strider flew the helicopter through the rain and fog, Alice explained to the crew the current version of his evolving plan to get back to Liftmaster that day. Instead of flying down the coast as they had discussed earlier, Alice's plan now was the same as everyone else's: fly, hover really slowly west-southwest until they came to QL1, and then follow it south until they recognized exactly where they were. Once they knew that, they would then fly/hover back on toward Liftmaster.

Based on where in the area of operation they were flying, the flaw with this plan was readily obvious to the entire crew, so much so that no one even had to say it out loud: antennas. When they had gone to Camp Evans for fuel earlier in the day, they were much further north than they would be on this trip, fewer military bases up there and correspondingly few antennas. Not true farther south, where there were lots of radio antennas between them and Phu Bai. Every one of those antennas was held up by nearly invisible guy wires, guy wires waiting for 506's rotor blades, and the crew didn't know exactly where the wires waited. Well, they did know where the antennas were, but the crew didn't know exactly where they were, as they headed vaguely toward Liftmaster. Alice was confident that they would figure it out before it became a real problem. Strider was not so sure, but since he was the copilot, he kept his mouth shut. ACs, being minor gods, are usually considered infallible. At least, they usually consider themselves infallible, even if no one else does.

"Sir, village at 3 o'clock. They don't look good" Powers called over the ICS.

It was time to go back to Phu Bai, past time really, but apparently they had one last rescue to do before they could go home. It was not one they intended to do, but when Strider turned the helicopter to the right so they could see what Powers was talking about, they discovered they had to do this one more before their day was over. As they flew around yet another small knot of people huddled together on a bit of ground not yet under water, trying to keep each other warm against the constant cold rain, something they had not encountered before happened. Instead of stoically ignoring the helicopter as it flew by, the people from this village were frantically waving anything they could to get the crew's attention, rags, hats, shirts.

From the air it looked like there were about 25 or 30 people in this group, but not all of them were standing up. Some waved from where they were laying in the mud. Were they too weak to stand up, Strider wondered?

Alice and the rest of the crew could not pass them by. Their mission was rescue, which these people needed, so instead of continuing on toward Phu Bai, Alice told Strider to turn back to help. The mission must be done. By now, well-practiced in the drill, Strider picked a spot and landed in the water as close as he could safely get to the people without blowing them away. As it turned out, the water was too shallow to float the Chinook, so their wheels were actually touching ground for a change, but the shallow water was a mixed blessing.

Yes, the aircraft was on the ground, so Powers could use the rear ramp to load and off load the people, instead of their having to use a boat to approach the Chinook. The bad part was that the villagers would have to wade through the water and knee-deep mud to get to the aircraft, something that took a fair amount of strength even in normal times. Right now it must be nearly beyond their capacity—even the young men and women appeared to be weak from hunger. The children and old people were in even worse shape, at or past the point of collapse. Apparently they had been out of food and water for some time and were about to start dying from exposure and hunger if help had not come at that moment.

Powers could see them start to struggle toward the aircraft, but it was clear that many of them would not be able to make it. Even the ones who could get to the helicopter would not be able to board without help from the crew. At Powers' signal, Crone and Crear immediately went down the ramp into the muddy water and began to walk over toward the small group of people, the first of numerous trips the two of them would make between the helicopter and the spot where the people waited.

They took the kids first, carrying two little kids at a time, one on each hip. Next they took the old people, carrying them in their arms, like a bride across the threshold. The younger villagers helped as much as they could with the children, but it was not much, since they too were at the limit of their endurance. Even so, there was no hurry in them, no panic; they were past that. Maybe they were all in shock, but exhaustion was probably the real answer. After five or six trips Crone and Crear had them all onboard.

Even with Crear and Crone's help, it took almost 20 minutes to get every-one onboard and settled in the cabin. There were only 27 of them, a light load by the standard of the last few days. Alice took the flight controls from Strider, since it was getting very difficult to see and as AC, it was his respon-sibility to get them down safely. He would do the difficult flying.

It was now dark enough in the cockpit of 506 that Strider reached up and turned on the instrument lights, in order to see the dash better. The lights came on, flooding the cockpit in a deep red, almost a startling event after the gray they had been looking at all day. He started to turn on the exterior top and bottom red anti-collision lights and their white tail-light, but Alice motioned not to. Those flashing lights would make them just too tempting a target for anyone with a weapon, and he didn't want to risk it. Besides, they knew for sure that there weren't any other aircraft flying out here right now, so a mid-air collision would not be a possibility.

Outside, darkness, which would preclude even hovering along, ad-vanced rapidly, so Alice made a decision. Given that they were in a war, it was a very difficult decision. He announced to the crew that they would find a patch of road out of the water and away from any villages and shut down for the night, alone and outside the wire. There was no time to find a safe spot for these people, so they would also stay onboard. Even if the CO had not been very specific about not bringing Vietnamese civilians onto a base, it was too late for 506 to get to one, and too dark to find one—Liftmaster, Phu Bai, Camp Eagle, Camp Evans—any of them. They couldn't even use their automatic direction finder to try to locate one, because the continuing flood had drowned out all the sending stations, shorting their electrical systems and shutting them down.

After Alice told them what they were going to do, Strider wondered if they should be afraid. A Chinook is a big, fat target, its aluminum walls offering no protection at all if the VC or NVA decided to shoot at them. Strider mused that they probably wouldn't have to worry about being taken prisoner. From what he had been told, the NVA rarely took helicopter crews prisoner. They were just too much trouble to front-line troops. It was not safe for them like it was for some farmer capturing a jet pilot float-ing down in a parachute up in North Vietnam where there were no other Americans around. Here, a missing helicopter drew many, many searchers in other helicopters and they were always within range of the Cobras and artillery. No, it was better to just kill helicopter crews on the spot, rather than risk getting spotted by other Americans looking for them.

Given that the weather made it virtually impossible to move around on the ground, Playtex 506's crew wasn't really afraid of being captured or killed by the NVA or VC. They were just wet and tired and stuck a long way from their base at Liftmaster Pad, or any base for that matter. It was time to call it a day and hope for the best.

Alice took off from the muddy spot and hovered west, looking for a place on the road to land. Just after takeoff, Alice heard Maas in Playtex 540 talking to the Artillery Clearance Agency. He called Maas and asked him to relay his plan on to operations, which Maas did without commenting. Maas was probably thinking, "Are you out of your fucking mind," but he wasn't going to criticize another AC right now. In a couple minutes, Maas relayed operation's acknowledgement and request that Alice check in with the Artillery Clearance Agency one last time when they were safe on the ground. He should call the artillery people first thing in the morning, too, for directions on what comes next.

It didn't take long to find a landing spot this time, a good thing since it was now dark enough that they had to use the landing light to see the spot where they intended to touch down. It was a stretch of paved road, maybe 200 yards long, and not under water, being maybe five feet higher than the surrounding terrain. In the gloom of the immediate darkness, it looked like a long, thin island in the middle of a huge lake, since both ends of it ended in water. Even so, it was the best they were going to do tonight.

Alice used the last moments of daylight to fly around the dry spot in widening circles until he was satisfied that there were no villages within at least a couple of miles. Even the one village they did see was dark, like everything else around them. Their makeshift LZ appeared to be well and truly abandoned to the floodwater.

Satisfied, Alice landed the Chinook on the road and they shut the aircraft down for the last time of the day. While he was still in the air, Alice gave the Artillery Clearance Agency their position as close as he could make it out. He was probably off by a few miles from where they actually were, but it was close enough for a search if things went badly. He told them that he would contact them on takeoff the next morning and requested they pass the information on up to Playtex and battalion operations. The artillery clearance people acknowledged Alice's request and said that they would pass on the information to the 159th ASHB. They did not say "good luck" before they signed off, but they were probably thinking it.

Normally, all passengers were off loaded for start and shut down, but neither Alice nor Powers said a word about getting them out of the helicopter before they shut the aircraft down. It just did not seem right to make these people get out into the rain again after what they had been through. It got very quiet as the auxiliary power plant came off-line and the big rotor blades spun slowly to a stop.

Taking his helmet off, Strider could no longer hear the rain hitting the aircraft's skin, but since the noise of the aircraft's transmissions and engines destroyed your hearing, helmet or no helmet, he probably would not have heard it even if it was pouring outside. He didn't really care about the rain now. All day long, for the last two days he had been damp, but not cold, too busy really to think about being cold, but now in the stillness of the cockpit, he felt cold for the first time. His right leg was wet, his flight suit trouser leg soaked where the rain leaked in around the window, and now it felt cold against his skin. Odd, Strider thought, how most of the people in the back made no sound at all. The only sounds from them Strider could hear were one baby crying and a couple of little kids sniffling.

RO1N—REMAIN OVER ONE NIGHT

In the cabin, Powers took stock of what they had left in terms of food and water. Not much, was the answer. There was one five-gallon can of water, a full case of C rats and a couple of individual meals, not enough for the "feeding of the 5,000," but enough to feed something to these exhausted people and the crew tonight.

After talking it over with Alice, Powers looked to see if he could figure out who was the leader of this group of people. He picked the oldest looking man, but that man pointed Powers to another bigger and younger man. Powers motioned for him to come to the ramp, which he did. Powers took three meals out of the C ration case for the crew to split, leaving nine for the people. The man took the C rat box without comment and passed it to a woman standing behind him. The crew all had at least a canteen full of water each, so Powers handed the man the last five-gallon can of water. He took it again without comment, passed it to another man and then, to Powers surprise, made motions with his hands indicating that the people wanted out of the aircraft.

When Powers told Alice that they wanted to leave, Alice replied that if they wanted to go back out in the rain, let them go, so Powers lowered the ramp. Following their leader, the villagers filed out of the cabin and into the rainy night, young helping the old, the bigger children carrying other, smaller children. He thought that perhaps they felt the Chinook was just too tempting a target for the VC or NVA, and would feel safer outside than inside.

The few minutes they had spent out of the rain seemed to have rejuvenated the villagers, somehow making them stronger. Maybe it had given them hope that they would survive this after all. In a few minutes, they were all clear of the aircraft, leaving the cabin as empty as if they had never been there. A few minutes after that, Powers stepped off the ramp and looked after them, but they were gone into the night.

Powers went back inside the cabin and set Crone and Crear to work, putting the troop seats down so that the three without stretchers would have a place to sleep in the Boeing Hilton. Troop seats made a very uncomfortable bed because the metal cross bars tended to dig into your ribs, but they were better than sleeping on the cabin deck. When they had finished, Powers dug down in his magic box of miscellaneous parts and came up with a bundle of rags, which he gave to Crone and Crear to dry themselves off a bit after their wade in the mud helping that last group of people.

Strider was stiff when he finally climbed out of the right cockpit seat and moved through the companionway into the cabin. Even though the cabin roof was 6'4" from the deck, Strider still touched his head on it if he didn't bend over, so he walked hunched over back to where the crewmen were gathered. He saw that both the crew chief and door gunner had taken off their boots and socks. They had already scraped off as much mud as they could, using a screwdriver as a tool, but that didn't do anything about the wetness of the boots.

Strider was surprised to hear Crone laugh, until he saw that Crear had pulled three pair of socks out of his helmet bag and was holding them up to the other two crewmen. He had seen this time coming and was ready for it. Powers also laughed as he took off his boots. Dry socks are always a luxury in war zones and all three of them looked happier, boots off, feet covered in dry socks, taking a moment before whatever came next, to relax. Crear was a hero, destined for great things, and they were deeply in his debt, at least momentarily.

Strider walked straight back out through the ramp to take a piss and stretch out some. He didn't stay long, it was too cold out in the rain. As he came back inside the cabin, the thought occurred to him that of all the people they had picked up and moved to higher ground, not one had made any kind of gesture of thanks. Maybe it was Vietnamese culture not to, he didn't know, but it still seemed strange to him. Maybe you lose face if you thank someone. Still, someone takes risks to bring you safety and give you food, water, yet you don't thank them? He decided that in the end, the only reason you do anything for anyone is that you want to do it. Never expect anything beyond personal satisfaction and you won't ever be disappointed. Besides, rescuing these people was Playtex 506's mission and the mission must be done.

But then, why would the villagers thank these foreigners? You, foreigner, are here today, knowing that you are in the right and making things so much better for the people who live here by what you do. At least in your mind you are. But you are gone tomorrow and things are the same as they were 100 or 300 years ago: the rice, fishing, governments that want taxes and young men for their wars. Nothing much changes for the people here, foreigner, no matter what you do.

Alice decided that they would not use any lights inside the aircraft now that it was dark. No point in making themselves an even easier target than they already were. Lights might be just too tempting to a sniper looking for a long-range kill or a bored VC looking to get lucky or some kid with a rifle he picked up somewhere. And, of course, they couldn't heat their C rations, because an open cooking flame, even a heat tab, inside the cabin of an aircraft is never a good idea. They could go outside into the rain to light heat tabs, they burn just fine in light rain, but rather than getting wetter than they already were they decided that they would eat their C rations cold. Again.

But tonight, even cold, the C rations tasted better than they normally did. Comradely warmth, perhaps, from sharing a meal with friends and colleagues, with whom you had just been sharing great danger, or was it a feeling that, for a change, they were actually accomplishing something, something just beyond bringing the weapons of war to the mountains? Strider didn't know, but the C rations tasted good that evening. Alice suspended the rule about smoking inside the shutdown aircraft, so Strider and Powers lit up, Strider his pipe and Powers a cigarette from the C ration four pack he had just opened, both leaving a pleasant cloud inside the Chinook's cabin. Somehow the smoke seemed to warm the inside of the cabin a little, too.

As often happened, the conversation among the crew swung from subject to subject, until it settled on what they were going to do after they got home. Some of them wanted to go to school; Strider, for example, was considering college, followed by law school. Powers was going to stay in the Army. He loved the machines and thought he would make an excellent maintenance chief someday. Crear and Crone were definitely not going to stay in the Army, but both agreed that going to school to pick up an Airframes and Power Plan Certificate from the FAA would be a good thing. That way they could stay in aviation and make some serious money at it.

Alice was more thoughtful than usual. Finally, when it was his turn, he said he would like to do medevac, but for civilians. Helicopters could get the wounded in Vietnam to a hospital much quicker than an ambulance could get people in a car wreck to a hospital back home. Why not use helicopters there, too?

Eventually, the conversation just died. They were too tired to go on with it for too long, so they called it a night.

"The Boeing Hilton," a.k.a. Playtex 506, was cold and damp, but they were in better conditions than that night's rescued Vietnamese were in, because it sheltered the five of them from the rain. Powers and Crone left two rows of troop seats on the starboard side of the cabin folded up, and placed their stretchers there to try to sleep. Alice picked out a section of troop seats on the port side and lay down, seemingly asleep in a moment. Crear sat at his normal duty station by the left-hand machine gun; he wasn't going to lie down. He ate his C rats in silence, looking to be deep in thought as he sat staring into the darkness. Strider tried to lay down on the troop seats, but one of the cross bars kept digging into his ribs and another into his hip, so he gave up. He decided the troop seats were just too uncomfortable and elected to climb back into the cockpit instead. He rotated his seat as far as he could to get some tilt to it and tried to get comfortable, but it was a losing battle.

Crear was not a former grunt, but as door gunner in this crew, he volunteered to take the first shift standing watch while the rest of the crew tried to sleep. Before everyone stretched out to sleep he re-mounted the right-hand door gun, just in case, and made sure the left-hand one was also operational before he took up his sentry post. He locked and loaded both of them so that if they were needed, all he had to do was pull the trigger to send rounds down range.

CHAPTER FOURTEEN

OCTOBER 30, 1970

DAY THREE: PLAYTEX 506

Strider must have dozed off up in the cockpit, wet and cold as he was, because it was just starting to get light outside when he opened his eyes. When he looked back through the companionway into the cabin, he could see Crear still at his post at the left door gun. He had not awakened anyone else to relieve him, because he knew that of the five of them, Crear's job was the least critical, that is, the least critical as long as they weren't under fire. He took the load so that the others could rest. Good man, Crear, Playtex 506's door gunner, Strider thought.

At this moment Strider needed three things. First, he needed to get out of this seat and stretch. His 6'4" frame was just about seized up solid from sleeping in the seat. Second, he really needed a smoke, the nicotine from his last hit on his pipe long gone. Third, and possibly most critical at this moment, he needed to pee.

As he walked outside through the open ramp to take care of the most pressing need, he could see no sign of the people they had dropped off here last night. Even any tracks they may have made were gone, the mud now smooth after still more rain over night. It was as if they never existed. As he filled his pipe from his tobacco pouch, he noticed that he was nearly out of tobacco, with perhaps enough remaining to fill it twice more. From now until they got back to Liftmaster he would either have to take it easy, smoke the cigarettes that came in C rations, quit smoking, or bum cigarettes from the crew, since Alice didn't smoke.

The rest of the crew was up too and moving around in the gray morning light. Powers had performed a miracle by coming up with another three C rations they could split from his personal, extra private, hiding place in the aircraft's cabin. They wouldn't start the day hungry—cold and wet maybe—but not hungry. As they sat there in the 506's cabin once more eating cold C rations, Powers noticed that the rain had finally stopped. Crone got up and walked out the back of the Chinook carrying materials for making coffee. He started up four small fires using heat tabs in C ration cans modified to use as stoves, and began heating water in four field expedient cups, also made from C ration cans. He didn't make five because he knew that Crear didn't like coffee. The coffee was instant from the C ration sundry packages and nasty by most definitions, but it tasted very good that late October morning.

It was strange, the five of them sitting there in the cabin of Playtex 506, drinking coffee in the middle of nowhere, Vietnam, with not a soul except the aircraft's crew to be seen. Outside, they could see only water, their little "island" cut off from everything else. As Strider smoked his pipe and drank his coffee he was pretty sure it was a unique situation, one that would not be repeated during his tour.

It was still heavily overcast, but the fog was diminished from yesterday, giving visibility of at least a mile or two, the first time that had happened in at least four days. The clouds looked higher too, so they quickly finished eating, gave the helicopter a hurried pre-flight inspection and fired up the engines. Alice made the takeoff, the aircraft climbing smoothly into the morning sky.

The mystery of what happened to the last villagers they evacuated was solved as they climbed out. What had appeared in the near darkness to be an island of road was not that, instead it was more of a peninsula. The villagers had somehow recognized where they were when the helicopter had landed last night, because Strider could now see them camped on a bit of high ground, maybe 300 yards from where they exited the aircraft. There were a couple of small huts standing there and they had sheltered through the night in them. As Playtex 506 flew past, Strider could see small cooking fires burning. He wished them well.

They were able to get to 500 feet as Alice headed the aircraft back toward the west and Phu Bai. As he leveled off, he called the Artillery Clearance Agency as operations had instructed. The artillery people told him that Playtex Operations had instructed all aircraft to come on back to Lift-master, the rescue operations were over and there were missions waiting for them.

NORMALCY

As they flew west, they went over one of the villages they had evacuated the day before. Even though the water had receded very little, if at all, it was obvious that at least it was no longer rising. Strider could see that some of the people they had evacuated had made their way back to what was left of their homes, since there was smoke from cooking fires coming up from some of the huts that had not completely gone under water. One or two of them might have looked up as the Chinook passed overhead, but no one waved. It seemed that to the people who lived there, things were back to normal, and if the helicopters came again, they probably would not be bringing good things, like food and water, but instead, just soldiers and the trouble soldiers normally bring with them.

The clouds continued to rise, so Alice climbed the aircraft a little higher, up to 1,500 feet. Visibility was still limited to less than two miles, but it felt good to be farther away from the trees. Even so, the world looked a little strange to the crew from 1,500 feet, after all those days of hovering around at 300 or 400 feet. It was almost disorienting. Then, over the ICS everyone in the crew heard Powers yell, "Shit!"

Something was wrong. Instantly, both pilot's eyes went to the caution panel and cockpit gauges, but everything there was normal. None of the caution lights lit up, either. Alice asked Powers over the ICS what the problem was, but got no answer. Strider adjusted the rear view mirror so that he could see down the companionway back into the cabin. When he did, he saw Powers sitting on the cabin deck, hurriedly removing his right boot.

In a minute Powers came up to the companionway and handed the boot to Strider. Sticking in the sole of the boot, just at the front of the arch was a bullet, probably an AK-47 round by the look of it. At 1,500 feet it was just about spent, but had enough force left in it to go through the outer aircraft skin and the cabin floor before hitting Powers in the boot. There it stopped, luckily for him. He was not really hurt and would not get a Purple Heart out of it because even though the bullet was hot enough to burn his foot a little, it did not break the skin. Powers wanted to leave the bullet in the boot, but Alice told him to pull it out and put the boot back on, which Powers did. He stuck the bullet in his pocket for "show and tell" later back at Liftmaster. The other flight engineers would get a kick out of this story. Strider thought to himself, "Fivelson, Mr. PAO, would love this story. He could even take a picture of Powers holding the boot with the bullet put back into the sole and pointing to the hole in the aircraft's deck, before he sent it off to Powers' hometown newspaper. Maybe he'd even get it published in *Stars and Stripes*." After Powers had both boots back on, he went to the back of the aircraft to check for further damage, like he always did when they took hits. There was none, just that one small hole in the aircraft floor.

It was a definite end to the rescue mission. It was quite clear to all that the war was no longer suspended. It was back on.

Strider's view of the brown water from the Chinook's cockpit was no longer exciting—it was just a sea of muddy brown water, broken by trees here and there. It was time to forget rescues and return to what Chinooks normally do. The people who lived down there were on their own again. The fire support bases needed ammo, fuel, water, and food.

The mission must be done.

CHAPTER FIFTEEN

OCTOBER 31, 1970—THE AFTERMATH

THE RLOS

Playtex's CO had the XO, the operations officer, the maintenance officer, and the S-1 officer in his office. All four had cups of coffee fresh from the CO's personal coffee pot, much better quality than mess hall coffee, since the grounds came from his private stash, not the Army issue stuff. The four RLO staff members were quiet, not sure why the CO had called them there. It was the first time since the major took command of Playtex that he had done so. Normally, they gave their reports to the XO, who in turn briefed the CO.

"Well," the major began, "We rescued a lot of people, but it cost us. I want you all to tell me face-to-face how we are doing. Let's start with you, maintenance officer, give us all a run down on the status of the aircraft."

"We've got one aircraft destroyed, one with some structural damage that's got to be looked at even though we have replaced the left wheel, and then we've got one that has holes all over the aft pylon and ramp from where the APU blew up. Those two are going to take a few days to get back into shape. We still haven't figured out why 820's number one engine is stuck at idle, but the Tech Rep thinks he knows the answer and we should have it back up tomorrow afternoon. Three others are down for scheduled maintenance, so we've got nine available for missions right now. Of those nine, three are going to be going in for heavy scheduled maintenance in the next 20 flight hours, but two of the three that are in now should be out by then. Bottom line, we should have nine aircraft available at all times for the next week. All in all, I guess we should be grateful that it's not worse," the maintenance officer said.

"Operations, what's it look like from battalion?" the CO continued.

"Sir, it looks like we are going to be going heavy for the next week. All the weather got things pretty well behind and division is going to want to catch up quickly. I'd say they'll want us to launch six to eight a day for at least five days. From what the maintenance officer just said, we should be able to handle that. I have heard rumors of a large operation coming soon up north, but they are only rumors right now. I will let you know when I have anything more solid.

Our crews are in pretty good shape, flight time wise. Some of the pilots are up around 90 hours in the last 30 days, but no one is pushing 110 hours, yet."

"S-1, how are things coming for replacements?"

"Sir, we are in good shape there, too. We are at 95% strength right now on the enlisted side and that's the best we have been since I've been here. Officer strength is at 90%, not bad either. Several of the warrants are getting short, but that shouldn't be a problem since we have two coming up for aircraft commander checks soon. Battalion tells me we've three newbies inbound from SERTC next week. The only unplanned loss we've had recently was the supply officer to that medical problem. Also, one of our best ACs, Alice, is short, but he has another month. We should be able to get at least another two weeks out of him. Cobb is the next to leave in two weeks," the S-1 Office replied.

"XO, how are things in general? Any problem areas we all should know about?"

The XO hesitated a moment before replying, "Yes, Sir, there are. Cobb may still have two weeks left, but he is also done flying, as far as I am concerned. I've flown with him a lot and I'm sure that the stress has gotten to him, so, I am hereby recommending to operations that he not fly any more as an AC, or for that matter, even as copilot. He needs some rest before he leaves. I am also concerned about his drinking. If he doesn't get that under control, he's going to have a lot of problems when he gets back home. We need to let him spool all the way down now, but somehow at the same time, get his drinking under control. Not really sure how to do that, but

I'm thinking of putting him in operations and working him hard."

The XO continued, "In that same hootch we've got Steiner. I looked at his flight hours record and he has been flying way too much. When he hit the revetment, he had around 50 flight hours in the preceding six or seven days. He was within the 30-day limit of 90 hours, but he was still too tired to be flying in all that bad weather. I'm not blaming operations; Steiner himself should have said something if he was getting too tired and he didn't. I do recommend that he not fly as AC any more, although he would make a good copilot for some of our newer ACs. He only has about seven weeks left now and he may be gun shy at this point, so let's take the pressure of flying as AC off him."

The operations officer chimed in, "Concur on both Cobb and Steiner. We have enough ACs to support missions right now, provided we don't lose anyone else. Also speaking of that hootch, at least Strider is ready for his AC check. Alice gave him a good report after the incident in the fuel pits. I will recommend him to the SIP (Standardization Instructor Pilot— the senior instructor) as soon as he gets another 25 hours in the air. That will put him over the top for hours in-country."

The CO just listened to them. He didn't need to say anything, because he already knew everything that his staff had just told him. They might think he just sat in his office, but really he listened everywhere and watched everything. Like he did with the warrants and their flying, he trusted the RLO staff to do their jobs, but he was always checking. There was no point in saying anything about Steiner taxiing into the revetment; the maintenance officer had already corrected that problem. No one would make that mistake again. No point in saying anything about Cobb either. Everyone knew that, too.

As for how things were going with the warrants, the CO often talked to the battalion operations officer to see how the missions were going from his standpoint. He always got the same answer: the missions were done as scheduled, with no complaints from division. This meant that the warrants were completing the missions just fine, exactly the right answer. It was his job as CO to see that it stayed that way.

With his RLOs, he watched for himself as things progressed day by day in each of their areas. He had no reason to complain about any of them. They all accepted and implemented his philosophy of keeping administrative pressure off the warrant's back as much as possible, keeping them free to fly, and that's the way it should be. One or two of the commissioned officers might do well in the Army, but mostly they had already reached as high as they were going to go. As the war ended, the Army was going to get much smaller, leaving room only for officers with the highest qualifications, like West Point diplomas. There was no hope for any of the Penny Postcard Lieutenants; they would all be reverted to their previous rank as warrants or be discharged as soon as they got back home. That was all right, most of them wanted to go back to being civilians as soon as possible anyway. As for himself, the CO was finished. He would retire as soon as he got back to the States.

The sergeant major kept him up to speed on the situation with the enlisted men. The drug and alcohol use did not please him, but the CO was smart enough to know that there was nothing he could do about it either. As long as the missions got done, all would be well. Always the mission, but sometimes he wondered what would come next for these men when the missions were done and they returned home. Life was going to be very hard for some of them, recovering from their problems here if they could, only to encounter new ones there.

Still, he had no complaints. The men of Playtex, RLOs, warrants, and enlisted, all did their jobs well and that made it easy and gratifying to be the CO.

"XO" the CO began, "I want every man, officer and enlisted, who flew in the rescue operations to get a Single Mission Air Medal for it, so make sure the Awards and Decorations officer gets right on it. And, even though he fell and broke his leg afterwards, our maintenance warrant should get a medal, too, the Army Commendation Medal or some such."

The XO nodded in confirmation and wrote it down in his notebook. He would make sure there was an awards ceremony for the aircrews.

The major asked if there were any more comments, there were not. The CO asked no further questions of his staff, nor did he make any further comments. Instead, he just thanked them and dismissed them. They filed out of his office to return to their jobs. Playtex would do fine.

The missions would be done.

THE ROOMMATES, PART TWO

STRIDER

When the missions were done and his aircraft was back in its revetment at Liftmaster, Strider was well and truly ready to call it a day. It was nearly dark when he finally got back to the hootch. He might have been 21 years old, but at that moment, he felt at least 60. The beauty of actually being 21 instead of being 60 is that with a good night's sleep, you are 21 again and ready for the next round. But now he was tired, so very tired and wet and dirty from no shower in three days. He was tired enough that he wasn't hungry, even though the C ration he had for breakfast was the only thing he had to eat all day. Neither of his roommates was there when he came in, they were probably at the Officers' Club. It was apparent that they had not been cooking that night, since there were no leftovers on the table, nor were there dinner smells coming from the hootch's backroom kitchen.

Strider dumped his flight gear on the poncho covering his bed, hung his wet rain jacket on the hook by his closet, and his holster on the hook next to his desk. All the things in his pockets went on his desk: his wallet, the checklist from his lower left trouser pocket, his pipe and tobacco from his lower right pocket. He sat and took his boots and socks off, leaving them both there on the floor beside his chair. He walked into the back room and began to run the hot water into the washing machine tub for a shower. He was tempted to fill the bathtub instead, but the thought of all the dirt mixed in with the water stopped him again. A nice hot shower would be fine, pure luxury, as always. He stripped off the rest of his clothes and dropped them on the floor next to his boots. Tomorrow he would do laundry, but tonight he just wanted to get clean. He wrapped a towel around himself, walked into the back room, and started to fill the washing machine's tub.

As he waited for the washing machine tub to fill, he looked in the mirror and saw three days' worth of beard. He ran some of the hot water into the sink, splashed his face with it and shaved. It made him feel cleaner already. When the tub was full he turned the washing machine to its drain cycle and climbed into the tub. He stood for a moment letting the hot water wash over him before he soaped up. He washed his hair, too, trying to get as clean as he could before bed. Climbing out and drying off, he saw that he had timed it just about right since the washing machine tub was nearly empty. Walking back into the front of the hootch he hung up the towel on the rack just above his bed before taking a light blue sweatshirt his wife had mailed him out from the closet. He put on the sweatshirt and a pair of white jeans, his only civilian clothes here in Vietnam. His flip-flops would serve as shoes for the rest of the evening. The wet clothes and boots went into the drying closet. He would deal with them tomorrow.

Now that he was clean, Strider decided he was hungry after all. He went back into the pantry and took down a can of C ration peaches and got a soft drink from the fridge. Thus equipped he went back to his desk and sat down. That was when he noticed the pile of seven letters on his desk. They were all from his wife, except for the one from his mother. One of his roommates must have dropped them off while he was in the shower. He started to read them, but was just too tired to both write a letter and read six letters. He wasn't on the schedule tomorrow so he could take care of both in the morning. He ate the peaches and drank the coke, enjoying the silence of the room.

Before he got into bed Strider loaded his pipe and lit up. As he sucked in the smoke, he thought about what he had learned about the Vietnamese people over the last three days, and decided the answer was very little. He learned that 12-year-old Vietnamese boys were just like 12-year old boys everywhere. Give them a chance to play with a big toy, like "flying" a helicopter, and they will jump at it. He learned that Vietnamese people love their children, just like all people do. He also learned that, at least in this case, Vietnamese people do not express thanks like the people back home do. It seemed to him that they just accepted what came, resigned that they couldn't change the outcome. Maybe rescuing them from the flood left them with good will in their hearts toward the Americans, but he doubted it. The overall impression he had was that the country people would rather the Americans just went away and left them to whatever fate had in store. Strider wondered if anything they did here made any difference in the long run, but he didn't contemplate it for too long, as it was too deep a question for a tired 21-year old.

On the morning of November 1, 1970, Strider's eyes clicked open at 0430 hours. He had not bothered to look at the crew list for that day, so he didn't know if he was on the schedule or not. He hoped he was not.

Was the duty clerk coming in to wake them up? No, no one was coming into the hootch, it was just his conditioning taking over: 0430 hours, time to get ready for the day's missions.

When Strider opened his eyes again it was 0630 hours. He could hear the sound of the Chinooks taking off from Liftmaster to begin the day's missions. Turning over, he could see both Cobb and Steiner still in their bunks. He had been so tired he had not heard them come in. Either that or they were being considerate and had been extra quiet. In either case, it looked like they were all three getting the day off, something that hadn't happened in a while. The operations officer must have figured they really needed it.

Returning the consideration his roommates had given him, Strider was as quiet as he could be as he dressed in a clean flight suit and dry boots before walking over to the mess hall. It was still heavily overcast, but at least it wasn't raining, a nice change from the last six weeks. The water standing around the officer's area looked like it had gone down since yesterday.

Strider had the six letters from his wife tucked in his flight suit pocket for reading while he drank his morning coffee. He would write one to her and date it yesterday first thing after he got to his desk. Today's letter he would write before he hit the bed this evening, so that she would know he thought of her every day. After breakfast he would go to the S-4 and get started in earnest on his new real job, a sad fact of life for all officers, warrant or commissioned.

COBB

Immediately after the meeting with the CO, the XO sent one of the S-1 clerks to tell Cobb to come to his office. The clerk found Cobb in his hootch but, Cobb being Cobb, he figured sometime before 1600 would be fine. He wasn't on the flight schedule that day, but then he hadn't been since the APU blew up on him. When he finally did stroll into the XO's office that afternoon, Cobb was prepared for a blow up, but was surprised when, far from blowing up, the XO just smiled, waved him into a seat, and offered him coffee.

"Jerry, you've done a great job here, but you are done flying effective immediately. We've got too many new ACs for short-timers like you to hog the stick time. What I want you to do now is help get operations squared away. Now, I know you think they're all assholes and out to get the pilots they don't like, but what's really wrong is that they are overwhelmed. So, get your ass in there this very afternoon and get started. Also, figure out who's going to take over the Glee Club when you depart. Oh, yeah, and turn over your song book to whoever that is so that they can get some practice before the next meeting."

As he spoke, he watched Cobb to check his reaction. He wouldn't swear to it, but there may have been a look of relief flash across his face. He did not mention Cobb's drinking. There was no point: Cobb knew. He had always known he was drinking too much, but just couldn't do anything about it. Or rather, didn't want to do anything about it. Two 1,000 flight hour tours in Vietnam only a year apart, with instructing at Fort Rucker in the middle, had burnt him out. Cobb knew that, too.

Cobb drank his coffee in silence. When he finally spoke he said: Yes, he would help operations out. Yes, he was glad there would be no more 0430 wakeups followed by ten straight hours in the air. No, he would not miss the missions. Mentally he added: No, he will not stop drinking. Slow it down a little, perhaps, but stop? Not just now, not yet. His mind was going through how he would end his tour in Playtex. It would not necessarily be in the way the XO expected it would. Much better a bang than a whimper.

After a week of working in operations, it was clear there was nothing left for Cobb to do, so he was relieved of all duties by the XO for his last week in Playtex. On the first morning after his release he was sitting in a chair on the patio of the Officers' Club, next to the ping pong table, at 0700 hours. He was wearing starched jungle fatigues, not a flight suit, and looking very military, complete with a fresh haircut. Under his chair was a packed duffle bag.

Strider found this all a bit odd as he walked by toward breakfast at the mess hall, but didn't say anything. Jerry was, after all, Jerry. Thirty minutes later, as Strider came back from breakfast, Cobb was no longer in the chair. He was now sitting on the ground with his back up against the Club wall. The duffle bag was leaning against the opposite wall.

"Jerry, what are you doing?" Strider asked.

"I'm practicing going home, so I get it right when the time comes. Before, I was waiting at Phu Bai Operations for the C-130 to Cam Ranh.

Now, I am on the C-130 and we are headed south." Cobb replied.

Strider just smiled and continued walking toward the S-4 and the dreaded real job. Cobb was truly just being Cobb. At lunch time, Strider walked by the patio again and there was Cobb, still in the jungle fatigues, but now with a beer in his hand as he laughed and talked with a couple of the other pilots. Before Strider could ask he said, "I'm at the holding station at Cam Ranh waiting on the Freedom Bird (a charter Stretch DC-8 that flew the soldiers to and from the States)."

After work at the S-4 was done for the day, Strider stopped by out of curiosity to see where Cobb was in his journey. This time he was wearing his dress green uniform trousers with a long sleeved khaki shirt and tie, and under the chair he was sitting in was a small AWOL bag (like a gym bag used by soldiers to carry small things on a trip). His dress green coat was folded neatly and resting on top of the AWOL bag. He had a soft drink in hand to go with the brown paper bag lunch scrounged from the mess hall. He was eating it with gusto as he sat there. "Don't tell me, you're on the Freedom Bird, headed toward Seattle." Strider said. Cobb just smiled and nodded in agreement.

After supper, Cobb was not to be seen on the patio, but as he went by the bar, Strider heard his voice. Sticking his head in, he saw Cobb, in full dress green uniform, complete with tie and jacket on, drinking a beer with the other pilots. "Jerry, where are you now?" he asked.

"I'm in the Officers' Club at McCord Air Force Base." Cobb said. "I've got a few hours to kill before I catch my plane back to Alabama, so I thought I would relax some."

After he finished his letter home for the day, Strider walked over to the mailbox to post it and there sat Cobb in his chair by the ping pong table. He had a full cocktail glass of what appeared to be whiskey on the rocks in his hand. He was wearing civilian clothes, slacks and a dress shirt this time, with the AWOL bag again under his chair. "I'm on the plane from Seattle to Dothan, Alabama." Cobb said helpfully.

Before calling it a night, Strider went to the Officers' Club one last time to check the flight schedule for tomorrow. He was not on the schedule, but there was Cobb, in the Club, drunk and happy, this time wearing cowboy boots, blue jeans, and a checkered shirt. Seeing Strider he yelled, "I'm home!"

The next morning as Strider walked to the mess hall at 0700 hours, there was Cobb, again wearing starched jungle fatigues, not a flight suit. Under his chair was the same packed duffle bag just as it had been yesterday. For the next five days he did exactly the same thing all day long, ending the day "at home." On the sixth day when Strider returned from flying, Cobb's portion of the hootch was empty and CW2 Martin Jerry Cobb was gone. Strider never saw him again. The Phu Bai Glee Club never met again, either.

STEINER

Steiner had seen it coming. As he stood contemplating the wreckage of Playtex 542 there by the revetment on Liftmaster Pad, he saw it quite clearly. When the operations officer sent the duty clerk to fetch him on the morning of the 31st of October, he knew in his heart what was coming next. The operations officer told him his AC papers had been pulled by the CO. It was just what he expected, even if he was not expecting what came next: Steiner was not through flying with Playtex after all. Being as gentle as he could, the operations officer explained that his job now would be to help get new ACs fully capable of handling the missions confidently and professionally, like Steiner always had for the last ten months. He was just too experienced and too good at it to lose him all together, so while he was not being made an instructor, he was being made a steadying influence. He would continue to fly until he had two weeks left, like everyone else did. Steiner was a bit flattered with the thought, since he figured night duty officer at battalion awaited him for his final seven weeks.

After he left operations, the depression that was beginning to build in him dissipated and Steiner again became "Super Jew." Then again, he understood that no one would pay any more attention to his self-proclaimed "Super Jew" status now than they did before, but he also knew that the crash had not removed all the confidence the senior RLOs had in him. He also knew the SIP (Senior Instructor Pilot) had put in a good word for him, so the warrants still trusted him, too. All things considered, it was a very good feeling.

Steiner, too, saw what Cobb was doing in his "practicing going home" routine and got a good laugh out of it: one more chance to yank the RLO's chain before he left. Cobb would be the odd one to the end, but that was

OK. At least it wasn't a mustache that resembled nose hairs this time. Cobb had survived two tours flying helicopters in Vietnam and that gave him all the rights he needed to enjoy the time remaining in Playtex by being just as strange as he wanted to be.

Now that he no longer had the pressure of being an AC weighing down on him, Steiner contemplated what he wanted to do after he finished his tour in Vietnam. Like Strider, he was "career indefinite" and would not be getting out of the Army when he went home. He went to the S-1 and talked to the XO about duty station options. Afterwards, he thought Europe would be the best choice, Germany for sure. Pilots were always needed in Germany. Maybe there, he could quit flying Chinooks and get into something smaller and more agile, OH-58 Kiowas, perhaps.

THE LOCALS

Sixty miles to the north of Liftmaster Pad, the villagers who had been evacuated by Playtex 506 and the other aircraft of the 159th ASHB were getting started on their day, too. They were making their way through the mud back to what was left of their homes, carrying with them the few things they had managed to bring when the helicopters came. They had no way of knowing how bad things were back in their villages until they got there to see for themselves. It really didn't matter, though. Life goes on and, as the water receded, it was time to start rebuilding.

In time they knew the Americans would recede, too. Whatever storm came after that they would endure and rebuild again.

EPILOGUE: THEY STILL LIVE

The everyday dangers that the men of Playtex and the rest of the helicopter crews in Vietnam faced were very real. According to the Vietnam Helicopter Pilots Association, of the 11,827 helicopters deployed to Vietnam, 5,086, or nearly 43%, were destroyed in combat or accidents. Of the 58,272 names on the Vietnam Memorial Wall, 4,914 are helicopter pilots and crewmen. During the company's time in Vietnam from 1969 to 1971, Playtex lost six aircraft, two in combat and four in accidents. In three of the losses the entire crew died—five aircrew men in two of the aircraft and six in the other. All of them, except one, were warrants or enlisted men.

Every man whose name was used in this no-fighting war story is dead. All but one of the men died in helicopter crashes, the exception dying in the crash of his personal, small fixed-wing aircraft. Some of the men were killed in combat, some of the men died in aviation mishaps, and four of the men died in crashes after surviving the Vietnam War. Always remember that no matter where or when or how they died, all of them died in the service of their country. They must be honored for that.

While they may be physically dead, I read somewhere once that people are only really dead when the living no longer say their names, so all the names used in this story are the names of real people with whom I served in Vietnam during 1970 and 1971. I have tried to render their personalities and deeds as closely as I can to how I remember them. Some of them were close to me, others I barely knew, but I count all of them as friends. I hope that, by using their names in this war story, maybe they will stay alive in some sense for a little longer, even if it's only in the hearts of those who loved them.

Every event in this story actually happened, just not necessarily in the order I wrote them, or to the men credited with them. Since this is a war story, not a history, the men named may or may not have done what I attribute to them, although in most cases I got events as close to correct as I could.

Please say their names out loud as you read them from the list below. James Taylor, Marvin Leonard, Barry Fivelson, John Powers, Don Crone, and Willis Crear all died when their Chinook, Playtex 506, was shot down by the NVA in Laos on February 15, 1971.

JAMES HARRY TAYLOR, 2LT
SERVICE DETAILS

Last Rank: Second Lieutenant

Last Unit: 1970–1971, 101st Airborne Division

Last Service Branch: Aviation

Service Years: 1970–1971

HOME STATE / YEAR OF BIRTH
Oroville, California / 1946

CASUALTY INFORMATION
Casualty Date: February 15, 1971

Cause: Hostile, Died while Missing

Location: Laos

Location of Interment: Arlington National Cemetery, Arlington, VA

Reason: Air Loss, Crash-Land

Conflict: Cold War

Wall / Plot Coordinates: 05W 109

UNIT ASSIGNMENTS
1970–1971, 1981: 159th Aviation Battalion/C Company
1970–1971: 101st Airborne Division

COMBAT AND OPERATIONS HISTORY
1962–1975: Vietnam War

MARVIN MAURICE LEONARD, CW2
SERVICE DETAILS
Last Rank: Chief Warrant Officer 2

Last Service Branch: Warrant Officer (pre-2004)

Last Primary MOS: 100C-Cargo Helicopter

Last MOS Group: Aviation (Officer)

Last Unit: 1971–Present, POW/MIA

Service Years: 1953–1971

HOME STATE / YEAR OF BIRTH
Grand Rapids, Michigan / 1936

CASUALTY INFORMATION
Casualty Date: February 15, 1971

Cause: Hostile, Died while Missing   *Reason:* Air Loss, Crash-Land

Location: Laos   *Conflict:* Vietnam War

UNIT ASSIGNMENTS
1970–1971: 159th Aviation Battalion/C Company
1970–1971: 101st Airborne Division
1971–Present, POW/MIA

COMBAT AND OPERATIONS HISTORY
1970–1971: Vietnam War/Counteroffensive Phase VII Campagn

BARRY FRANK FIVELSON, WO1
SERVICE DETAILS

Last Rank: Warrant Officer 1   *Last Service Branch:* Aviation

Last Primary MOS: 100C-Cargo   *Last MOS Group:* Aviation (Officer)

Helicopter Pilot   *Last Unit:* 1970–1971, 100C,

Service Years: 1969–1971   159th Aviation Battalion

HOME STATE / YEAR OF BIRTH
Evanston, Illinois / 1950

CASUALTY INFORMATION
Casualty Date: February 15, 1971

Cause: Hostile, Died while Missing   *Reason:* Air Loss, Crash-Land

Location: Laos   *Location of Interment:* Arlington

Conflict: Cold War   National Cemetery, Arlington, VA

UNIT ASSIGNMENTS
1970: Warrant Officer Candidate School, Fort Rucker
1970–1971: 159th Aviation Battalion

COMBAT AND OPERATIONS HISTORY
1970–1971: Vietnam War
1971: Counteroffensive Phase VII Campaign/Operation Lam Son 719

JOHN LYNN POWERS, SP4
SERVICE DETAILS
Last Rank: Specialist 4
Last Service Branch: Aviation
Last Primary MOS: 67U-Medium Helicopter Repairer
Last MOS Group: Aviation (Enlisted)
Last Unit: 1970–1971, 67U, 2nd Attack
  Reconnaisssance Battalion (ARB),
  159th Aviation Regiment/C Company
Service Years: 1970–1971

HOME STATE / YEAR OF BIRTH
Mackay, Idaho / 1949

CASUALTY INFORMATION
Casualty Date: February 15, 1971
Cause: Hostile, Died while Missing   *Reason:* Air Loss, Crash-Land
Location: Laos   *Conflict:* Vietnam War
Wall / Plot Coordinates: Panel W5, Line 107

UNIT ASSIGNMENTS
1970–1971: 67U, 2nd Attack Reconnaissance Battalion (ARB),
159th Aviation Regiment/C Company

DONALD EVERETT CRONE, SP4
SERVICE DETAILS
Last Rank: Specialist 4
Last Service Branch: Aviation
Last Primary MOS: 67U-Medium Helicopter Repairer
Last MOS Group: Aviation (Enlisted)
Last Unit: 1971–2001, 67U, POW/MIA
Service Years: 1970–1971

HOME STATE / YEAR OF BIRTH
Whittier, California / 1949

CASUALTY INFORMATION
Casualty Date: February 15, 1971

Cause: Hostile, Died while Missing   *Reason:* Air Loss, Crash-Land
Location: Laos   *Conflict:* Vietnam War
Location of Interment: Arlington National Cemetery, Arlington, VA

UNIT ASSIGNMENTS
1970–1971: 159th Aviation Battalion/C Company
1970–1971: 67U, 101st Airborne Division
1971–2001, 67U, POW/MIA

COMBAT AND OPERATIONS HISTORY
1970: Vietnam War/Sanctuary Counteroffensive Campaign
1971: Counteroffensive Phase VII Campaign/Operation Lam Son 719

WILLIS CALVIN CREAR, SP4
SERVICE DETAILS

Last Rank: Specialist 4   *Last Service Branch:* Aviation
Last Unit: 1971–2001, 67A, POW/MIA   *Service Years:* 1970–1985
Unofficial US Army Certificates: Cold War Certificate

HOME STATE / YEAR OF BIRTH
Birmingham, Alabama / 1950

CASUALTY INFORMATION
Casualty Date: February 15, 1971
Cause: Hostile, Died while Missing   *Reason:* Air Loss, Crash-Land
Location: Laos   *Location of Interment:* Arlington
Conflict: Vietnam War   National Cemetery

UNIT ASSIGNMENTS
1970–1971: 67A, 101st Airborne Division
1970–1971: 67A, 159th Aviation Battalion/C Company
1971–2001, 67A, POW/MIA

COMBAT AND OPERATIONS HISTORY
1970–1971: Vietnam War/Counteroffensive Phase VII Campaign
1971: Vietnam War/Consolidation I Campaign
1971: Counteroffensive Phase VII Campaign/Operation Lam Son 719
1971–1972: Vietnam War/Consolidation II Campaign
1972–1973: Vietnam War/Cease-Fire Campaign

Jerry Cobb died in Vietnam, he just didn't know it. The end finally came when he crashed his personal Aeronca airplane in Alabama on May 9, 1971, within months of coming home from his second Vietnam tour.

JERRY COBB
Photo courtesy of Jerry's daughters,
Lynn Hoxit and Kelli Owens

Jerald Carter, Joe Savick, Mike Crawford, Ray Trujillo, Willie Oaks, and 28 other men died when their Chinook, Playtex 866, crashed into a mountain in bad weather on November 28, 1971 in Vietnam.

JERALD WAYNE CARTER, CW2
SERVICE DETAILS
Last Rank: Chief Warrant Officer 2
Last Service Branch: Warrant Officer (pre-2004)
Last Primary MOS: 100C-Cargo Helicopter Pilot
Last MOS Group: Aviation (Officer)
Last Unit: 1971, 100C, 159th Aviation Battalion/
    C Company
Service Years: 1969–1971

HOME STATE / YEAR OF BIRTH
Daleville, Alabama / 1946

CASUALTY INFORMATION
Casualty Date: November 28, 1971
Cause: Non-Hostile, Died while Missing
Reason: Air Loss, Crash-Land
Location: Thua Thien
Conflict: Vietnam War/Unspecified Operation
Location of Interment: Riverside Cemetery, Fort Morgan, CO
Wall/Plot Coordinates: 02W 074

JOSEPH JAMES SAVICK, JR., CW2
SERVICE DETAILS
Last Rank: Chief Warrant Officer 2
Last Service Branch: Warrant Officer (pre-2004)
Last Primary MOS: 100C-Cargo Helicopter Pilot
Last MOS Group: Aviation (Officer)
Last Unit: 1971, 100C, 159th Aviation Battalion/C Company
Service Years: 1969–1971

HOME STATE / YEAR OF BIRTH
Akron, Ohio / 1944

CASUALTY INFORMATION
Casualty Date: November 28, 1971
Cause: Non-Hostile, Died while Missing　　*Reason:* Air Loss, Crash-Land
Location: Thua Thien　　*Conflict:* Vietnam War
Wall / Plot Coordinates: 02W 079

UNIT ASSIGNMENTS
1969–1970: Warrant Officer Rotary-Wing Aviator Course (WORWAC)
1970–1971: 062B, CH-47 Transition Course
1971: 100C, 101st Airborne Division
1971: 100C, 159th Aviation Battalion/C Company

COMBAT AND OPERATIONS HISTORY
1970–1971: Vietnam War/Counteroffensive Phase VII Campaign
1971: Vietnam War/Consolidation I Campaign

MICHAEL ALAN CRAWFORD, SGT
SERVICE DETAILS
Last Rank: Sergeant　　*Last Service Branch:* Aviation
Last Primary MOS: 67V-Observation/Scout Helicopter Repairer
Last MOS Group: Aviation (Enlisted)
Last Unit: 1971, 67V, 159th Aviation Battalion/C Company
Service Years: 1968–1971

HOME STATE / YEAR OF BIRTH
Henryetta, Oklahoma / 1951

CASUALTY INFORMATION
Casualty Date: November 28, 1971
Cause: Non-Hostile, Died while Missing   *Reason:* Air Loss, Crash-Land
Location: Thua Thien   *Conflict:* Vietnam War
Wall / Plot Coordinates: 02W 075

UNIT ASSIGNMENTS
1971: 67V, 159th Aviation Battalion/C Company

COMBAT AND OPERATIONS HISTORY
1971: Vietnam War/Consolidation I Campaign

RAYMOND ANTHONY TRUJILLO, SP4
SERVICE DETAILS
Last Rank: Specialist 4
Last Primary MOS: 67U-Medium
   Helicopter Repairer
Last MOS Group: Aviation (Enlisted)
Last Unit: 1971, 67U, 159th Aviation
   Battalion/C Company
Service Years: 1970–1971

HOME STATE / YEAR OF BIRTH
La Puente, California / 1952

CASUALTY INFORMATION
Casualty Date: November 28, 1971
Cause: Non-Hostile, Died while Missing   *Reason:* Air Loss, Crash-Land
Location: Thua Thien   *Conflict:* Vietnam War
Location of Interment: Queen of Heaven Cemetery, Rowland Heights, CA
Wall / Plot Coordinates: 02W 080

UNIT ASSIGNMENTS
1971: 67U, 101st Airborne Division
1971: 67U, 159th Aviation Battalion/C Company

COMBAT AND OPERATIONS HISTORY
1971: Vietnam War/Counteroffensive Phase VII Campaign
1971: Vietnam War/Consolidation I Campaign

WILLIE JAMES OAKS, PFC

SERVICE DETAILS

Last Rank: Private First Class   *Last Service Branch:* Aviation
Last Primary MOS: 67A-Aircraft Maintenance Apprentice
Last MOS Group: Aviation (Enlisted)
Last Unit: 1971, 159th Aviation Battalion
Service Years: 1971

HOME STATE / YEAR OF BIRTH

Beattyville, Kentucky / 1949

CASUALTY INFORMATION

Casualty Date: November 28, 1971
Cause: Non-Hostile, Died while Missing   *Reason:* Air Loss, Crash-Land
Location: Thua Thien   *Conflict:* Vietnam War
Wall / Plot Coordinates: 02W 078

UNIT ASSIGNMENTS

1971: 159th Aviation Battalion

COMBAT AND OPERATIONS HISTORY

1971: Vietnam War

Dick Steiner (left) died in the crash of an OH-58A Kiowa in Germany on December 7, 1972.
Author's collection

Alex, a.k.a. "Alice," Kelly (right) died in the crash of his LifeNet medevac helicopter in Arizona on July 29, 2010.
Photo courtesy of Alex's daughter, Paige Kelley

Steve Maas died in the crash of a UH-1H Huey in Texas on April 24, 1973.
Author's collection

*Robert, a.k.a. "Strider,"
Curtis is the narrator of
this non-war war story
and, to my great surprise,
I am still alive in 2015.
I miss my friends who
are not.*

ACKNOWLEDGMENTS

The greatest of thanks to my brother Army Aviators & Air Crewmen from our Vietnam days: Jim Scott, Jim Morrical, Chuck Magaw, Deane Wiethe, Lee Grossnicklaus, Ken Werenko, Rickie Owens, Bill O'Conner, and Paul Carter. Thanks to all of you for the memories you shared in our various emails, text messages, and phone calls. Thanks to Jim Morrical, Bill Smith, Bill O'Conner, Ken Werenko, Rickie Owens, Paul Cater, and sisters Kelli Owens and Lynn Hoxit for the use of your pictures. Thanks to *Together We Served* for supplying photos of my friends who I could not otherwise locate. It is from their website, togetherweserved.com, that I was able to get the service profiles of the men featured in the Appendix.

To all of my aviator friends who figure unnamed in this story, I am glad I did not have to use your names in this no-fighting war story. Finally, great thanks, as always, to my editor, best friend, lover, and wife, Mariellen, for reading this many times and for inspiring me to write it. Without you I would not have written it.

GLOSSARY

1LT	—	1st Lieutenant
2LT	—	2nd Lieutenant
AC	—	Aircraft Commander
APU	—	Auxiliary Power Unit
ARVN	—	Army of the Republic of Vietnam
ASHB	—	Assault Support Helicopter Battalion
C-rations	—	Combat rations; usually canned meals for use in the field
CO	—	Commanding Officer
CW2	—	Chief Warrant Officer 2
DI	—	Drill Instructor
DMZ	—	De-Militarized Zone
Duce and a half	—	two-and-a-half-ton trucks
FSB	—	Fire Support Base
GCA	—	Ground Controlled Approach using precision radar
Hell Hole	—	the hatch in the floor in the center of a Chinook cabin that opens to allow the crew to look down at an external load.
IP	—	Instructor Pilot
ITO	—	Instrument Takeoff
KP	—	Kitchen Police
KY-28	—	scrambler for radios
LZ	—	Landing Zone
medevac	—	medical evacuation
nav aids	—	radio aids to navigation
NCO	—	Non-Commissioned Officer
NVA	—	North Vietnamese Army

OD — Olive Drab

OH-6 LOHs — Light Observation Helicopter, pronounced "Loach"

PAO — Public Affairs Officer

Pintle — upright pivot pins on which other parts turn

PSP — Pierced Steel Planking; rectangular sheets of steel that lock together to make a temporary road or runway

Punji Stakes — wooden or bamboo spikes

PZ — Pick-up Zone

QA — Quality Assurance

RLO — Real Live Officer (A lieutenant, captain, major, etc., as opposed to a warrant officer

R&R — Rest and Recuperation

S-1 — Personnel Office

S-4 — Supply Office

SEA — Southeast Asia

Seabees — Navy Construction Engineers

SERTC — Screaming Eagle Replacement Training Center

SFC — Sergeant First Class

SIP — Standardization Instructor Pilot

SOP — Standard Operating Procedures

Spec 4 — Specialist 4th Class

SPP — Special Purpose Packs (cellophane packet containing toiletries and cigarettes, sometimes given along with C-rations to soldiers in the field)

VC — Viet Cong, the National Liberation Front

VFR — Visual Flight Rules

WO1 — Warrant Officer 1

XO — Executive Officer

IFR — Instrument Flight Rules

RUFF/PUFFs — the Regional Forces/Popular Forces, a South Vietnamese and U.S. sponsored, lightly armed militia, a sort of home-grown National Guard.